Chapter 1

My life began, perhaps as all lives do, as a blank sheet of white paper—no markings, no wrinkles—just a clean canvass with infinite potential.

The hope of new life is boundless. When children are born, people celebrate, not because they know what that child will become or how she will elevate herself in life, but because they don't. Nobody knows what a baby will become and that's precisely the cause for jubilation. Pure innocence means a chance to start anew, uninhibited by the scars that everyone watching has already been limited by. So people celebrate new life, and for good reason, because maybe, just maybe, that blank sheet of white paper can begin to be painted with the most beautiful things imaginable. Maybe, just maybe, that life can take on a quality beyond that which we've ever seen in the past.

That hope is the derivative for our inspiration. It is the cause for art and love and dreams of peace.

Yet, it is always the baby within which these hopes reside. Only through time does life's brush begin stroking her paper. Only then do her memories begin to take shape. It is these memories through time that weather our dreams into form and illustrate that intrinsic energy within each of us that we are forced to define as our life.

And I guess this is the problem for me.

For many, life begins painting beautiful images, and our earliest memories are of fairy tales and magic and stories that end with *happily ever after*. For them, the world is fanciful, filled with promise and joy and opportunity—lovely pictures to show the world.

Those were not my first memories.

And some of the first things that would be drawn onto my blank white sheet of paper were images that I wish I could erase. Yet, the metaphor is that for a reason.

Life is a lead-based paint.

You can smudge and smear and paint over it, but it will never actually go away. The marks will always be there, lurking beneath the picture that you show to the rest of the world. And nobody else might know that it's there, but you know.

You see it every time you look in the mirror.

It takes two good deep breaths before I can even open the door.

When people look at me now, they see a New York fashion designer. I am the Design Director of Women's Footwear at *Tommy Hilfiger*.

Ever since I woke up this morning, I've been contemplating what version of me I want to present today. I didn't sleep much last night, and to offset the *blah*, I slip on a bright yellow t-shirt with an embroidered blazer, dark denim jeans, and cowboy boots. I have makeup on to make my face look as lively as possible, and my hair is metallic silver, sculpted to perfection.

It's all part of the job.

When I open my front door, the quiet recesses of my private world are drowned out by the sights, sounds, and smells of Manhattan in the morning. As I take my first few steps, a flurry of unnerving activity greets me. An ambulance blares its sirens, car horns fire off indiscriminately, and the distant sounds of traffic are fused with the faint whistle of the sweeping wind rifling through the towering, iconic buildings of the city.

I pop in a set of ear buds and turn on my iPod, to dampen the chaos.

Every day, the walk to work takes about thirty minutes, and it's a refreshing opportunity to get my head straight. Once I exit home, this walk will be the only calming part of my day.

Turning left at a street corner, I see the imposing Chrysler building off in the distance—a breathtaking sight. It is a beautiful and classic white brick skyscraper that narrows at the top and is adorned with chrome and flying buttresses shaped like Chrysler's hood ornaments. Today, the chrome is glistening in the winter sun, and the needle atop the building appears to be piercing a low-hanging, wispy cloud.

As I ramble down the sidewalk, I feel a powerful, stinging emotion. With thousands of people milling around, gigantic billboards, and traffic crammed in like a fat kid in an airplane bathroom, you get the sense that you are in the midst of something important.

When most people envision a male fashion designer, they probably think of some super-excitable chatty gay guy who uses his hands to emphasize every point.

I am gay. But I'm not that guy.

I'm reserved, insecure, and cynical to the touch. I don't like being around people, especially if I don't know them. So, when I walk through Times Square, I always wear an eye-catching pair of shades. Today, I'm wearing vintage-inspired, bamboo James Dean-style glasses with dark lenses that I bought on one of my recent trips to China. With these, my translucent presence allows me to safely and anonymously scan the landscape of humanity before me without giving myself away.

I've got a Lady Gaga song, *Bad Romance*, blasting through my ear buds as I walk through the crowd. If people stare at me, whether it's because of my gigantic diamond ring, my silver broach, or my metallic hair, I know that I'm a success today. What you present to others is what they think of you, and what people think of me determines whether or not I have a job. So, if my appearance doesn't garner attention, I'm in the wrong business.

I am eternally captivated by the eclectic collection of individuals that I pass on my way through the city. When you're here, people seem so ant-like—zigging and zagging through crowds on their way to their plotted destination. I know where I'm going and they know where they're going. People don't bother each other and avoid eye contact like the plague. You can be totally invisible without feeling alien. Everyone who melds into the routine and culture of New York Life is welcome, even if they aren't greeted with a smile.

As I weave through the never-ending stream of crowds, I keep my eyes focused very closely to the front—never up at the spectacular skyline above or over at the masterful storefront windows. They are merely the enduring background to the innumerable lives that scurry about within the city's womb. And all I ever remember, from my daily walk to work, is the choppy vignettes of people and scenes with which I collide.

With a new Lady Gaga song on, this stroll through the multitudes feels like a giant orchestrated dance for a music video.

New York is, as it has always been known, the great melting pot of the world. But I know that what appears on the surface doesn't even come close to explaining the true diversity of the people in this city. We are only what we choose to represent to the world. Beneath that, the painting gets much more complicated. The city functions as a powerful veneer—a cloak for all those yearning souls who don't care to reveal the images of their past.

As I approach my office building, the people are packed as tightly as ever. The subways, apartment high rises, freeways, taxis, and office buildings repetitiously pump people through the streets as incessantly as your heart passes blood through your veins.

My building is fifteen stories high and the size of an entire city block. It is made of red brick that has faded over time into a deep, dark blood red. Each corner of the building is rounded so that the large glass windows featured on every floor can wrap all the way around without interruption. The front of the building is accessed by large glass revolving doors framed by reflective chrome.

Walking into the building, I see a sign that says "Hugo Boss Model Check-In." Beautiful people are shuffling through every day hoping for their shot to be featured in a magazine advertisement or catalog. Our building is home to Hugo Boss, Tommy Hilfiger, Martha Stewart, and Bodum. You could create an entire wardrobe and decorate your home without buying a single thing designed and marketed outside of this building.

At the center of the cavernous marble lobby, I make feigned eye contact with the guard, who gives a subtle recognition that he knows me and I can proceed to the elevators. On the way, I glance over to notice that a tall, blonde businesswoman just hurriedly walked past wearing a pair of Coach Shoes that I designed four years prior.

I smile, but only on the inside.

In the crowded elevator, I squeeze through to press the 6. When the doors open, I try to smoothly glide through, without accidentally molesting someone and causing an awkward separation from our short *ela-lationship*. That's what I call my elevator relationships, which consist mainly of nausea, paranoia, and social incompetence.

I turn right and realize that to be the wrong way, as I usually do, and spin around nonchalantly, only to find that the door has yet to close. I failed miserably to avoid the awkward exit that I had dreamed of, and I put my hands up in *flusteration* (flustered frustration) to show my discontent.

Life goes on.

The hallway leading into the Tommy office is painted in wide Navy blue stripes of different texture, and on the walls are about a dozen photographic interpretations of the American flag. Tommy Hilfiger is built around the theme of Americana. Originally, it was just t-shirts, but the company has been continually blossoming and evolving into new areas of the fashion industry, like women's shoes.

I have to walk about half a city block to get to my desk once I walk through the large glass doors of the Tommy office. A large flat screen TV flashes a slideshow of Tommy Hilfiger's accomplishments over the years.

The long corridors lead me past the cafeteria, which is catered daily by a private chef. A large dining room was built inside with large crystal chandeliers and an impressive view of the Hudson River. The company pays half of all food expenses so breakfast and lunch cost two to three dollars per meal.

But I never eat at work.

Nearing the end of the marathon to my desk, I pass through another long corridor that will one day come to a *T*. On the left is the outsourcing department, which comprises all of the products that are not made in-house, like sunglasses, watches, and small leather goods. To the right are in-house products, where I work.

When I finally arrive in my office, I look out at a massive room, with cubicles lined through all sides and over 100 employees from various departments. Accountants, marketers, salesmen, visual merchandisers, and others combine with designers to make up the component cogs of the industrial machine that is this room.

In calm moments, I look through the expansive windows at the Hudson River gently flowing through the infinite metropolis and marvel at the world I am a part of.

Unfortunately, my painting has not always looked like this. The events and characters and stories of my life were not predestined for greatness. My life was not cut from the fabric of *The American Dream*. I don't even know what the hell that means.

All I know is that, well, things look different now. People always try to give me encouragement. They tell me that my life is vogue and enviable. They tell me that my life is great—everybody's dream. I never can find a way to believe them. To me, it all functions as an exterior.

Beneath the exterior resides a recurring episode of fear, flashes of angst, and a lifetime of insecurity. There is a reason that I take two deep breaths before I can walk out my own front door. There is a reason that I didn't sleep well last night. There is a reason why I don't eat while I'm at work. And there's a reason that, no matter how hard I try, I can't fully enjoy my grandiose Manhattan life. We all have something painted beneath the picture we choose to show the rest of the world. Here are the images that are drawn beneath mine.

This is my story.

Chapter 2

On the surface, I was part of a pretty stereotypical American family, except we were Mexican. Yeah, Mexicans can be Americans too, dick. We had a house, a mother, a father, four sons, and a busted up old Chevy truck. My Dad had a job and Mom had dinner ready every day by the time he arrived home.

The neighborhood—Cypress Park in Los Angeles, California—had the appearances of a decent community. The homes were packed tightly together. Some had porches and a teeny little façade of a lawn. The school was two blocks up the street. The grocery store was just around the corner on the main road, Cypress Avenue, and along the same thoroughfare were family-owned Mexican restaurants and a local liquor store. It was home to the urban working class.

Towering above the neighborhood in the distance to the north was Mount Washington. Mount Washington was home to the wealthy outsiders with which we had no connection whatsoever. From the top you could peer out over the sprawling city of Los Angeles, and its millions of little homes tucked into its hundreds of little neighborhoods, never too far from some jammed up freeway that cut sections through the city.

For those of us living at the base of the mountain, the thick grey Los Angeles smog acted as a hovering blanket to remind us of our place in society.

During my early years, our neighbors were the component parts of the Mexican working class in Los Angeles, living the typically hard-fought lives of first, second, and third generation immigrants. There was little to no racial integration. Los Angeles was composed of Latino neighborhoods, African-American neighborhoods, Caucasian neighborhoods, and Asian neighborhoods, creating powerfully insular inner-city cultures which developed in little pockets.

Gangs thrived on the ethnic, racial, cultural, and territorial xenophobia that pervaded each subgroup.

Just to the south of our home was the busy San Fernando Road and a train track that ran alongside the Los Angeles River—a concrete-banked, waterless river that wound through the urban expanses of Los Angeles County and south to the Pacific Ocean. Beyond the river and across the freeway to the south was Elysian Park, which was set on top of the same mountain as Dodger Stadium. With this slope to the south and Mount Washington to the north, our neighborhood was nestled into a little enclave that made it impossible to recognize that we lived within ten miles of Hollywood and five miles of Downtown L.A.

Cars whizzed by on the freeway. Planes cruised overhead. And nobody from outside of our little enclave knew that I existed.

The people in Cypress Park spoke some combination of English, Spanish, or Spanglish. Our food, language, and celebrations all reflected Mexican heritage, although my family's ethnicity is quite a bit more confused.

The Serna family used to live on lands that were once a part of Mexico. Then, as westward expansion in the United States pushed the population across the Mexican border during the 1830's and 1840's, a war ensued when the United States government and its western settlers decided to challenge Mexico over its right to maintain its own land. When America won—you know, the whole "Remember the Alamo" thing—the *Treaty of Guadalupe Hidalgo* was signed and Mexico ceded the modern day states of New Mexico, California, Arizona, Nevada, Utah, and parts of Colorado and Wyoming to the United States. With the stroke of a pen, my ancestors went from being Mexican to American.

It's better to be on the winning side of stupid wars.

Our skin is lighter in complexion than most Mexican families, and I've often been mistaken as a white kid. After doing some research, I found out that most people with the name Serna originated in the mountains of northern Spain, making it more likely that my Serna ancestors were conquistadors than native Mexicans. So my family probably won a few wars before we lost.

My supporting cast of characters went something like this:

My Mother was a loving, compassionate woman who always put her family ahead of herself. Loyalty was her most endearing quality and her tragic flaw. She taught us to read, made sure we were well dressed, and was definitely the one in charge of the house. She was particularly concerned with holding up appearances. She would clean the house dressed to the nines, in full makeup and high heels. Her family was the same way. During these years, my three brothers and I looked like this.

(Insert family picture?)

Mom's maiden name was Chance, and her mother was a very traditional Mexican lady with a strict, carefully designed household. Mom was the second oldest in a family of six that was comprised of four girls and two boys. The family was pretty poor, living off of one meager salary. My grandfather Edward worked in a naval shipyard, which was hard work without much pay.

My grandmother's name was Aurora Chance—acronym, A. Chance—and her core belief was that *a woman must be loyal to her family above all else*. I named this book after my grandma Chance because of that core belief, and for its hidden meaning in this story unfolding before your eyes.

Like my mom, A. Chance did all of her housework in heels and would frantically clean and scrub the home every day, making sure that everything was perfect, with dinner on the table, by the time my grandfather arrived home. She knew that even though they didn't have much money, it was her job to keep the family presentable, so that everyone felt good about themselves and their home.

Grandma treated my Grandpa Edward like he was the most important person on earth. She bent over backwards to make sure he was always satisfied. Just like my mother, she never graduated from high school, and had no skills or experience that would allow her to work a job outside of the home.

And she would never abandon her husband, no matter what it meant to her life.

A. Chance raised my mom in Highland Park, which is the northeastern neighbor to Cypress Park, where my dad grew up.

Their two families couldn't have been more different.

My dad Peanut—yes, that's really what everyone called him—was a pretty ordinary working father figure when we were very young. When I began Kindergarten, which is about as far back as I can remember, Dad worked in the *Farmer John Meatpacking Factory* in Vernon, just south of Los Angeles. The plant was an integral part of my family's history. His father, my grandfather Refugio, started working there immediately following his return from the Korean War. They were famous for producing Dodger Dogs, the scrumptious extra long hot dogs served at Los Angeles Dodgers baseball games.

Grandpa had experienced intense and traumatic battle during the war and settled down with his family in Cypress Park. For better or worse, he never looked back, and his daily work routines at *Farmer John* became his way of coping with the difficult things he had seen.

Grandpa Refugio was an enigmatic man. At times, he was cheerful and warm. At others he was strict, almost militant in his manners. He was among the most hardworking people I've ever met. Perhaps this is why he found such success at the plant. After many years of labor, they made him a manager, and he made an excellent salary that more than allowed him to raise his family of five—one daughter and four boys.

His wife, my grandmother Serna was also quite successful. She was a proofreader at the Los Angeles Times, an exceptionally professional job for a woman in the 1950's and '60's. Grandmother was a severe, but gorgeous, woman. I can most accurately describe her as the evil queen from *Snow White*. She was harsh, critical, and unrelenting toward her husband and children. As a result, she was feared by the kids because they felt as if they always had to be perfect in order to win her approval. If they weren't, they could count on a life of condescending and hurtful condemnation.

Grandma and Grandpa lived five houses up from us on Losemore Street. Their house was like a museum, everything spotlessly cleaned and adorned to perfection, with everything kept tidily in its designated place. Their bedroom contained two tightly made twin beds, parallel to one another and separated by six feet of cold, unoccupied space.

They were devoutly catholic, attending church habitually and unwaveringly. They showed it off in their home with grave images of Jesus Christ and crosses intentionally smattered throughout the house so that you could never get too far without feeling the burden of guilt.

My mom's side of the family was loving and open—my dad's side reserved and authoritarian.

But, I guess the common thread between the two divergent home environments was that appearances meant everything. What you show to the outside world is what they will think of you.

And image is what matters most.

My parents found one another at Franklin High School in Highland Park. On the first day of school, my mom was standing at the entrance of the school with a group of girls when she spotted a boy walking across the bridge that led from the physical education building to the main campus. He was wearing a leather jacket and a wife beater on top of a set of well carved abs.

She turned to the girls and said, "Who is that guy?" with dreamy curiosity.

As it turned out, she would see him again, later that day, in her sixth period social studies class. They never spoke to one another, but after developing a mutual habit of furtive glances, she noticed that she was seeing him around more often. He would keep his distance, but followed her around like a puppy.

But he hadn't yet summoned the courage to talk to her.

Then one weekend afternoon, when my mom was packing up the car in preparation for a family road trip, she spotted the boy through the window. Wearing a bandana and scrubby sweats, she panicked. She had been trained never to be seen by men, particularly ones that she was interested in, wearing anything but her finest. Futilely trying to hide behind a parked car, he spotted her, and, not wanting him to leave with his only impression of her being her shabby attire, she approached him for the first time.

"Hi," she said excitedly.

"Hi."

"What's up?" she wondered aloud, trying to start a conversation.

He nervously tossed his feet from side to side. "Oh, nothing. I'm just taking a walk."

He was lying. He had walked all the way over from his home in Cypress Park just to see if she was home.

"You know, there's a dance coming up at school. I, I don't have anybody to go with. You know, whatever." He stammered incoherently.

My mom helped him out a little.

"So, do you want to go with me?" she asked.

"Well, that's. I mean. That could be cool. Yeah?"

"Ok, sure."

That's how they met. They developed a passionate relationship, and, not more than one year later, she was pregnant at the age of seventeen.

Then, a moment—a decision point—arrived that would eternally alter the course of their lives.

Grandma Chance had been through a turbulent batch of years. Her husband Edward had several mistresses and they had been divorced and remarried. When that marriage didn't work out, Grandpa

Edward came back to my grandmother and begged her to take him back. And she did. Every time. She even moved their family out of the neighborhood to follow him.

But none of them yet knew that my mother was pregnant at seventeen years old.

Understanding her family's strict, Catholic feelings about sex out of wedlock, my mom packed all of her things into bags before she shared the news. When she approached Grandma Chance about it, there was no ambiguity to her response. With Grandma shouting and crying, all of my mom's siblings rushed into the living room to see what had happened.

"She's dead now. She doesn't exist," my grandmother exclaimed deliriously.

With her brothers and sisters crying, Mom took all of her belongings and left—right then and there, never to return.

Right before their child was born, my dad's parents offered them a small home down the street. Though my mom didn't like the offer, because it implied that Grandma Serna would have total authority over them, my dad convinced her to accept the house.

It is the home where I spent my childhood. They live there to this very day.

Over the course of the next four years, my parents would get married and engage in a frenetic pattern of sex and birthing that would eventually lead to a family of six by the time she was only twenty-two—literally as fast as humanly possible.

I am now the youngest of four boys, and this is a reality that I will never escape for as long as I live. You see, in our household, age dictated the hierarchy. Whatever the oldest said was the law of the land. To understand us, you have to understand the brother structure and the characters that built its power.

Richard was the oldest—the man in charge. He was born in 1975, not even four full years older than me. Ten months after Richard was born, the second oldest, Armando "Mando", introduced himself to the world in July of 1976. 1977 was an off-year for my Mom's expeditious birthing, but the next child was soon to follow in May of 1978, when my brother Ruben arrived.

Then, 360 days later, on May 26, 1979, it was my turn. I entered the scene as the youngest of four—the final piece to the Serna family puzzle.

The four brothers made up two perfect pairs. We lived in a house that was scarcely larger than 1,000 square feet. It had two tiny bedrooms and one large master bedroom that had formerly been known as a two-car garage.

Two boys per room.

Mom had this planned out very deliberately. We were placed into living pairs that would be maintained for the rest of our childhood. The three rooms were all connected in a row.

In the room next to my parents, Richard, the oldest, was paired with Ruben, the elder of the young pair. Richard slept on top bunk and Ruben was on bottom. In the room next to them, Mando was on top bunk and I was on bottom.

In many ways, our personalities developed according to our role in the hierarchy, and once we were old enough, my parents really left us to ourselves. The older brothers were responsible for watching out for the younger. My parents would become very hands-off, treating us as adults, free to make our own choices.

Richard became the sternest of the brothers. He was very concerned with protecting the younger siblings and he was often very deliberate in making sure that we understood his power as the oldest. He was probably the most complex of all the characters because he was both strong willed and compassionate, bossy and loyal. Since he had more responsibility, he also learned to wear many hats—just like a parent.

Mando was quite a bit more laid-back. Perhaps because Richard was always acting as the authority figure, Mando found that he was more successful as the peacemaker of the bunch. He was nice, non-confrontational, and a people-pleaser. For these qualities, he too became powerful because when things went wrong, we could always turn to Mando to help make us feel better or resolve a problem.

Ruben, as the youngest middle child, was the mercurial protagonist for trouble. He was short, but wanted to prove he was tough—funny, but also intense and eager to show that he wasn't just a jokester. He always wanted to gain approval from Dad and the older brothers, and he was never fully comfortable with being a subordinate in the family. The only one that he had authority over was me. He often took that power to extremes, and I have the scars to prove it.

Beneath these three characters was me, the low man on the totem pole. We didn't even have a dog that I could order around. You can judge for yourself what I'm like, but all I need to say is that, as the youngest, I was an observer. I could watch everything taking place, but had no control over it. In the beginning, I was as innocent as a lamb, an adorable sheet of blank white paper—a fresh opportunity for creation and hope and life.

Chapter 3

The first thing I can remember was the ritual my family went through in the morning before school. I was four years old and didn't have to go to school yet.

Every night, Mom would lay all of my brother's school clothes out in the living room and iron them to perfection. In the morning, the other three would leave and I would basically have the house to myself. It was just Mom and I—a perfect, calming arrangement with which I was entirely content.

All day long, I would tinker around with toys while she kept up with the housework. Every day around noon, she would exercise in the living room to a Richard Simmons video, and I would jump in gleefully to dance with her.

You know how I know you're gay?

You like to stay home with your Mom and dance to Richard Simmons videos.

Yeah. Seriously.

When my brothers would get home, the house would get loud again and it was harder for me to keep to myself. We had a lot of fun as kids, but it was a struggle for me. I really thrived when I had space to myself, devoid of interruption.

Then on one fateful evening, when all seemed right in the world, I walked out into the living room and saw the clothes strewn about in methodical order and counted.

One. Two. Three. Four.

Four sets of clothing. My five-year-old mind churned and fired and raced, recognizing a critical difference.

Oh, no. I think I'm going to school tomorrow.

When I heard my parents talking about it in their bedroom, I knew. My first day of school is tomorrow. I tossed and turned and wondered.

Can't I just stay home for one more day?

I barely slept. I dreaded the thought of going to school. All of the other kids, the teachers, the noise, just seemed like too much for me. I was only five years old for god's sake. How could anyone do this to a child?

On the morning of my first day, Mom helped me slip into my clothes. She ordered us all into a neat little line, wetted her hand, and stroked the clumsily configured strands on top of our head until we all looked like miniature 1970's game show hosts. Then, she led us to the door like a row of ducks behind Richard, the door creaked open, and she said those fateful words.

"Have a great day at school, Mijos."

My stomach turned into knots. I grimaced as I took my first two steps off of the stoop.

I'm not ready. It's too soon.

To an outsider, we must have been quite the sight to see—four boys with backpacks, finely pressed clothes, and well manicured hair marching in lockstep up the hill toward school. That is, until I started heaving and stopped to puke on the sidewalk. My Mom came running out.

"What's the matter Ray?"

"I'm sick. I feel scared."

She shouted ahead, "Richard, when you get to school, take Ray straight to the nurse's office. You understand?"

"Yes Mom."

"Have a great day at school my love. Feel better. Ok?" she pleaded sympathetically.

Not even puke was going to delay my attendance at school. My brothers kept walking steadily up the sloped sidewalk. I stopped about four more times to heave and groan and hyperventilate.

As we walked up to Aragon Elementary, just two blocks up the street, the fear and anxiety got worse. It was a big, cement building with a fence surrounding a large asphalt play area.

Richard took me straight to the nurse and left to report to his own class. The nurse let me sit there until she determined that I felt well enough to attend class. Then she escorted me to the correct room.

I was a fish out of water. Mom wasn't there. My brother abandoned me. The nurse dropped me off with a bunch of people I had never met without the slightest sense of condolence. This, I determined quickly, was not fun. Nevertheless, I took my place amongst the students as instructed and waited to find out what the hell these people wanted from me.

I was further disheartened to find out that our first lesson was to learn the *Pledge of Allegiance*. It confused me more than anything. Every single day we had to do the stupid Pledge of Allegiance. It was very much like being in a Catholic Church mass service. You stand up, regurgitate a bunch of stuff you'd been taught, irrespective of meaning, and you have to say it anyway. Back in those days, you'd be sent to the principal's office if you didn't recite the pledge.

I hated having to do something—anything—which is probably why I hated the idea of going to school in the first place. Once you start giving into mandatory activities, a little bit of your freedom, a little bit of your creativity, is usurped for the sake of routine and continuity.

The teacher stood before us, with hand on heart, like George Washington would smite her if she didn't, and said, "Ok, ready, begin."

And it would sound something like this:

"I pedge a regence to the flag of the United States of Ramerica. And to the Repub-ic, for which it stands. One nashion, under god, in va-visible, with li-burty and just is for all."

Out of a class of twenty-five, I think only three kids knew what ten of those words even meant: I, the, and, to, for, it, one, under, with, all.

Zero students understood any of the other words.

Yet, we said it every single day and would be scolded if we seemed to lack the proper enthusiasm. God bless America or God save the king, or whatever.

A little later in the day, as I was sitting innocently at my desk coloring in bubble letters, I was attacked by what felt like a clothes pin. The baby fat on my arm was scrunched together hastily.

"Ouch!" I shouted.

I turned around to see a little chubby girl giggling. She sounded like a squeaky chew toy being mauled by a Rottweiler.

False alarm.

Later, I would ask Mom why she did that to me, and Mom told me, "That girl just has a crush on you Ray. She likes you!"

"Oh, god," I exclaimed. "Gross!"

Ironically, that's as close as I ever got to having a girlfriend, and my straight friends tell me that I got off with relatively little pain.

After several hours of routine—recite the pledge, color some things, listen to the teacher read a book, get assaulted by a she-devil—the teacher finally let us leave.

My mother was there to greet me at noon, after my first few hours in the torture chamber they called *Kindergarten*. I could always tell when she was coming. The echoing clack of stiletto high heeled boots down the hall was a dead giveaway.

The factory where Dad worked was about a twenty minute drive from home. Dad was gone in the morning and returned in the evening—a typical nine to five working father. When he came home, he smelled of blood and death and fat from the meatpacking plant. Mom made him take off his boots before he trounced inside, and demanded that he take a shower on account of his stench.

Dad was hard to get a feel for. He was very stern, and, when he came home, I remember that everyone had to be very serious and act perfectly. Mom, as was tradition in her family, would bring us all into the living room about the time Dad was expected to come home to make sure our hair was properly combed and our outfits looked pristine for his arrival.

Dad's mood really dictated our behavior. If he seemed to be in a quiet or serious mood, we would act the same. If he seemed to be joking a little, we could lighten up. My brothers and I kind of remember him acting like Fred Savage's dad from *The Wonder Years*. Nobody ever wanted to say anything to get his panties in a twist.

Every morning, Dad told Mom exactly what he wanted for dinner and she would faithfully prepare his dish of choice, regardless of how much we despised it. On this particular morning, my Dad had requested *tripas de leche burritos*, or milk intestine burritos—the most vile piece of a cow hidden amongst traditional burrito toppings.

We hated milk intestine burritos.

When Mom prepared them, she periodically gagged while dissecting the intestines that once led into a cow's utter. Yet, after the dirty work was done and they were fried to perfection, Dad would tackle them with the reckless abandon of a hungry jackal. We looked on in horror, knowing that we too would be expected to clean our plates of the filth he called food.

We never got to choose what we ate for dinner. From the beginning, everything revolved around Dad and his wishes, just as it had in Grandma Chance's household.

After dinner, we did our chores—cleaned up after dinner, did the dishes, and made sure the house was back in order for the following day. Then, the boys sat down on the couch in the living room and watched *Family Ties*.

I went into Mom and Dad's room and watched *Jaws* on cable.

The brothers complained, "Why does Ray get to watch cable with you, Mom?"

She responded, "Talk to your dad about it. Watch your show."

Sometimes it was good being the baby.

Chapter 4

As the youngest, I had been conditioned to share my opinion only when absolutely necessary. Whether it was at home or at school, I tended to be the quiet one, the observer in the crowd.

Every day in Kindergarten, my teacher put a sentence up on the board that was at a first grade reading level. It was like a bonus question. If you could read it in kindergarten then it meant that you were ahead of most of the other kids. As a kindergartner, I looked at the sentence every day and read it to myself.

"The dog ran happily up the hill on his way home."

Pretty simple. Yet, every single day, when the teacher would give us a chance to read it aloud, I kept my mouth shut.

And the room was drowned in awkward silence. Crickets abounded.

I didn't think it was my place to speak up, but day after day I read it to myself, alone, in secret.

"The dog ran happily up the hill on his way home."

And every day I kept to myself, until, about two weeks later, something snapped. I could no longer stand the agony of silence. I finally raised my hand, and the teacher called on me.

Cautiously, I read, "The dog ran happily up the hill on his way home."

Whew. What a relief!

"Very good, Ray! I had no idea you could read like that," the teacher exclaimed, clapping her hands at me with a smile.

The revelation called for a parent-teacher conference. Oh Joy!

I sat there as Mom explained that she had taught my brothers and I many things, such as numbers to 100, the ABC's, and some basic reading skills.

Shut up, Mom! Shut up!

Those words would be the undoing of my complacency.

"I'll have to get you more advanced material to read," my teacher told me, which was adult-speak for having to stay inside to read while the other kids went out to play. Great move, genius!

I was showing promise in school when I was struck with a tormenting twist.

With mounting pressure building in my bladder, I informed the teacher that I had to go to the bathroom. The ensuing events seemed to be more of an ordeal than they should have been. She went over to her desk and picked up the phone, and about a minute later an older boy walked in.

I could have gone to the bathroom by myself and been back already.

"Ray, this is Eric. He's your bathroom escort. You go with him," my teacher guided.

You've got to be kidding me.

Eric was a fourth grader, four years older than me. He was white. No, he was sallow—disgusting, like a slimy mole. He was a good head taller than I was, very slender, and kind of wimpy looking for his age. He had a haircut that looked like a bad mix between Elvis and Vanilla Ice. I remember he was wearing splotchy, light-colored jeans and a red leather jacket with an unreasonable number of zippers on it, a Michael Jackson type of thing.

I walked to the door as instructed and followed Eric out of the classroom. The hallways seemed so big, like everything must to a five year old. We travelled down two flights of stairs to ground level, around a corner, and through a door leading to the outdoor schoolyard. The schoolyard was lined with a row of peppercorn trees.

The outdoor area was surrounded by silver chain-linked fence. On the top level there was a covered cafeteria area with picnic tables, where the kids ate lunch. On the bottom level was a rectangular space with basketball hoops, tetherball poles, and a painted area for baseball games.

All of this was set upon heat-radiating black asphalt.

Eric led me past the peppercorn trees and to the left where the outdoor entrance to the bathroom was located. The bathroom was a hollow, concrete room with two stalls and two urinals. It was dingy and smelled of must and mold and urine. There were no doors on the stalls and the door to the bathroom was propped open. Rivulets of light made their way through the grime-encrusted, bar-covered windows high above our heads. The faint droplets of light painted the dank walls pale yellow.

It was the only light in the room.

I looked up at Eric, who had stopped in front of the urinal.

He glared back at me.

Just before I unzipped to do my business, I heard his voice.

"What you got there?" he said.

"Huh?" I responded.

"Why don't you show me what you've got in those pants? I'll show you mine if you show me yours."

It is very hard to explain the feelings that were coursing through my body in that moment. I remember my mind raced and my stomach was queasy. My eyes darted frantically from one direction to the next. I wanted to ignore him.

"Show me," he insisted.

At five years old, I was so vulnerable. A bigger, older boy had asked me a question. He demanded that I do something. And everything that I ever learned was to listen to older boys. That's how my family hierarchy worked. That's how it was in school.

Respect your elders. Do what you're told.

Feeling pressured, I looked back at Eric, hoping for a smile, a laugh—anything that would help me to know that he was being friendly or just making a joke.

"Go on. Show me," he said with a stern, antagonizing tone.

His face was blank and intent.

Inside of me, a sensational conflict erupted—in my gut, in my mind, and in my heart—as I nervously unbuttoned my pants and exposed myself to him. He looked down at me, at my privates, and he smiled. I could tell he was satisfied, and he grew more excited as he pulled open his pants, gripped his naked crotch and showed himself to me.

"You see that."

He didn't say it as a question.

Eric knew I saw. And I knew that he had seen me. We stood there exposed to each other, and I didn't understand what was happening. At five years old, there was nothing sexual about the encounter to me. Yet, it wasn't like playing hopscotch with someone either. I didn't know why, but I sensed that I had done something wrong.

And I felt humiliation for the first time.

Eric pulled his pants back together quickly and buttoned up again. I did the same.

I never even used the bathroom, I was so distraught.

Without a single word, Eric led me back past the overhanging peppercorn trees. The crunching of the tiny pink pepper berries beneath my feet sent a spicy, stinging aroma into my nostrils as I followed him through the door, around the corner, up the flight of stairs, and back into my classroom.

I looked up to him. He peered back at me angrily.

I felt like we had been away at the bathroom for too long. What had seemed like an hour lasted only fifteen minutes. But the teacher wasn't upset with me when I walked back to my seat. She went on teaching like everything was normal.

A feverish panic snuck into me. I checked my pockets like I had lost something. I had one pencil and an eraser in my right pocket and nothing in my left—same as before. I hadn't lost anything. Everything, on the exterior, remained in place.

Later that day, as I followed my class back from lunch, I saw Eric on the other side of the hall. He was travelling in my direction. I looked to up to him as he passed, feeling strangely curious at the sight of a familiar face. I wondered if, even though I felt so strangely about our encounter, maybe he was my friend.

Was that something that friends do at school?

As he eclipsed the shadow I cast onto the tile floor below, Eric delivered his left elbow into the back of my ribs, and I buckled to the ground in pain.

He was definitely not my friend. But what was he? My face flushed, as the unmitigated anger quickly transformed into a new wave of embarrassment. Nobody noticed me on the ground until the final classmate behind me in line offered his hand in assistance. I jerked my hand away nervously. Who could I trust in this place?

No words were spoken.

In this series of unspoken actions I was left confused, nervous, and afraid. The way Eric looked at me, the way the teacher just went on without recognizing what I had been through, the way he knocked me to the ground without making a sound, and the questions, thoughts, and feelings that I didn't have the tools to explain, were translated by my five-year-old mind into a simple repeating mantra.

I don't belong here.

When I got home, and Mom asked about my day, I told her that everything was fine. I didn't know what to tell her. I didn't know how to tell her. The jarring pressure, the unsettling emotions, were abandoned in the echoing cavern inside my head.

For the next couple of days, everything at school proceeded routinely. I didn't like it, but it was a lulling, unremarkable monotony that, much like Los Angeles traffic, becomes bearable to the weary, beaten down travelers who no longer have the energy or motivation to exert any energy toward protest. We students were prisoners with dwindling notions of escape.

Then one day, as it does to all people, I felt that mounting pressure again, and informed my teacher that I needed to use the bathroom. Just like before, she went to the phone and, once again, about a minute later, an older student appeared at the door.

It was Eric again.

"Is he always going to be there?" I mumbled to myself.

I stayed seated as if I had never asked to use the bathroom.

"Ray, Eric's here. Go on now," my teacher directed firmly.

I got up hesitantly and looked around the room. The students were all seated upright in their chairs with their heads focused intently downward. The pencils were moving around like little bobbers, floating smoothly up and down with the flowing current of their hands. Not a single person looked up. Not a single person noticed the concerned look on my face as I meandered through the room toward Eric.

When I reached the door, Eric turned his back and began walking toward the stairs, as if I didn't even exist. I took one last look back into the classroom, using my eyes to search for help. No contact was made, with anyone. And I turned to follow along, like a good little boy—sinking down the stairs steadily, disappearing from the surface of supervision.

Eric said nothing as we walked past the peppercorn trees once more. The beaming California sun belted down upon the back of my neck and I felt a chilling sensation as I slipped into the dark, musty shade provided on the other side of the bathroom door.

"Just go to the bathroom and leave," I whispered to myself.

I tried darting quickly into one of the stalls instead of heading for the urinals, hoping, praying that Eric would just let me go.

Then I felt his clenched hand on the collar of my shirt. He redirected me past the stalls. Leaning toward the urinals, he grabbed me again and thrust me past them and into a narrow corridor to the right of the sinks.

There was a janitor's closet in the boy's bathroom that was hidden beyond the toilets and the sinks at the end of a hallway. The corridor was dark, dingy, and stunk of mold. Nobody who came in to use the bathroom could know if people were back there because it was tucked into the little elbow by the janitor's closet.

We were completely alone.

Eric shoved me into the dead end corner at the end of the dark hall. I felt the walls and ceilings closing in on me, as if the room were shrinking. I developed a heightened awareness for sights and smells. The moist, moldy air closed in on me and I began breathing heavily. My heart raced. Eric hadn't said a single word since we left the classroom, and he was holding his hand against my chest, controlling me by force.

My back was pressed against the dead end wall.

"Unzip my pants," he said methodically.

The discomfort and uncertainty I felt during our first encounter was replaced by pure, unadulterated fear. My stomach in knots, sweat dripping onto my tiny patch of eyebrows, I did as I was told.

"Now pull down my pants and put your mouth on my underwear."

He pushed me down onto my knees against my will. The floor was soaked with shallow puddles of putrid water and piss and God knows what else.

"Lick my balls and rub me with your hand," he commanded.

He forced my head into him with his hand.

I did as I was told.

His thin, white underwear felt coarse on my tongue. The taste and smell was disgusting and it grew worse as my mouth moistened the thin layer of cloth separating him from me. I coughed and my face scrunched up in displeasure.

"Keep going!" he shouted.

The room pulsed, becoming smaller and smaller—time, slower and slower. I became twitchy and quick in my movements, subconsciously moving faster and faster, hoping that time would follow suit. But it didn't. I was stuck. With my eyes closed, I waited and waited as he pressed me helplessly up against the wall.

"Please be over soon. I hate this so much," I pleaded internally without making a sound, meanwhile submitting to his sick commands. As he looked down on me with his mouth tightened in either anger or ecstasy, he broke the silent interaction.

"I know you like it, you little bitch," he groaned sickly.

Tears were now running down my cheek. My chest grew smaller and tighter, my arms cowered to the center of my body as I knelt in the corner.

"Ah, yeah. Oh. That's it. Ahh."

He stopped pressing against me and moved away. I remained in the corner, my arms now folded in my lap, my legs curled helplessly behind me. I looked up at him, and he looked up at the ceiling. He pulled up his pants and signaled me to get up.

I did as I was told.

He stood there and let me walk by, back into the bathroom past the sinks, past the urinals, and past the toilets. Eric followed closely behind, as I walked out the door.

Again, I never got to use the bathroom.

The sun shone brightly onto the front of me and the expansive blue sky would have provided a sense of freedom had I not been so keenly aware that I remained trapped. Eric walked past because I was walking slowly, aimlessly.

Where do I go? What just happened? What should I do now?

I stopped beneath the speckled shade of the peppercorn trees in protest.

"Come on twerp. Let's go," Eric demanded.

Neither my feet nor my lungs moved as I delivered an impulsive statement.

"I'm going to tell the teacher what you did," I said squeakily, overwhelmed by unspeakable emotions.

Eric paused, eyes intensely glaring at me through the effervescent rays of light seeping through the wavering peppercorn trees. He stepped slowly toward me. I stood stiff and erect, like a granite statue frozen in time. I heard a rip, some squeaking, and a shuffle as I watched him remove his zipper-laden Michael Jackson-style jacket.

Without a single word or sound exiting his mouth, he took two quick steps to my side, raised his jacket high above his head, and swung the metal and leather jacket with all of his might until it whipped into the back of my soft, skinny legs.

I crumpled to the ground in agony, my arms striking the asphalt. As I rolled over onto my stomach, my cheek pressed against the ground, crushing pink peppercorn berries with my cheek. A pungent whiff of spicy pepper infected my sinus as I rolled around on the ground before freezing face down.

I don't belong here.

Looking up, the sun bouncing in and out of my eyes, Eric stood dominantly above.

Noticing that my eyelids were welling up, he said, "What? You gonna cry about it baby?"

I insisted that I wasn't, but he knew I was in pain. He knew I was crying. I knew I was crying.

"If you tell anyone about this, I'll kill you next time, baby," he promised.

I stood up, and, trusting that he meant what he'd said, followed him past the peppercorn trees, around the corner, up the flight of stairs, and into my classroom.

Nobody said a word to me when I walked back to my seat. My lips tightened. My eyes welled up again. I grabbed my pencil from the edge of the desk.

I don't belong here.

Chapter 5

As I lay in bed, my mind won't stop, can't stop. No matter what I do. No matter what I try. It won't stop. I think. I whisper things to myself. Most of all, I remember.

With a twitch I am running. It's so dark outside and I'm so small. The sky above is pressing down against me as my breaths get shorter and shorter. My feet move faster and faster. To each side is a wall and in front, a long narrowing path.

It stinks of garbage all around. I'm so tired. But I hear footsteps coming from behind. They are long, loud slams against the pavement. Beneath me are short, frantic smacks, and I know that I'm not fast enough. I know that whatever is behind me is closing in.

And yet I run.

The walls are behind me now. The steps are even closer. I don't have time to look up, and I'm so afraid to look back. To the right and to the left are evidence of my life—tires and scrap metal, wrappers and soiled diapers—heaps upon stacks of human emptiness.

And yet I run.

The air is suddenly cold as I extend my legs, feeling my hamstrings tighten to their full potential. I want to quit but I keep demanding:

One more step. Just one more step.

And I run.

I can hear his breath now, as I can see mine plume fleetingly before my face. I hear him grunting as he gains quickly upon me. The sounds become so loud that I can feel it before it happens.

The slamming, the breathing, the grunting.

I let off two loud breaths and two long steps before I crumple to the ground in agony, my arms striking the asphalt.

Pink peppercorn berries crush beneath my cheek as he rolls me over to face him.

He has me pinned to the ground, with his body straddling my torso. His hands wrapped tightly around my neck, he leans over so that his face is six inches from mine.

His eyes are dark, nearly black, and beady and bloodshot. His face is worn old far beyond his years with blotchy skin and veiny discoloration on his cheeks. His beard and mustache are ragged and unkempt, with dried up spit and food and powder hanging from their gnarly locks. His clothes are torn, stained and faded, and he smells like a plastic bag filled with old dirty mops and sponges, soaked for months in muddy water and the summer sun.

He is the epitome of ugliness to me when he leans over with total control—total dominance.

My heart skips and sputters and stops in fear when he opens his mouth.

With uncontrollable fury, He squeezes at my neck and declares, "It's never going to end! It's never going to end!"

It's never going to end.

A faint buzzing enters into my mind followed by a series of quick beeps. A horn sound begins growing closer with every beat.

I open my eyes.

I'm in New York. I'm thirty-one years old. And my cell phone is ringing at nine in the morning on a Saturday.

I pick the phone up and answer.

"Hello?"

"Hi Ray, it's Bornie," she answers.

She's my boss at Tommy Hilfiger.

I roll over and frantically search the room for a few seconds, trying to focus my eyes. I'm groggy and still dripping with terror.

Hi Bornie, what's up?"

"I just got off the phone with the President of Tommy and he wants the newest line of women's shoes to begin design on Monday. Will you be ready to go?"

"Of course. Thanks for letting me know."

"Okay, great. See you on Monday."

"Okay, bye Bornie."

I hang up the phone, set it on my nightstand, and roll onto my back, staring drowsily, in that way that makes your vision so blurry that it seems as if you're looking beyond the objects in front of you. It was hard to reassure myself that my world is real.

I'm still afraid that it's not.

"Who was that Ray?" My husband Ben asks.

With a tired, pained groan I respond, "It was Bornie. We begin our newest collection on Monday. She was calling to let me know."

"Well that's cool," he says. "I know you'll do great."

I'm glad he thinks so. I seldom do.

Ben and I met eleven years ago in Chicago. It was my first time at a gay bar. When I turned twenty-one, about a month prior, I wanted to start taking advantage of my new citizen perks, but until that day I was too nervous to even walk by. I was insecure and skeptical of all the things it might entail. Who knows what kind of psychos I might find in there?

One random evening, against my better judgment, in June of 2000, I was riding alone on the train and felt this sneaking inclination to get off seven stops early to try my luck at a place called Spin. Amazingly, I went with it. Fifteen minutes later, I found myself alone at a bar with a beer.

And I hate beer.

A girl with crutches stumbled in and awkwardly gravitated toward me. When she approached the bar, she asked if she could sit next to me.

Clearly seeing her full leg cast, I sarcastically replied, "Are you sure you don't want to dance?"

She giggled and we started talking.

Great, now I'm officially part of the socially awkward and handicapped section of the bar! Leave it to me to hang out with a straight, one-legged woman on my first trip to the gay bar.

When she asked me for my phone number, I seriously thought I was in the wrong place. Had I walked in on straight night or something?

"You do realize I'm gay don't you," I asked confusedly.

"It's not for me, it's for my friend Ben," she insisted.

Not thinking much of it, and not wanting to give my number out to a crippled stranger, I rejected her offer, but waited a few minutes, not wanting to be completely rude and bitter.

As I began to walk away, she said, "Wait! Hold on. My friend Ben is right there."

Wonderful. More people to join the socially handicapped section.

However, I was pleasantly surprised to find that Ben was really nice—perhaps a little too nice. He bought me beers for hours, and I never mustered the nerve to tell him that I hated beer and just didn't know what else to order. By the end of the night, I had eight full beers sitting at the bar, warming by the minute.

He asked for my number.

I refused, and wondered if he was a serial killer.

So I said, "I'm not giving you my number. You're probably a serial killer."

Ben giggled, probably assuming (wrongly) that I was joking. He danced excitedly with a cocktail in his right hand and a smile on his face. There was something alive about him that I really admired.

So, despite my suspicion that he was a deranged mass murderer, I took his number at the end of the night. And, after several days of quietly questioning my already questionable judgment, I called.

We went on a date, bowling, which I also hate. Yet, somewhere along the way, he grew on me. I had fun every time I was with him.

And we've been together ever since.

Ben is now the Regional Marketing Director for Dave and Busters in Times Square. He is my advocate and support system. Ben has always admired my talent and has always encouraged me, the perpetual cynic, to say yes to new things that come along. He always pushes me to do what I'm passionate about.

I would never be as far along in my career if I didn't decide to get off the train seven stops early that night. And I know I wouldn't be as happy. It's too bad that Ben entered my life so late, so near the end of this story I have to tell.

But, while we're at it, you should know what I do now—if for no other reason than to distract you from the pain and regret inherent in reading about a five year old being sexually abused at a public school.

Every new fashion season I'm tasked with developing a new collection of shoes. The first steps are ultimately the most difficult because there are so many component pieces that must fall into place. The fashion concepts, the timing, and the production process need to be just right.

When I get started, a myriad of essential questions plague my mind. Where should I begin? What is *in* this season and where are the trends heading? What materials should I use? What colors are hot right now and what colors are on their way out? Who's using what hardware and why?

I don't have much time to process these questions. Decisions must be made quickly because deadlines are tight. There is little time to second-guess myself, especially once I get started.

The first step is to start pounding the pavement. I venture out with a battle plan in mind. A variety of upscale stores are my homework. I will carefully inspect the styles, materials, and designs being sold at the time. I must study not only competing shoe brands, but also fragrances and accessories, like handbags. I have to sum up the whole market that will accompany my shoes in store.

The best (and most fun) way to research the market is to walk around the city. I glean inspiration anywhere I can—on the street, in the stores, in magazines, and on the internet.

First, I head out to the Meat Packing District of Manhattan, where I can find really unique, handcrafted, fashionable designs at stores like Jeffrey, Stella McCartney, Alexander McQueen, Christian Louboutin, and Scoop. Here, I can see what the high-end shoe, clothing, and accessory designs are looking like and use them as a compass for where I will choose to go with my line.

I never want to go into a fashion line copying someone else. That would be career suicide. But if I don't know the ins and outs of the other brands, I might step on toes or feature apparently unoriginal concepts without knowing. That's why I have to know *everything*.

What are people wearing now? And what are people going to wear next season?

That's what it's all about.

You see, the design industry is about always knowing, or at least convincing people that you know, which direction the trends are heading, so that you can predict what people are going to want before they know they want it. The line that I am beginning right now for Tommy Hilfiger won't hit stores until next year. So I have to produce something people *will* crave—something that is fresh, but not so exotic that it is unmarketable.

As I approach my favorite boutique, Alexander McQueen, I know that appearances are everything. In here, you aren't going to find a pair of shoes for less than $1,000. Arrogance overtakes me as I saunter through the doors, playing it smooth, as if I drop $10,000 on a pair of runway shoes all the time. Dark shades make me look fierce and unapproachable.

I examine the items flippantly, as if they aren't impressive, making clear that I'm not just some tourist. I'm looking not only at what is on the shelves, but also what the women in the store are wearing. What colors are dominant in the clothing? What fabrics are used? Are women wearing silk or cotton? Is gold or silver used more? Do I detect a touch of bronze and rose gold hardware colors? Are they high-shine, brushed, or antique-finished? The details say everything.

I draw a picture in my head.

Street culture matters a lot. Sometimes I learn more walking the streets outside of the stores than I do on the inside. The information that I'm looking for, after all, goes beyond what women are wearing. How they wear it, where they are wearing it, and what they wear it with, are all vital pieces to the fashion puzzle.

And I have no more than three days to put it all together.

I'm looking for reasons, red flags, repetition, continuity, originality, and relevance. If I see one really interesting shoe that's kind of wild, kind of out there, it tells me nothing. Maybe someone will buy it. Maybe I even love it, but it doesn't help me to figure out what the Tommy Hilfiger line for next year should include. That's why I'm on the lookout for noticeable, even if subtle, patterns.

From an established fashion pattern I can extrapolate and say, "Ok, if people are wearing shoes with spikes this year then I know that they will love a shoe with some type of similar, yet unique, variation on the spike next year." Maybe it's adding a different color to the shoe. Maybe it's wrapping the leather in a different way—something to look new enough to get attention, but not so totally different that it doesn't fit their paradigm.

Making variations on existing trends works like a charm—unless, of course, it's not actually a trend.

Many times in fashion, something is wildly popular one month and totally dead the next. It has a very short shelf life. I call this a 'flash in the pan.' It happens all the time.

As a designer, if I misinterpret a 'flash in the pan' as a continuing trend, it comes at a very high cost. An incredible amount of money and resources go into every shoe line. If just one of my lines bombs, it means my job. Countless design careers have been ended permanently for designing an entire line around a false trend that nobody wanted the following season.

But no pressure.

Next stop, Time Warner Center.

I'm going Uptown to peek into JCrew, Hugo Boss, Swarovski, and Anthropologie. I'm here to scout accessories and shoe ornamentation. Do the shoes have beadwork? If so, do I see more wood, crystal, or metallic beads? What types of laces are on the shoes? What type of buckles? What stitching patterns and colors are popular on the shoes? What about the handbags?

After visiting those four stores and combining the information with my stops in the Meat Packing District, I have confirmed that people are gravitating toward more deconstructed looks, such as sun bleached fabrics, frayed edges, and multi-colored shoelaces. Also, there seems to be a trend toward nautical looks like, awning stripes, military-style buttons, and nautical map printed fabrics. There is a demand for heavy-welted rubber soles with stacked heels inset, and I'm seeing a lot of silk screened graphic elements on the uppers of boat shoes. These, I know, can look great with the Tommy brand.

I've seen a lot, but it has been a long day. Time for a cocktail—or seven.

On my second day of research, I'm going to stay home for the morning to flip through fashion magazines, like Vogue, L'officiel, Harpers Bizarre, V, Cosmopolitan, and Vanity Fair.

These magazines, among dozens of others, are the fashion manuals for millions of women. The presentations in these pages will make impressions on people that will lead to shoe purchases. I look to see what stands out. Sometimes it's the shoes, but many times it's where the women are in the advertisements or photographs that make the biggest impact. Are the heels on women at work higher or lower? Are women at the club wearing platform-raised heels or stilettos?

I draw a picture in my head.

Then I head out to Fifth Avenue to check out some of the other designs. Here I can find the *en vogue* companies of the day like, Prada, Gucci, Lois Vuitton, Henri Bendel, and Bergdorf Goodman.

Walking through Prada and Gucci, I'm going to be particularly mindful of how the uppers (the top of the shoes) look as I peruse. Are sling backs in right now? Are ankle wraps in? Are other designers going lower with their top lines?

Then, I'll consider sole designs. Are they using a feminine-typical sole like you'd normally see on a dress shoe? Or something that's completely outside of that box such as tire tread or really heavy lug soles?

Then, finally, when I'm done doing all of my shopping and I've appropriately scoured the fashion magazines and the internet, I have to ask myself the following question: How do the styles, constructions, and materials that I found patterns of in all of those different places fit into the company's footwear that I'm designing?

This is an incredibly daunting task. All of the component parts of each fashion season add up to something that I can recognize and then get creative with. However, I first have to weed out a lot of elements that are unrealistic for the Tommy Hilfiger brand. Tommy is a very diverse company and that's one of the things I really love about working here. You can create a lot of different types of shoes with a lot of different practical uses. But, it's not Alexander McQueen. We're not selling shoes for $1,500 a pair. It's not Prada either.

And brand identity, for me, is the most important thing, and what I've built my career on.

My new line, and my future, begins tomorrow when I show up at work.

It takes two good deep breaths before I can even open the door.

Today, it's time to get to work, and my outward appearance makes that clear. I'm wearing a non-descript, black Calvin Klein button-down shirt, a pair of dark denim blue jeans from H&M, a belt with a rhinestone-encrusted buckle, hand-carved Lucite sunglasses from Japan, and silver metallic hair, sculpted to perfection of course.

I flip on my Ipod, pull my vintage leather, bright orange messenger bag over my shoulder, and open the door for another day. The usual anxiety-riddled rush courses through my body as I take my first steps onto the cluttered street.

For a half an hour, I dance and dodge through the New York streets. Step-by-step, song-by-song, my anxiety becomes subdued by the immediacy of Manhattan. I take one more deep breath as I enter the building, and after walking my little marathon and embarrassing myself getting off the elevator again, I arrive at my desk—only to find a pile of blank white paper staring me in the face.

It's almost time to draw the line.

First, decisions must be made. My Vice President has left a sales report on my desk, which reveals the sales record for all the shoes from my last collection. I need to scrutinize this report and decide which shoe constructions I need to revisit and which shoe constructions I should scrap in the next line.

Now comes the fun part—choosing construction styles. The constructions run the gamut from athletic sneakers to pumps. There are literally thousands of variations to choose from and I have to narrow it down to about twenty-five. Sometimes the season dictates the choices. For example, every winter line has a snow boot and every summer line has a sandal, but, beyond the obvious, it's all up to me.

I'm designing right now for spring of the next season. My research from the past couple of days indicates that I need to include a boat shoe, a good moccasin, and a sneaker. The rest will be constructions that I find interesting and slightly different from last year in toe-shape and overall appearance. My main focus is to combine the designs that have worked for the company in the past with more relevant constructions that I think people would like to see out of Tommy.

Once I've established our line of constructions, it's time to turn it into something real. I pull out 'Ole Blue,' my blue leather-bound sketch book, and begin to organize the page into one-and-a-half inch squares. In each, I will draw a basic outline, or silhouette, of each shoe that will be part of the collection—editing and merchandising as I go.

As each picture in my head hits the paper, I have to recognize patterns, like a certain buckle or ornamentation, and make sure that I include it in several of the shoes. In order for a collection to be a success, it has to have continuity and make sense together. This phase in the design process is all about identifying characteristics that make up the Tommy Hilfiger DNA.

I keep drawing, my creativity hard at work, mapping out all of the little things and bringing them all together.

After all the thumbnails are sketched, I scan the collection several times. Any styles that don't belong stick out like a sore thumb. I discard them and start over. Some styles seem questionable, but I'm not ready to give up on them yet.

These little thumbnails I put together will soon be made into full-sized sketches, steadily navigating the process from fleeting idea to a tangible prototype that will, one day, transform into a final sample to be presented to hundreds of big market retail buyers all around the world.

After I finish scanning the thumbnails and envisioning the final concept of the collection, I close my sketch book and recline in my chair. I take a second to look around at all of the people milling about their day.

I smile for a moment, realizing that for the past few days I've been looking at fashion items and drawing. And I actually get paid for it.

My Product Coordinator Natalie breezes by my desk and says, "It's time to go *botch*." That's Natalie-speak for bitch. We have our own language and nobody has any idea what we're talking about most of the time. We like it that way.

I grab my bag and she grabs her yoga mat and water bottle and we walk towards the elevator together. As we make our way through the lobby, a man passes by. Natalie looks at me with a raised eyebrow.

I know exactly what she's thinking and I say, "Did you leave any in the bottle?" referring to the ridiculous amount of cologne he's wearing.

As we are inundated by his perfume cloud, I pick up a strong scent of pepper.

"Uggh. I love Marc Jacobs but I can't stand that pepper smell," I tell Natalie.

"That's weird," she replies. "Why not?"

I changed the subject.

The elevator door opened and we got in. For those few brief, quiet moments in the elevator I felt a stinging pain in the back of my legs. The elevator walls felt like they were closing in on me.

Los Angeles had jumped back into my mind.

"See ya tomorrow Nat."

"Totes. Later."

Chapter 6

I'm standing outside. It's dark. A cement alleyway with graffiti on the walls and trash cans upended surround me. I hear footsteps—long, loud slams against the pavement. My chilled breath plumes before my face as I turn to run.

The narrowing alley disappears behind me as I continue rushing down an infinite path through a trash heap filled with used tires and diapers and cigarette butts. I feel his presence closing in and I know that I am moving to slow.

And yet I run.

The sounds grow louder—the grunting, the slamming, the breathing. He is not far behind now. I can feel his breath on the back of my neck.

I let off two loud breaths and two long steps before I crumple to the ground in agony, my arms striking the asphalt.

Pink peppercorn berries crush beneath my cheek as he rolls me over to face Him.

He smells like a plastic bag filled with old dirty mops and sponges soaked for months in muddy water and the summer sun.

His face enraged, eyes bloodshot, He draws my face six inches from His and shouts, "It's never going to end! It's never going to end!"

It's never going to end.

A ray of light pierces through the blinds and into the left orbit of my skull. I blink, and my right eyelid pries open. I turn my head and stare through the blank white wall to my side. My breathing is frantic.

I'm in Los Angeles. It's my sixth birthday, and it was the first time that I ever had that dream.

I lay in bed silently for what felt like eternity. Gripped in terror, I covered myself in my blanket and froze motionless. None of my brothers were awake yet.

I was alone.

Kindergarten was winding to a close. After several new encounters with Eric, I grew too scared to use the bathroom at school. I learned to avoid making contact with other students, and that, for whatever reason, I attracted the ire of troubled people.

The day was my brother's birthday. Since my parents had been so consistent with their sex habits, my Brother Ruben and I shared birthday weeks, one year apart. He was born on May 31, 1978. I was born on May 26, 1979. To simplify the whole process, we just had a party for both of us on his birthday.

Great! On my birthday, everybody says, "Don't worry Ray. You'll get your cake and presents in five days."

For Ruben's birthday, friends of my parents, aunts, uncles, and cousins alike show up in droves, dressed in their finest with packages and food, to have fun in his honor.

Jealous much? Yeah, just a bit.

Still shaken from the nightmare, I stumbled languidly into the kitchen to find Mom already in the kitchen preparing food for our party. She had *carne asada* marinating in beer for tacos. Paper party plates and cups were divided neatly on the table for the guests when they arrived. She wore high-heels, an apron, and a house dress, as usual.

"Good morning *Mijo*!" she exclaimed.

She always called us *Mijo*, Spanish slang for son. It's a very endearing term. She always showered us with love, even in difficult times. She never used curse words or said anything to cut us down. Her tone, her words, and her expressions were always dripping with love, even at times when it may have seemed disingenuous. She wanted to make sure that, no matter what, we knew that she loved us.

"How did you sleep, my love?" She asked with a smile.

Thinking through my nightmare, I flashed through the moments of emotion, captured by my brain as colors and heat and light. I thought of what I saw, but I didn't have words. I thought of the pain I felt being dragged down and the pink peppercorn berries flashing before me as I struck the asphalt.

"I had a bad dream. I fell and there was pink," I said, sensing that this description was insufficient.

"Like The Pink Panther?" Mom asked.

The Pink Panther was one of my favorite shows.

Hesitantly, I responded, "Yeah, like that I guess."

"That's nothing to be worry about Ray. You don't have to be afraid, *Mijo*."

I couldn't explain what I felt.

Before long, my brothers were awake and playing in the house. The noise rose steadily. The ice cream truck outside sang loudly as it cruised through the neighborhood. The TV turned on and the silly melodies of *Looney Tunes* bounced around in my brain and propelled it into a frenzy of distracted thoughts. And my dream drifted further and further from consciousness.

The first guest to arrive was my Aunt Lilly.

"Happy Birthday, Ruben! You're getting so big. Happy Birthday, Ray! You look so nice today," my Aunt Lilly said gleefully.

She placed a card on the table and began talking to my mom. My dad was still in his room.

Every time we had a birthday party it seemed like the adults without kids showed up first and we would just wait around for more kids to show up, watching TV and running into the kitchen to grab snacks. When the kids finally did show, we would go out into the street behind our house. Usually the boys would play baseball.

If I had my way, I'd sit on the grass and try to catch bugs.

I loved nature and science from a very early age. I could just look at an insect or a lizard or a flower and be entertained for hours. I loved trying to figure out how things worked. I was curious about how things were put together. How do they fly? Why are lizard scales so rough? Why does a flower always have a colorful thing poking out from the center?

Baseball, however, is what I was left with because there usually weren't enough kids to play. So my brothers would demand that I help them catch the ball. I stood timorously behind the batter, and the ball would usually bounce right off my chest and down the street. Then the whole process started over again, until someone new showed up to relieve me from my position. I hated baseball.

Bugs were much less terrifying.

The party continued casually—the adults inside drinking beer and talking and the kids outside playing games—until Mom came outside to inform us that it was time to eat.

The house filled with the rich smells of Mexican cuisine, rice and beans, steak and guacamole. The sounds were joyful and warm with a welcoming family atmosphere seeping through every doorway.

We ate and opened presents. I remember getting a pair of Airwalk shoes from one of my dad's friends. Except, ironically, I hated shoes—not as much as I hated baseball, but still. I preferred going barefoot, but had to pretend that I liked the gift anyway.

Mom taught us to always be polite.

After presents, we gathered behind the house to take swings at a piñata because, yeah, that's what Mexicans do. We had no trees in the gravel driveway behind our house, where all the adults were sitting, so Dad had to climb up onto the roof and hang the piñata from the rain gutter attached to the house. I was no better at this game than baseball, but at least I got candy at the end.

Slowly, as people began slipping into their food and cake-induced comas, the family members began to leave and the party transformed into a drinking party with my dad and his friends. The people with kids left, and it was me, my brothers, and the partiers. The smells of food slowly wafted away and the rich family atmosphere turned into a circle of adults smoking and drinking.

It grew louder by the minute.

The sun set over the modest, cookie-cutter houses across the street and, as was always the case in Cypress Park, the daytime smells of oil and dirt and smog gave way to the crisp, refreshing scent of night jasmine flowers.

My mother came inside and helped the boys and I get ready for bed.

She guided me into my pajamas and said, "Goodnight *Mijos*! Sleep well my loves," before shutting off the lights to our room.

She left our door open and the hallway light on, so that she could check in on us and we could find our way through the dark.

For a while, my brothers stayed awake. Mando liked to make me giggle. Richard and Ruben would shout silly things. But it didn't take long until all of them drifted to sleep. Steadily, the quiet would rise over the room, until I could sense that I was the only one left conscious.

I was always the last one left awake.

Perhaps I was still rattled from the nightmare I'd had the night before, and didn't want to have a repeat performance. So I listened. Every once in a while, I'd hold my breath trying to make out what my parents were talking about.

Dad's loud voice boomed through the narrow doorway. He was the only person whose voice I could distinguish.

After a while, everyone was louder than normal and speaking strangely. I noticed that they started using the bathroom a lot more. This gave me an uneasy feeling. I just kept my eyes wide open, staring out at the hall—waiting for something to happen.

A Pink Floyd song, "In the Flesh," started playing on the record player. When I held my breath, I could hear a metallic flicking sound spark off periodically. A light, skunky smell drifted into the hall. And the music played. On and on, the songs kept coming and going. I struggled and thought of going to sleep, but my mind was clogged with irrational thoughts and curiosities. I wanted to know what was happening on the other side of the wall.

For a while, their voices grew quieter. Then, after I heard some rustling, a medley of shouting ensued, like they were celebrating something.

I was pretty sure it had nothing to do with my birthday.

When I lay totally still, I could hear that they were having trouble breathing—like they were taking quick, hard breaths, but their noses were stuffy. They sounded like a bunch of asthmatic kids in a pollen cloud.

I could see random feet walk by for a split second, as they wandered in and out from the bathroom. They were so erratic, turning the light on and off and fiddling with the lock. Mom would peek back in every once in a while to see how we were doing, and I would quickly close my eyes and pretend to be asleep.

I have no idea why I did that.

As the pitch black shades of night began evolving into gray, I heard a sudden twist in the tone of my dad's voice. It was like the rotation of the earth had crossed a line and his mood flipped in an instant. Where he was once happy and jubilant, filled with laughter and exuberant stories, his voice began to seep with antagonism and bellicosity, challenging and arguing in his loud, overwhelming howl.

My jaw locked and I grew rigid in an effort to stay quiet during the conflict.

After several minutes of this newly combative tone, I no longer had to hold my breath to hear, "What the fuck would you say that for? You must be crazy! Why don't you leave me the fuck alone, you bitch?"

The sound rippled through the neighborhood and echoed into the hallway outside of my room.

My dad's friends mumbled at him, trying to cease his tirade, and Mom tried to reason with him. But it didn't work. He had transformed into an angry, marauding beast.

The door to the front of our house opened, then slammed, and I heard footsteps walking outside. My dad kept up the shouting from inside the house, louder and louder each time.

He told my mom that she was "stupid."

My barely six-year-old heart raced beneath the covers I held tightly to my chest. I kept staring out at the manufactured light in the hallway, hoping for something, anything, that I could see. But there was nothing, just the same view of the hall and the dark walls of my room—my brothers all around remaining peacefully unaware.

I am completely alone. What's going to happen to Mom?

The yelling went on for about an hour. My dad simply lost his mind, and he took all of his frustration out on her. He pummeled her with cruelty.

And I didn't understand.

Shades of blue and yellow light began painting the wall opposite from me, as the shouting turned to silence. Quiet once more, I grew calmer, but was not at ease.

After hearing that my parents had also fallen asleep, I too hoped to rest. My young eyes eased their way shut and minutes after dawn I slipped away into a world of dreams.

I awoke only about an hour later, when my brother Mando jumped off of the top bunk. He was laughing and messing around with Ruben. I saw Richard lazily wander into my parent's room. I heard my mom preparing breakfast in the kitchen. Everything seemed normal again. Nobody was talking about the fight. Nobody seemed to be on edge, like me.

When I walked out into the living room, a couple who had stayed the night on the couch was packing up their things to leave. They had stayed through the whole fight. Bleary eyed and quiet, reeking of alcohol and cigarette smoke, they said goodbye to Mom and walked out the back door.

When I walked into the kitchen, Mom said, "Good morning *Mijo*! How did you sleep, my love?"

As I rubbed my eye with my left fist I replied, "Pretty good."

It would be many years before I would tell her that I heard the fighting. It would be many years before I told her that I was scared for her. And it would be years until I could honestly tell anyone that I slept pretty good last night.

On the very next day after my birthday party and the big, senseless fight that my parents had in the middle of the night, I went into their room to play with the Crayola Caddy that I had received for my birthday. It was a school bus yellow art organizer that had crayons, markers, paint, watercolors, and paintbrushes. It would spin around so you could grab your art supplies more easily. I had it set up in my parent's bedroom since the day before, waiting for everyone to leave so I could use it.

But just as I got out a piece of paper and grabbed a crayon, I looked over to see Mom with a very concerned look on her face. She was looking up at the TV, one hand over the top of her mouth. Standing statue-like, she gasped.

"Oh my gosh, who would do something like that?" she wondered aloud.

Just as my dad started to make some sarcastic remark, Mom shushed him and demanded that he watch along with her.

I looked up at the TV to see what she was watching. On the screen I saw a pencil sketch of a man with a long face, curly hair, and dark, intense eyes. The TV speakers blared with the following announcement:

> "In the last three days, 'The Walk-In Killer' has broken into two different residences in the Los Angeles area. On Wednesday, May 29, the suspect broke into a home just outside of Monrovia, bludgeoning 84-year-old woman Mabel Bell to death with a hammer and brutally raping her 81 year old sister Florence Lang. The Walk-In Killer drew a pentagram, a

symbol for devil worship, on Lang's inner thigh. Then, two days ago, on

May, 30, the suspect broke into a Burbank home through a doggy door

and attacked 41 year old Ruth Wilson. He dragged her out of her bed,

took her into her twelve year old son's room and brutally raped and

sodomized her while her son listened to the entire incident from a locked

closet. 'The Walk-In Killer' remains on the loose. This composite sketch

outlines a Mexican man in his twenties. He is approximately 6 feet, 2

inches and has been seen wearing a black sweatshirt and black hat. He

is armed and extremely dangerous. If you have any information on this

case, please contact your local police department."

To this day, I remember that news report very vividly. I remember seeing the crime scenes with people crying outside of homes surrounded by yellow police tape. Things seemed chaotic, as if everyone's dreams had been broken, their misery on display for all to see. A sinking sensation crowded my stomach.

I had never seen my mother with such fear in her eyes. She was always very cautious not to show negative emotions or anxiety in front of us because she worried that it would hurt us or make us scared. In most instances, Mom sugar-coated things to protect us, but, with the 'Walk-In Killer,' she was taken so off guard by fear that she didn't have the wherewithal to hide it.

When the report was over, she turned off the TV and went straight over to the windows in her bedroom to begin locking up the house. We had those old hand-crank windows that you had to give yourself a hernia just to work. She wound all of them shut as if the killer were outside pounding at the door.

That night, she brought us all together after dinner in the living room to tell us that we were no longer allowed outside of the house unless we were with my oldest brother Richard.

Ruben, frustrated by the prospect of a new rule, said, "Why Mom? That's not fair."

Mom, pained and without words for a minute, used a very matter-of-fact tone.

She said, "Well, Mijos, there have been some crimes committed by a man in Los Angeles. The police don't really know why he does this, or how he chooses his victims, but he enters into people's homes at night and hurts them. I'm so sorry. I don't want to tell you these things," she justified, wrought with emotion. "But you need to know that it is very important to be with your brothers at all times. Nobody should be alone right now."

With darkness soon shading the walls of our home once again, I knew that it was almost time to go to bed. Pressure mounted in my chest. I became more aware of my breathing, more aware of the seemingly infinite selection of miniature sounds that drenched city life.

I didn't want to go to sleep anymore. I didn't want to go to sleep ever again!

In an effort to avoid my fate, I snuck into my parent's room when they weren't there and hid underneath a chair in the corner. I hoped they might not realize, and I could stay the night with them instead. Mando and I's room was the farthest away from my parents, and the closest to the windows.

What if the 'Walk-in-Killer' came to our house? Wouldn't I be the first he'd hurt?

A few short minutes went by, giving me faint hope that my plan was working—until Mom opened the door. She discovered me immediately.

"What are you doing under there, my love? You're so silly. Come on out and get ready for bed," she said.

Darn. Plan failed.

I reluctantly squeezed my way out from under the chair and proceeded to follow orders. This was going to be another long night. I brushed my teeth and put on my pajamas before slipping beneath my covers. My brothers, as usual, didn't seem to be troubled one bit. Mando made a fart noise and Ruben started laughing uncontrollably. Richard scolded them for acting stupid. Then, as the minutes passed, the inevitable happened. They drifted to sleep once more.

And I was completely alone again.

It was a combination of things. With a family of six, I was never physically alone—ever. That's not what I'm talking about. No, it was this growing sense of isolation that was building inside of me, especially at night. During the daytime, distractions abounded. The daytime helped to quiet the incessant ticking in my head. But at night, when everyone else had gone to sleep, I heard it once again.

Tick. Tick. Tick.

There was a Mickey Mouse clock that sat on the small table across from my bed, and I consciously listened for it, every second of it.

Tick. Tick. Tick.

Each sound seemed longer than the last as time slowed in my brain. Yet, it was not the clock that I actually heard. It was the enigmatic thoughts flaring to life in my brain. They lay dormant until it grew dark and quiet around me. Then they surfaced, before sinking back to their origin. But I could feel that they wouldn't go away. They were never gone. And when the gyrations of life gave way to a drifting respite, they reemerged, more alive than ever.

Fearful at home and at school, 'The Walk-In Killer' investigation made it so I didn't feel safe anywhere. Days later, two more women had been killed when he crept into their homes and slit their throats.

The neighborhood was on high alert.

One day at school lunch, I remember a girl running full speed down to the asphalt play area screaming, "*El Matador*! *El Matador*!" meaning 'the murderer' in Spanish.

Within moments, the noon-duty aides, our supervisors during recess, began blowing whistles and herding children back toward their classrooms.

Everyone was running and shouting, "*El Matador*! *El Matador*!"

With my eyes looking up at the blue concrete schoolhouse, I saw a mob of frantic, running children streaking as fast as they could into the building, blocking up the entrance like a bunch of hillbillies cramming into Walmart on the day after Thanksgiving.

As it turned out, the girl had been outside of the school fences and a woman approached her with a knife shouting, "*Te voy a matar*," or 'I'm going to kill you.' The girl wasn't lying or anything, but when people heard '*El Matador*,' everyone automatically thought it was 'The Walk-In Killer. His killing spree was causing widespread panic, and the school started sending home leaflets with information about how to protect your family from him.

We were instructed to lock all of our windows and doors, to not go out after dark, to call the police immediately if anything unusual were going on in our neighborhood. The scariest part was that there was no rhyme or reason to his approach. He killed men and women, old and young, suburb and city, with weapons ranging from knives and guns to tire irons and hammers. There was no pattern, and many of the murders happened within a few miles of our house.

Nobody was safe.

As Kindergarten finally came to a close in June, I had become keenly aware of a reality that I could not shirk. With a molester preying upon me at school, nightmares terrorizing my sleep, parents partying and fighting late into the night, and an indiscriminate murderer on the loose in the area, it seemed like there was nowhere to hide.

Yet, the most troubling thing might have been that I didn't have it in me to tell anyone what I was feeling. I just wanted all of it to go away, as if none of it had ever happened.

But all of these things did happen. Every time I felt some of the weight lifting from my mind, it would turn to night, and the cycle would reboot. A creeping, incessant tension had flooded my brain, as a hard rain overflows a riverbank, and I didn't know how to cope. I didn't know how to express myself.

My parents didn't talk to me about it. My brothers didn't talk about it. The kids at school didn't seem to have a care in the world. All of this convinced me that I was different—a misfit, an oddball— from the group. I wasn't quite like my family. And I wasn't quite like the rest of the kids at school.

I couldn't place my finger on it.

I seemed to be aware of everything, like an adult in a kid's body—the smells, the sounds, and the deviations from normal patterns. I wanted to rationalize. What does my nightmare mean? Why was Dad yelling at Mom? Why did Eric choose me?

And all I could do is watch the time creep by slowly, as it always had. All I could do was dream of a place that wouldn't be so harrowing, so absent. What I wanted was a time machine that could take me away from my time and place. I felt deep in my soul that this body, this home, this life, did not fit.

It didn't feel like, me.

Chapter 8

On a muggy Los Angeles summer day, like any other, news came that would change my family forever. The structure, the daily rituals, the rules, all began to slowly fade from its effects.

My brothers and I were out in the street playing freeze tag when my mom told Richard to gather the four of us and bring us into our parent's room to talk.

We were never all called into their room for a talk at once, so it was painfully obvious that something strange was about to occur. Richard and I climbed onto my parent's bed. Mando and Ruben found a seat along the bedside. My parents had a waterbed, and every time Richard moved I was swept upward then rocked down. I sat with my hands in my lap, my head tilted up at my mom and dad, bobbing like a duck in choppy waters, anticipating the news to come.

There was clearly a tense feeling because my brothers, who almost always started joking about something whenever presented with a prolonged moment of silence, sat quietly like me. It was as if we had all unknowingly been Survivor contestants and one of us was going to get voted off the island.

Please let it be me!

The dim lights shone faintly through the wafting smoke that filled the room from Dad's cigarette. It seemed to me as if they didn't know what they were going to say. Did someone die? Are we in trouble? Are they getting a divorce? Oh God, we're not getting the sex talk are we? Our young minds did all the things that young minds do.

Mom, as usual, was the one to initiate the conversation. Dad rarely communicated to us directly.

Mom said, "Ok, Mijos. I know that you have been a little confused lately by some things that have been going on around here."

No shit Sherlock. What's your next case?

She continued, "There have been some funny smells, and Richard has been asking us why we always have our door locked. We want to be honest with you about everything. We don't want you to think that we're hiding things from you."

Pausing and looking over to my dad with her ever-loving, sympathetic eyes, she said, "Your father lost his job at Farmer John last month, and he hasn't been getting paid like he used to. That means that we have needed to find other ways to get money."

The sound of The Doors emanated at low volume from the record player, fostering a groovy, smoke-filled 1970's aura. Usually, my dad would make some tension-breaking inappropriate comment, like a racial joke or something. However, he said nothing, just looked away from us blankly. And The Doors were the soundtrack to the awkward nonverbal exchange we observed between Mom and Dad. They were silently arguing about who would speak next.

Then, Mom begrudgingly took over the conversation.

"Mijos, we have to make money in whatever way we can. For the last month or so, one of the ways we have been getting money is by selling things to people that some people do not think is okay. It's not legal to sell these things. That's why we have to lock the door, and these things are creating the smells that you have been wondering about."

"Peanut, do you have something to show them?" she asked in my dad's direction, clearing her throat with an insinuative tone.

My dad grumbled a bit as he stood up to reach for a wooden box sitting on top of the large headboard at the end of their bed. He lifted a wood-framed mirror with Garfield, the cartoon cat, on it and placed it on the bed. His hand reached inside of the box and pulled out a little plastic bag with herbs in it. He pried open a little box, pulling out a tiny square of paper. When he dumped the herbs into the box, I could see that they were light green with tiny little red hairs wrapping all the way around. They smelled like a complicated mixture of sweet chocolate and pungent skunk. My dad skillfully wrapped the greenery up into the square of paper until it looked like a thin little cocoon, narrowed at both ends. He lit it on fire and pressed the other end up against his lips. A wispy cloud of rich smoke grew from his hands and stretched gracefully toward the ceiling.

As my dad went through all of these steps, Mom narrated like an airline stewardess explaining the appropriate way to fasten a seatbelt.

She said, "What you do is you take the herbs out of the baggie and place them on the paper. Then, you use your hand to roll it tightly so that it is all held securely inside and roll it up. Your father is licking the paper right now so that it will stick together. Then he will light it on fire and inhale it. That's the smell that you have been noticing around the house."

"This is herb," he said in a raspy, breathless tone, the smoke billowing steadily from his mouth. "It's a naturally growing plant that people use to make themselves feel good and help them relax."

As kids, we sat and watched, hanging on every word of this Bizzaro World lecture they offered on how to smoke pot the right way.

Dad handed me the baggie filled with the greenery and said, "Here, you can smell it."

I gingerly grabbed the edges of the plastic, and leaned my head in to inspect and study the composition of this strange vegetation. With the smoke in the air and my nose in the bag, it smelled familiar from nights past. And for the first time I had put the smell to a tangible thing, something I could understand—relatively speaking.

After I passed the bag over to Richard and he passed it back to Mando, my dad said, "If you ever want to try this, if some of your friends start doing it or you are curious, I want you to come to me first. You hear?"

"Yes, Dad," we replied in a scattered, imperfect attempt at unison.

"I don't want you ever going out and buying this from someone else or trying it on the streets."

Dad confiscated the bag from Ruben and placed it back into the wooden box. Still puffing on the cigarette thingy that he had just rolled for himself, he pulled out another baggie. He held it up in front of us.

It looked like a bag filled with clumps of sugar.

He poured the bag out onto the Garfield mirror, and, with a flat-bottomed metal cup, he began pressing the stuff up against the mirror. It crushed gently and easily as it dissipated into an expanse of crumbled white sand.

Continuing the demonstration, he showed us a normal dose and he showed us the point at which the chemical would become too dangerous. He explained what it should look like and what it shouldn't look like.

Mom said, "This is a different chemical that your dad sells to people. When people use it, they feel happy and excited, but, just like the other stuff, it isn't legal to have or sell. You can get in trouble, and it can be dangerous."

My dad then chimed in. "People used to use this stuff for medicine. It helps get rid of pain and stop people from feeling down in the dumps. They even used to use it in Coca-Cola! Kids would drink it and get all hyper and excited. Some people got addicted to it so the government decided that people shouldn't use it anymore. But people get addicted to pain killers too. People get addicted to alcohol, and they can die from it. Either way, people can't get it. It's against the law, but people still want it. I help them."

Then, Mom took a crack at it.

"Even our friends use these things, Mijos. Their kids do not know and they won't tell, but we want to be honest with you. We want you to be aware because if you don't know all of this then we could all get in a lot of trouble," she explained.

Now that the conversation became more open, my parents went back and forth as we listened intently, not knowing exactly what to think of the whole conversation. Honestly, as a kid, it didn't seem like a big deal. I didn't really understand what they were telling us.

Richard, who was ten years old at the time, was the first of us to chime in.

"But Mom," he said. "I heard at school that these things are bad and that people who sell them are criminals who hurt and kill people."

"No, my love," she interrupted, not wanting my brother to get carried away. "All kinds of people do these things, and we're only telling you about this because of the *D.A.R.E.* program that all of you are going to go through at school. Police officers are going to come in and tell you that people who do drugs are all violent, like mobsters, but it isn't true. If you tell them, though, then we would get in major trouble."

"If you talk about these things at school with teachers or police, or even if you tell our friends and family, then strange people will come to our home and take you away from us. They might even put us in jail and we wouldn't get to see each other anymore," Mom told us.

Now, beginning to talk a little faster, in a slightly desperate tone, she got emotional. I became scared that somebody was going to take me away from her.

My dad said, "Look, you guys aren't going anywhere and we aren't going to get into any trouble. Just make sure that when the police come in and your teachers start talking to you about these things that you just stay quiet and don't talk about any of the things we showed you today."

"Do you understand?" he asked, finally making eye contact with me.

"Yes, Dad," we said softly, clearly overwhelmed.

"I just love you so much, Mijos," Mom exclaimed, bringing us all in for a group hug. "Now, go back out and play. Everything will be just fine."

We all walked out uncertain about what we had just seen. Stepping out of the back door and into the driveway, an ominous feeling hovered over me. How am I supposed to take that? What does this mean? Are my parents going to be in trouble? Will I be sent away to live with strangers?

I didn't know. Again, I was left with a secret—another thing that I knew would have consequences if I shared with the outside world.

As a family, we never talked about drugs again. The only thing that changed is that they would be used and distributed openly in front of us from that day forward because my parents no longer had anything to hide.

Sure enough, two weeks into first grade, my teacher announced that we were having a special guest. With a knock on the door, she went over to answer and in walked one police officer, named Officer Wong, and a gigantic bird mascot wearing a *D.A.R.E.* t-shirt named Officer Byrd. He was a multi-colored macaw.

Mr. Bird cawed loudly, and, in a cartoonish voice, said, "Hi kids, I'm Officer Byrd and I'm here to teach you that drugs are bad!"

"Raaw!!" he crowed.

The police officer stood there stoically with his arms pinned tightly on his hips, scanning the room slowly as if searching for little six year old druggies.

When it was his turn to talk, Officer Wong took one step forward and raised his hand into the air.

"People who use drugs are criminals. They come after children and steal to get money to pay for their habit. Dealers bring guns into your neighborhood and your schools and they will shoot anyone who doesn't pay. They don't care who gets hurt. Drugs destroy the body and the mind. Worst of all, they ruin lives. If you are ever asked by anyone if you want to try drugs, just say no," Officer Wong demanded sternly.

Then, in a corny, methodical tone he said, "If someone asks you to use drugs, what do you say kids?"

"No!" all the students shouted loudly.

I felt like I was reciting the Pledge of Allegiance again—blank minded drones repeating what we were told.

Not knowing exactly how to react to all this, I played along, but I was really conflicted. This big, stupid bird and his dorky "'Sergeant Cop'" buddy were ridiculous. And so were all the kids who were getting a charge out of it.

Officer Wong and his awkward bird friend began their presentation on the different types of drugs and how they affect people.

What is wrong with people? I'm six years old and this is the second time in a month that I've been shown mind-altering chemicals and how they're used. Don't people ever think that if they show all these kids what drugs are and how they are used that they might actually use them?

Duh. Hello? Anyone?

Then I began to feel indignant about the discrepancy between what my dad taught me and what the police officer saying in class. My dad described the drugs as medicines that people used to make themselves feel better. The cop and wise-cracking Officer Byrd were saying that these substances were used by criminals to fool children into throwing away their brains. Of course I believed my parents. It wasn't that bad. Right?

All I wanted to do was just raise my hand and tell that dumb bird and his gorpy friend that they were wrong, but I knew I couldn't. I remembered back to the conversation that I had with my parents. It would have to just stay in my head.

Don't raise your hand, Ray. Don't blurt anything out.

I just repeated that refrain to myself over and over, silently in my mind. I resisted the urges, and, like a sheep, faithfully waited it out.

At long last, the big macaw loped away and it was all over. My secret was intact.

The first grade began with some changes in my appearance. During kindergarten and before, I had been a really cute kid. I mean look at this:

(insert picture)

Yeah, I know. Pretty cute, right?

However, on the day before I started the first grade, I had gone through my dresser to try on the clothes I could wear. Rummaging around for a second in the drawer, I grabbed hold of my favorite shirt. Pulling it out with my round, little hands, I unbuttoned the top button and began drawing it over my head. I yanked at the bottom of it and wiggled my torso a bit. I gave it another good tug. To my dismay, it was way too tight.

I then tried on my old corduroys. As they were around my thighs, I jumped and squeezed my belly in. I jerked at the waist, trying desperately to make the button slide into the little slit on the left hand side. I couldn't.

"Mom!" I shouted, with a pair of pants clamped tightly around my thighs and a shirt bursting at the seams above my chest.

In a moment she walked into my room. "What is it my love?"

"My clothes don't fit," I scoffed in frustration.

She inspected the situation, drawing at the bottom of my shirt and grasping the waist of my pants.

"Oh my, they sure don't," she said.

With my dad out of work, this was a major problem. We didn't have any money for new clothes. What was I going to wear to school?

Mom started searching through Ruben's drawer and grabbed a pair of pants for me to try on. Slipping my feet through the pant legs and guiding them up around my waist with my mom's assistance, I was able to narrowly encapsulate my flubber and button them. Ruben was one year older than me and I was barely able to coerce myself into his pants and shirts.

I had gotten fat over the summer.

My mom said, "Ray, we're going to have to watch what you eat."

When my dad found out that I didn't fit into my clothes anymore, he offered some helpful wisdom (sarcasm intended).

"We're going to have to get you some big checkered pants now, Ray. We'll call you 'Chubby Checker,'" he quipped.

Hilarious, Dad. Thanks for making me feel great about myself!

And, though it didn't hit me at first, I began to grow uncomfortable with this new idea of being fat.

When I got to school and sat down at my desk I could feel Ruben's green, striped polo shirt tugging at my jiggly breast. I squirmed and yanked at the cloth, trying to loosen it up, but every time I moved I could feel the shirt getting tighter and tighter around me. My already shaken confidence at school grew worse and I felt increasingly self-aware.

It sure didn't help at all to discover that my new figure would win me the attention of one of my classmates. A kid named Vinny, who was a rambunctious, outspoken Mexican kid that liked to wreak havoc upon the weaklings in class for his own sick amusement, started to pick on me. He was a tiny little kid—flea-like in his ways—that I could have easily swatted away if I had any level of aggression, but I was meek and reserved, insecure about the way I looked.

Sitting right behind me and to my right, he threw his pencil into my back. Then he mockingly whispered, "Hey fatty, give me my pencil back."

I just sat there trying to ignore him, but he wouldn't relent.

"What's the matter fatty? Too fat to bend over?" Vinny taunted.

Feeling pressured, I leaned over to my left and grabbed the pencil. I set it neatly on my desk, making sure not to make eye contact with him and thinking that I now had the upper hand in his stupid little game. With a sudden jerk from behind me I heard a screeching sound, and Vinnie slid his desk into the back of my chair.

The teacher, appalled by the interruption to her lesson, scolded quickly. "Vinnie, what is going on back there?"

"The fat kid stole my pencil and won't give it back! I asked him nice," he said like a monk.

The whole class erupted in laughter. Surveying the room shyly out of the corner of my eyes, I could see a little boy rocking uproariously back and forth slapping his thigh. In front of him a little girl looked back at me, giggling with her hand over her mouth.

"Vinnie, it's very rude to call someone fat. Don't say that in my classroom anymore."

"Ray, do you have his pencil?" the teacher questioned.

Without saying a word, I slowly reached my arm back in his direction and dropped the pencil on his desk. The teacher, happy to see the situation resolved, made sure to correct Vinnie.

"Now Vinnie, if he ever takes your pencil again I want you to raise your hand quietly and just let me know. Do you understand?" she asked with a raised eyebrow.

"Yes, Mrs. Williams. I'll do better next time," Vinny said apologetically.

"Good. Now, when you see a comma like this one in the middle of a sentence, it means that you pause for just a quick second before you continue reading. It is there to help you know when there is a short break in the words," the teacher continued, droning on with her lesson.

Awesome! I get in trouble for getting called *fatty* and he gets to apologize and act like he's a little angel.

That day after school, I walked home alone. The school had sent home our schedules for the year during the summer and I was placed on a different track than my other three brothers, which meant that I had to start the year early. Walking down the hill toward our house, I kept my eyes peeled firmly on the concrete in front of my feet.

"I just want to be left alone," I muttered to myself.

I kicked a pebble down the street as I sulked along.

These hopes would continue to be a struggle for me in first grade. The more I kept to myself, the more bullies like Vinnie and Eric would hassle me. Vinnie ended up becoming a regular. Every day, he would sneak in some remark about how fat I was. He picked and prodded at me whenever he could, trying to get me to show the slightest bit of fear or anger.

Eric, just like last year, sought out opportunities to force me into the bathroom to molest me. One time, about a month into first grade, he even took me into the corridor at the back of the boy's bathroom and peed on me. It was the most disgusting thing that I have ever had happen to me. Again, because he was a total *perv*, he was aroused by it. Afterward, I had to walk back into class with my shirt soaked in urine and try to make it seem like nothing was wrong.

Nobody helped—nobody even noticed—even when I was soaked in piss.

Thankfully, about three months into the school year, I noticed that Eric was not at school. And the next day he was gone too. Day in and day out, I showed up and Eric was absent. He had bullied me one last, sick, disgusting, perverted, unbearable time.

I never saw Eric again; I don't even know his last name.

I hope that he one day came to understand pain and suffering and anguish that he afflicted upon me. All I knew was that he was gone and I felt relieved that, even though the pain and humiliation of his actions would never leave me, I would not have to confront him again.

I just wanted it all to go away.

But still, and this lasted through college, I never used public bathrooms. I just held it in all day, every day.

The school bell rang, indicating that we had to go somewhere else.

The clock struck noon, meaning that it was time for lunch. As usual, I walked straight past the picnic tables, where all the kids ate, and meandered my way to the back of the playground. Away from the other kids, I could often spare myself the torment of fat jokes.

To increase my chances of being invisible, I gravitated towards the other outcasts—the special needs kids, ESL students, and the enigmatic Asians who were constantly misunderstood and unappreciated within the dominant Mexican culture. There was a sloped slab of concrete at the far end of the blacktop play area where the misfits and I would assemble. The Asians played Chinese jump rope, the special needs kids would usually run around pinching each other, and I would sit down and watch. I just sat in the corner to reflect—to get away from people who could hurt me.

I didn't eat lunch either. I found that when I ate at school I was much more vulnerable to the bullies. A bully seeing the fat kid eating a bologna sandwich is like a bear finding a salmon in an inflatable swimming pool. It's just too easy.

Another bell went off after a little while and all of the kids from the lunch area flooded down into the play area where I was hiding, inducing my blood pressure to rise along with the onslaught of terror I imagined when I saw more kids. As they started to make their way into their respective cliques, a basketball game broke out near the area where I was sitting. Hunkered down in place observing things, I caught a glimpse of Vinny in the corner of my left eye. He was at the top of the stoop in front of me, and he had a fresh victim caught in his talons. He was holding a kid from my class by the scruff of his shirt and taunting him. Then he would strike at him, twisting his nipples aggressively through the cotton of his shirt. For about five minutes, this went on, and the kid pleaded and pleaded for Vinny to stop. His head was hanging in defeat, trying to avoid eye contact and hoping the situation would soon come to an end.

I knew exactly what he felt like.

Confrontation with Vinny was the kiss of death. On the few occasions when I tried to be defiant, Vinny would lash out violently, punching, kicking, and pinching his victim into submission. It was best to just play dead.

Finally, after this poor kid had endured enough humiliation, Vinny got bored and hopped off to seek other poor sap to toy with.

His victim started walking away, and I could see his face turning red. He had tears in his eyes. When Vinny was out of sight, I decided to cautiously wander over to console him.

When I got close, I hesitantly asked, "What's your name?

I already knew his name because he was in my class, but I didn't really know him so I thought I'd be redundant. He was distrusting at first, embarrassed with his face in his hands.

"Sergio," he replied after taking a few seconds to compose himself.

I knew that crying on the playground was the worst thing for anyone in his situation. He was totally vulnerable to the Vinnys of the school. Tears were to bullies as blood is to a shark.

"Do you want to go get some water?" I asked.

"Ok," he responded shyly.

And in total silence, without making any contact with one another, I led him over to the drinking fountain by the schoolhouse, a place where I often found solace. The area was a bit of a hiding place because it was in the shade and above the play area, out of sight from the chaotic mob.

When we got up there, Sergio washed off his face and began to feel better.

Despite feeling nervous, I tried to start up a conversation.

"Does he pick on you a lot?" I asked. "He picks on me too."

"Yeah. Pretty much every day," Sergio sniffled.

Wow. For the first time at school, I had something in common with another kid.

"Yeah, he's an ass. Just don't make eye contact with him and try to stay on the other side of the playground," I advised.

I noticed that he had a Trapper Keeper with him and a couple of books, so I asked him what they were.

"They're drawing books," he responded. "Do you like to draw?"

"Yeah, I guess so," I answered. "I draw in class sometimes. Where did you get them?"

"My dad works for a paint store and he brings them home for me all the time," Sergio said. "You wanna see?"

"Sure."

He started flipping through the book, and it had instructions on the inside for how to draw all kinds of still life pictures. I saw that he had drawn a cartoon inside, and I told him that I liked it.

"Do you want it?" he asked, perhaps noticing my curiosity.

Shocked at the prospect, I didn't know what to say. Nobody had ever talked to me before unless it was about class work or something.

"No, it's yours. You can keep it," I said uncertainly.

"Seriously, if you like it, I'll get you one. I have lots," Sergio insisted.

"Ok."

I didn't know what else to say. I didn't know how to react. He seemed nice, but could I really trust somebody at school?

The bell rang again, and we parted ways.

I always remembered that peaceful conversation we had near the drinking fountain. Could it possibly be that I have a friend?

Constantly a cynic, based on some horrific past experiences in that department, I took the interaction with a grain of salt, and figured that we would never talk again. But I was wrong. The very next day, when Sergio walked into class, he spotted me, came right over to my desk, and dropped a drawing book off.

"Here you go Ray. This is one of those books we talked about," he said sheepishly.

"Thanks."

From that one kind gesture, helping Sergio get away from the playground when he was crying, I had made my first friend. To my surprise, we talked throughout the rest of the year, mainly discussing how much Vinny sucked when he wasn't around.

But then there was art. When I got home the night after Sergio gave me the drawing book, I pulled it out of my backpack, went into my parent's room to snag a sheet of blank, white construction paper, and began to draw a flower that was printed in the book. For an hour, I gazed into the paper, hearing nothing but the scraping sound of my markers from my Crayola Caddie on the page. It seemed as if time sped up and the room around me expanded.

The next day, I brought my picture in to show Sergio. "Check this out," I said.

"Wow. That's pretty good. Look what I drew," he answered.

Chapter 7

It's just a stack of blank, white paper and I stare at it for a couple hours. There is so much that I think—so much that I have to think in order to do what I do. Part of me wants to just leave it alone, to let it be so that it can remain pure—an unrealized dream.

But I know that I have to create.

Once a mark has been made, I know the dream will never be the same again. All of the hope behind the idea will succumb to the struggle of reality, and time will begin to take its toll. Idealism will take form, and, no matter how great, how beautiful the end result of that creative process becomes, it is always disappointing, because nothing has more potential than a sheet of blank, white paper.

I don't know if these are rational thoughts that I go through, but every time I am tasked with starting the full sketches for my latest collection of shoes, the hardest part is always getting started. Anxiety racks my brain as my heart races alone at my desk. And I think that those fears of tarnishing perfection are the biggest reason why. In my mind, the ideas have all become so vivid and, in there, the shoes are as beautiful as anything I've ever imagined. But when they take form on paper, things get so technical, and my once pure ideas are forced to collide with the industry within which I work. After all, I get paid not based upon the purity or ingenuity of my design, but by how well they sell with the label Tommy Hilfiger stamped on the final product.

Do I know what I'm doing anymore? Are people going to like this? Am I going to have to redo this entire collection? Are my ideas getting tired and dull? What if I stop getting better?

These insecurities plague me over and over when it's time to begin.

With all of the conflicting images that I have in my mind, it often takes me days just to get started. I have about two weeks to turn the twenty five blank constructions that I've decided upon for this year's collection into somewhere between 100 -125 technical sketches, complete with measurements, material specifications, color schemes, and descriptions of the most minute details imaginable on a shoe—from the way a sole pattern needs to be pieced together to the size and shape of the eyelets. Even if you think this sounds incredibly difficult, it's not that easy.

The main problem is that all of my work as a design director is cumulative. Projects from previous seasons continue coming back to me. For example, the winter collection that I just made two months ago remains in the factory. We have already sold those shoes to major retail buyers, but the specifications for mass production often get confused. So while I am trying to map out what the spring sketches have to look like, I'm getting emails from a factory in China, and it gets presented to me something like this.

Natalie walks over to my desk and says, "The upper on the Maria shoe, is it supposed to be new masters navy blue or peacoat blue? And should the sole be three millimeters or five millimeters?"

First of all, I don't even remember what the Maria shoe even is. We start all of the names of our common shoe constructions with the same letter to help organize them, but there are three or four different designs per construction, not to mention several different seasons. So we have to go back and look through sketches from previous seasons and figure out how to make the shoe right.

"Masters navy or peacoat? Really? Are you kidding me? They are basically the same color and nobody could tell the difference anyway. And, when it gets to the factory they have to make every color from scratch, meaning that there's always a five to ten percent margin of error between our reference sample and their final version of the color," I say to Natalie.

"Please use standard navy blue," I say to her in an annoyed tone.

"K," she says casually as she darts away.

All I can see is a wisp of blonde hair.

Remembering the second question she asked, I shouted across to her cubicle, "and that's a fivemillimeterthicksole.com"

"K.net," she bellows from another cubicle.

Natalie emails the information back to China in very literal, specific language. It is critical to be clear because the Chinese factory managers usually know only very literal, textbook versions of English and miscommunication occurs all of the time, particularly in the jargon-heavy fashion world.

Additionally, the marketing side of things from the previous season is still in full swing. This means that I'm constantly getting bombarded by others in the company who are wondering if we can use more cost-effective materials or if we can change the color patterns of certain shoes at the special request of large scale buyers. It is quite tedious and extremely boring.

Essentially, I am always juggling two fashion seasons at once. And, the business side of shoe design always has to take precedent over the actual design of new collections. I have to drop my pencil and attend to business and production problems on a regular basis, making it very hard to stay focused on my upcoming deadline for the sketches.

Deadlines are as finite as they sound. They are everything. Business is expecting to move on specific dates with very specific achievements and I simply don't get any more time, no matter how many distractions I had during the two week period allotted to me for sketches. This means a lot of late nights when deadlines are approaching. You can't leave the office until your responsibilities have been met on time.

If by some chance I failed to meet the deadlines that the company established, it means that I would be interrupting the schedule for my boss, and her boss, and his boss, all the way up to the top of the company. And if that happens, I'd be in a spot where my job is on the line. You don't get second chances in fashion.

After just a few hours in this environment, my head starts spinning. Memories of conversations that I had a couple hours ago begin integrating into the office chatter going on all around. Forms outlining design specs are strewn about my desk right alongside the thumbnail sketches of the constructions and color catalogs to which my designs are supposed to adhere.

Sitting down in my chair, I reach for a pencil and stare deeply at the blank piece of paper centered neatly onto a clearing in my desk. My eyes pierce almost through it, and I scan the catalog of designs that are toggling around in my head.

It is time. I must begin.

The anxiety is fierce. I try to convince myself to wait, just put it off for a little while longer. Don't make a mark. The insecurities are rampant, making me question the very premise of my job. Beneath it all I have to ignore the negative impulses. I have to move on.

Just breath. Just breath.

Once the pencil strikes down on the paper, it flows smoothly, and the cluttered sounds of conversation in the office dull into a monotonous, audible drone that slides quickly away from my consciousness. All I can hear is the scratching sound of my pencil. And the lines being drawn beneath begin to take form. With precision and structure, ideas turn into reality before me and I can see the collection taking shape.

While it sometimes takes hours upon hours, the drawing phase feels as if it lasts only a moment. The clock speeds as my mind comes into harmony with my hand. The room widens as my creative senses continue expanding. The solidarity of my mind with my environment reassures me that I'm not alone. I am confident that this is where I belong.

I flip through to the next drawing, then to the next. I pin each one up on the wall when it's finished, creating a sprawling collage of shoes for all to see. Taking a seat again, I hear the grinding sound of my pencil sharpener preparing my weapon for battle, and I continue. Another drawing gets posted on the wall.

As the usual office interruptions take me away from my desk to deal with issues in the production of my last line, my thought process gravitates back to those blank pieces of paper sitting on my desk. I remain in a state of creative peace while I navigate the office and its inherent obstacles. It has to be that way because once I'm in the zone, I can't quit. Who knows how long it will take me to get back to that place again?

In three days, my vice president Bornie has scheduled me for a meeting with all of the decision-makers regarding the spring 2012 collection of women's shoes. On that day, I need to have all of my sketches in order, complete with color schemes, measurements, and a presentation that explains the choices that I made during the drawing process. This is one of the hardest parts of my job—to explain to others why my art looks the way it does and what elements went into my decision-making process. When I start to draw, it becomes a stream of consciousness type of experience. I put in the time for research. I studied the constructions to make my best estimation about what is going to be popular. But when I start drawing, all of the science, all of the reasoning, goes out the window. It is just me and my pencil and my paper.

When I finish the drawings, I look at them as a whole, as a unit, and try to make sense of the collection so that I can explain why I drew what I did. What are common accessories on the shoes? What shapes, patterns, and prints occur most frequently? Are any of the shoes unexpectedly out of context from the others in the collection? All of these questions, along with literally hundreds of others, must be answered before I walk into my meeting. In the end, I am selling the people at Tommy on why the shoes I designed fit the company's vision for this season.

Every new season begins with a company-run marketing presentation on what Tommy is supposed to look like. It occurs in a big meeting room and everything, down to the temperature in the room, is calculated to sell the image that they are trying to project. There is music flowing through surround sound speakers to set the mood. A professional marketer reads a carefully worded script in an excited, almost inspirational, voice. And masterful graphic designs are posted on every inch of the wall along with live models that set the standard for this season in Tommy fashion.

The theme of the spring season is nautical, with prints of anchors and thick navy blue stripes. It is sort of a vintage theme as well that plays on some historically successful looks that Tommy has used in the past. My job in designing the line of women's shoes is to replicate the feel of this room and compliment its image.

Unfortunately for me, integrating these themes and designs into footwear is not so easy. With clothing, there is a lot of space to print and cut and design thematic elements into the product. Jean designers can put anchor stitching into the back of the pants. Shirt designers can have bows and prints and broad stripes. The challenge for me is that shoes are so small. How much crap can you put on a shoe without making someone look like a clown?

For one of the flats I designed this season, the initial idea was to have a preppy upper with a navy patent leather base with ivory patent leather binding and a nautical striped lining. This fit the overall theme without overdoing it. On others, I featured frayed edges on the fabric to give it a worn appearance, as if it had been someone's old favorite beach shoe for years. These simple techniques allowed me to achieve a look that appeals to the customer and falls in line with what the company stands for.

When my deadline for sketches and design was up, the moment of judgment had arrived. This is my single least favorite part of being a designer. At the end of every line a presentation meeting is scheduled, including Bornie, the Vice President of handbag production, Betsie Grass, and a Sales Director. At this meeting, all of the sketches that I drew are up on the wall behind me. The three sets of judging eyes bear down on them and me, and everything is naked before them. Their role is to critique what I have produced, and the presentation revolves around two questions. Why did you design these shoes in the way that you did? And how is it valid for the company?

I always arrive early on presentation days. It makes it easier to be early when you never sleep. On those days, it takes a little extra time and a couple extra deep breaths before I can walk out the door. Anxiety and doubt force my inner voice to fight back and shout some encouragement.

You can do this, Ray. You can do this. Let's go.

I have to turn my Ipod up a little louder on days like this and walk with a little extra swagger. It's the only way I can make myself feel confident on a day in which my whole creative process is being dissected and examined by the people who have the power to squash my hopes and dreams—insert overdramatized sarcasm, I know.

Arriving at my desk, I sit for about thirty minutes before most of the people in the office have arrived. I try to stay calm, listening to the deafening silence of my thoughts as I run through the collection in my head. I look at the sketches on the wall and continue seeking words and making connections between the shoes that I've created on paper and the Tommy Hilfiger image.

When Natalie arrives, we meet together for about an hour, comparing the notes we had planned together and going over each shoe, one-by-one, making sure that we will be speaking with one voice at the meeting. My palms are sweaty and I feel a nauseating pressure in my chest. Looking over at Natalie, I notice that she's totally fine.

"Aren't you nervous?" I ask.

"No, we're ready. Everything's going to be great," she says nonchalantly.

She is totally comfortable with confrontation. I, on the other hand, am completely terrified by it. To me, confrontation is fear. It means raising your hand in class and realizing that you should have kept your mouth shut. It means being vulnerable to the whims and judgment of people who don't really care about you.

My watch reads, "9:55." The meeting is at ten and it's time to walk over. Natalie and I gather our things and move to a meeting room across the hall. The other three are yet to arrive. Waiting, even for seconds at this point, makes me a nervous wreck.

Right before the clock hits *10*, my mouth goes dry.

After the excruciating minutes pass, the three people who will be inspecting my proposed collection enter the room ten minutes late. They formally shake our hands and have a seat about six feet away from the wall of sketches. I'm standing in front of them, as if on stage, with Natalie standing to my left with a notepad. A terrifying moment of silence ensues and Bornie signals to me silently, as if asking, "Okay, what do you got?"

And then the moment is upon me, the moment that I hate more than anything. All eyes are focused on me, beating down like rain on exposed pavement. The walls seem to be closing in and I feel shorter—small and helpless.

But that feeling can't get the best of me now. I know my collection. I know what I did. All I need to do is find my voice so that I can rise above this moment. I try to lighten the mood. Humor and sarcasm always make me feel better.

With a quick glance out the window, I can see rain cascading down, smattering the window with surges of water. "Beautiful day isn't it?" I ask sarcastically.

And they chuckle lightly, as you might after a nervous comedian horribly bombs his first joke. When you are sitting front row to such a disastrous spectacle, you have to laugh so you don't feel the deep, crushing sadness right along with them.

I move on, regardless. I'm not a comedian, okay?

And, I begin. With a slightly broken voice, I explain the ways in which I took the nautical theme and applied it to my collection of women's footwear. The anxiety makes it hard for my voice to catch up. I describe the color schemes for each sketch and how the collection offers a variety of different looks and personalities to fit a diverse customer base. Once I get flowing with things, my voice corrects and I begin to feel slightly more comfortable.

They jump in with challenging questions about each and every aspect of my shoes. I have learned that it is absolutely imperative to answer each question in a confident, matter-of-fact way. If I waver at all about a design, my audience can tell. They will ask, why did you put that upper with that base? Shouldn't the strap be thinner on that shoe?

If I'm confident in the shoe, that's when I will break out the technical jargon. I will start referring to everything in specific millimeters with very precise details about the materials and color schemes. I have to justify the thought process that I went through when I began design on that particular model. I try to comfort them, promising that the proportions of the shoe will come together when the prototype returns from the factory. And any corrections and modifications will be presented to them before anything is finalized.

If they continue to have doubts about a shoe in question, and I agree in some way, I will tear it off the wall right then and there and tell them that I will rethink it. But sometimes, I have a very strong feeling about a shoe and I need to defend it.

One such shoe that the panel challenged was the flat espadrille with a cotton canvass upper. It had an embroidered Tommy Hilfiger logo on the front of the shoe and all of the edges were frayed. None of them liked it.

"Why is it frayed?" they asked. "Doesn't it just look sloppy?"

During my research phase, I had seen this frayed look on a lot of different collections at a lot of different stores, and I had seen a lot of women wearing a similar style on the streets of Manhattan. I was very confident that when it was all finished, it would look really cool and go with a continuing trend that I had noticed in fashion. This encouraged me to keep explaining it to them and keep describing the vision that I had going in.

Natalie jumped in. "I would totally wear that."

After some back and forth about whether the shoe was valid or not, the group approved it and gave me the chance to at least come out with a prototype.

And, before I can catch my breath, the meeting ends.

Blood rushes into my head, and I can feel my temples throb. Gathering up our stuff and exiting the room, I hope that I never have to do that again. But I know that I will. And the terror will strike again. It is part of the job, and I'll never get used to it.

It is like that feeling that you get when you're walking down stairs in the middle of the night and you miss a step. Your foot slips off the ledge. Your stomach drops. Your heart stops. And even though you land safely on the next step, you pause, disoriented and horrified. Since you know that nothing is wrong you can continue, but you are still gripped with an eerie sense that you got away with something. And you just feel like going back to bed.

Insecure about the events that just transpired, I turned to Natalie. "Did that go ok?" I asked, scratching my head.

"Way to go betch. You nailed it."

Out of about eighty-five sketches that I presented that day, only seven were thrown out to be redone. The company supported my vision, almost unanimously.

But why did I feel such anxiety? Why was I so fearful, so defensive? Why did I feel naked and alone when speaking before even the smallest of crowds?

Have I always been like this?

Chapter 8

The noon Los Angeles sun beats down on the back of my neck. Sweat slips beneath my collar as my head turns upward to see where I am.

I'm standing at a microphone, holding a piece of paper, overlooking a crowd of over 400 people. I'm in sixth grade. I'm six feet tall, and I weigh 210 pounds. My husky pants are waist high and held up by a pair of broad, red suspenders. My elementary school principal is standing tall to my right, and, as I peer over at her, she beams back a look of pride.

I have no idea why.

My weight shifts back and forth uncontrollably over the balls of my feet, and I tug uncomfortably at the belly of my shirt, stretching the fabric away from my moist, flabby skin.

I'm uneasy about this whole thing and don't trust myself or anyone out in the crowd. My mouth hasn't opened yet, but I know that when it does, the fear will take over.

I feel completely alone.

How did I get here? Well, that's an interesting story.

Throughout all of elementary school I clung to the only things that made me feel like I belonged, which means that I avoided people like the plague. My friend Sergio and I still hung out together at school, sharing art and talking about the assholes who picked on us. We stayed isolated from the other kids, although our group of misfits had grown by a couple of people over the years. Up until this point, however, I had never gone over to anyone's house to play or have a sleepover. I always went straight home, and, as was my ritual, found my way into the back corner of my parent's room to draw pictures and be alone.

It was now a fully formed habit. I knew all too well how dangerous and harmful other people could be.

My parents, despite engaging in several unsavory habits that would normally disengage people from mainstream politics, were real news junkies—no pun intended. Every night, around five o'clock they would turn on the local news and watch together. Oftentimes, this would lead into long conversations about the world, history, and politics. I would sit in their room and overhear the things they were saying. If I had questions about what they were talking about, they would never hesitate to include me.

They never treated me or my brothers like we were children. To them, we were like little men, free to think and make decisions on our own.

For the past month or so, my dad had been particularly animated when the news came on. He would shout all kinds of sarcastic things like, "Yeah, so go bomb a bunch of camels you fuckin' idiot," or,

"At least spare us from these bullshit comments about how, 'this aggression will not stand' and just tell everybody that you want their oil. At least be honest, you cocksucker."

I don't give my dad a lot of credit, but I should take this time to thank him for exposing me to such an expansive vocabulary at an early age.

Even my mom had been getting pretty excited by the news lately, and I hadn't seen her like this since the 'Walk-in-Killer' was on the loose. Considering that his killing sprees helped kick start a lifetime of insomnia for me, I felt that I too should be somewhat conscious of current events.

As it turned out, the 'Walk-in-Killer' had kept all of southern California on vigilant watch for half of a horrific year, and new information about his crimes inspired him to be redubbed, the 'Night Stalker' because his crimes were almost uniformly committed at night. Due to an eyewitness spotting him leaving a home and reporting a partial license plate number, the police were able to locate his stolen vehicle and find a fingerprint that identified the mass murderer as Richard Ramirez.

When his picture was released to the media, he was spotted after getting off of a bus at a liquor store and fled the scene. He ran into an East Los Angeles neighborhood and tried to steal a women's car. The woman, who was pregnant, started screaming. Her husband hustled out after him and chased him with a lead pipe. Screaming, "*El Matador, El Matador*!" the neighbors also took to the streets. The husband and a mob of neighbors beat Ramirez senseless until the police arrived to arrest him for his heinous crimes. The peasants rejoiced!

"Hey, it's the first time anyone in East L.A. actually did something good," Dad remarked after watching it on the news.

Ramirez' reign of terror had a huge impact on my early life and after he was caught I felt relieved, even though I remained afraid at night.

Watching my parents get all wrapped up into another news story put me on edge again, and after avoiding the subject initially, I decided to ask what all the fuss was about.

"Dad, what is going on in the news? Why are you so upset?"

Still looking up at the TV, he never really made any eye contact with me, but he did provide an answer.

"Fuckiiiin,'" he drew his f-words out for emphasis. "George Bush and his oil men are about to get us into a war in Iraq."

Not sure what to think, I responded, "Where's Iraq?"

"It's like thousands of miles away, in the Middle East—in Asia. They are going to send tens of thousands of young people, only like five years older than your brother Richard over there to fight their war."

"Are people going to get hurt?" I asked sensitively.

"Oh, yeah. Lots of people are going to die. It's going to be a bloodbath. Hell, when I was your age we did this same damned thing in Vietnam and there was a draft. Boys had to go fight a bunch of rice farmers in the fuckiiiin' jungle even if they didn't want to. Tons of people died Ray."

An uncomfortable silence got between us as he pulled his lighter out of his wooden box and lit one of his skunky cigarettes on fire. The smoke wafted across the dark room and I could see the rays of light from the TV piercing through the smoke in fantastic shades of green and red.

"Uggh," Dad groaned. "Why do we gotta keep doing this shit? What the hell is wrong with this country?" he reckoned.

I can't say that I ever cared too much about politics or whatever. I mean, I was only eleven years old for god's sake. But for some reason, peering through the smoke at my dad staring off into the ceiling as if it were thousands of miles away, I felt a tingling sense of unfairness rising from my stomach.

Maybe it was just a contact high, but it inspired me somehow.

Why should people have to die?

So that night, I decided to write a letter expressing my feelings about the War in Iraq. I addressed it to the President of the United States because that's who my mom and dad seemed to be so mad at all the time.

With the clock ticking in the back of the room behind my head, my pencil touched the page, making a mark on an otherwise perfect piece of lined white paper. It read something like this:

Dear President Bush,

I am writing because I don't know why you are sending our country to war in Iraq. Why are you doing that?

I know that you are upset with one another, but that is no reason to kill people. My dad told me that lots of people are going to die because of this war and I think that is wrong. My brothers are older than me and I don't think they should go thousands of miles away to fight people they

don't even know. I love my brothers and I don't want them to die.

War is wrong and nobody wins when things get violent. As President of

America I don't know why you don't know that. Didn't you ever learn

about war in school?

I just wanted to write to ask you why this is happening and tell you that I

don't think it's correct what you are doing.

Ray Serna

I took my letter, folded it twice, and walked into the kitchen where I grabbed a stamp and an envelope from the drawer where Mom kept stuff like that. Neatly placing the letter in the envelope, I licked the back side and sealed it together. I put my address up in the top-left corner, and, in the center, with a black marker, I encrypted the following in big bulky letters:

The White House.

No address. No zip code. No city. Simply: *The White House*.

I dropped the ignorantly addressed letter off in the mailbox outside of the school and went about my daily business.

I had completely forgotten about it until about three weeks later, when my Mom walked in the door with the mail. She shuffled through the stack, making unhappy faces every time she saw a piece of mail she didn't like, until she reached the final envelope. It was a large, paper-sized manila envelope with butterfly tabs in the back to keep it sealed. Her brow furrowed and her head snapped back gently.

"Ray, you have some mail," she said.

In total disbelief, I froze. I had never received any mail before.

With a very confused, hesitant voice she finished her comment.

"It's from the White House?"

I was excited, but not for the reason you might think. I thought it was cool just to get some mail. Who cares where it's from?

I got mail!

My dad walked out from the bedroom and Mom told him the news. "Peanut, Ray got a letter from the White House."

"From the White House!? Ray, what're you doing getting mail from the White House? Did you kill somebody or something?" he asked with somewhat legitimate fear.

Not grasping the gravity of the situation, I replied, "No, I just sent a letter."

Mom jumped in, "When did you do that?" Her voice screeched when she asked.

"A little while ago. I don't know."

"Why didn't you tell us, Mijo?"

"I don't know why I would. I just wrote a letter," I explained naively.

My dad snatched the envelope from my mother's grasp.

"Let me see that," he said.

Tearing the neatly fastened envelope open at the seams, Dad's eyes lit up when he looked inside.

"It's on their official stationary and everything," he shouted. "And look. There's a signed picture of Bush in here."

He let off a quick, hysterical laugh, and behaved like a kid that had just won a trip to Disneyland.

There were two typed letters in the envelope, one was smaller and addressed to me personally. The other was full sized and explained why America had to take on such a central role in the war.

My dad started reading the smaller one. It went something like this:

> Dear Ray,
>
> It is so exciting to see a person of your age take such great interest in your country. We need people like you to keep writing, keep caring, and pass along our great tradition of citizenship to future generations..."

The letter continued on in this tone and I obviously failed to get the point. What is he talking about?

"I just wrote a letter. What's the big deal?" I wondered aloud.

My dad kept reading and moved onto the larger letter, which outlined America's role in Iraq. He scoffed and sarcastically played along, reading certain points with unnecessary emphasis like, "Oh, yeah, Kuwait is one of our closest allies."

Then going off script, Dad exclaimed, "Where would America be if not for the mighty nation of Kuwait?"

He was way more excited than I was, although I had not yet been given a chance to even see the mail because he was so enthralled. When he finally set it down, he gave me a pat on the back and said, "That's really cool Ray."

And he walked out the door to go buy a frame for the letter.

My mom kept trying to explain how special it was that I would just send a letter to the president without any prompting from adults, but I didn't really get it.

All I knew was that, the next day at school, I got called into the principal's office over the intercom.

Excellent. What did I do this time?

It was never good to be called into the principal's office. My whole goal in school was to mind my business and hope everyone left me alone. Now, everybody hears my name over the intercom.

I creeped through the halls, down a set of stairs, and took my seat inside the bland, grey room with sharp brick walls. When the secretary got off the phone, I told her my name and she told me that the principal was waiting.

Her name was Mrs. Wilkins. She was a tall, imposing person who had a strange fusion of firmness and compassion, a balance that only a former teacher could master. Her office was very traditional looking. All of the chairs were wooden, there was a typewriter on her desk—there were no computers back then—and there was one small wood framed window tucked on the other side of a large American flag she had hanging from a pole in the room.

I had a seat in one of those wooden chairs. Just sitting in it made me feel like my ass had already been paddled, it was so uncomfortable. Sitting quietly, I waited for her to explain why I was there.

"Ray, some things have been brought to our attention," she began.

Oh, god. Oh, no. What happened?

"I never realized how outgoing you are," she continued.

This lady's totally crazy.

"What do you mean?" I asked, hoping for clarification.

She pulled out the big manila envelope that I had received in the mail from the White House, and Mrs. Wilkins then explained how unusual it was for a child my age to send a letter to the President of the United States.

"What made you write this, Ray?" she asked.

Still under the impression that I was about to be in big trouble, I defensively responded, "I had just heard about the war and I didn't know why we were fighting it and I didn't want to see my brother Richard get drafted and go off and die. Is that okay?"

"Oh, yes Ray. It's wonderful. I'm so impressed that you just decided to send the letter and wanted to ask you if you would do something for me."

"Ok, what?" I asked.

"Well, I don't think many of the students at this school have much of an understanding about what it means to be a good citizen. Letter writing to our political leaders is a very important thing to do, as you know..."

I didn't know that at all. I just wrote a letter. Why are adults so ridiculous?

"So I am wondering if you would be willing to share the letter you received from the president at a school assembly on Friday. Will you do that Ray?" she asked.

Her hands folded together and she looked at me intensely, examining my response.

Here is what I didn't say: "Oh boy. There is no way in hell that I'm getting up in front of the whole school—me, the fat kid with glasses and suspenders standing up there reading a stupid letter in front of every single kid that goes to this school. That would be the most humiliating thing ever."

Here's what I did say: "Okay, Mrs. Wilkins."

"Thank you Ray, this will be a wonderful opportunity for you to show everyone how smart you are. You may go back to class now," she said.

Silently—shellshocked, flabbergasted, befuddled—I wandered out of the office and on my way back to the classroom. What was I thinking?

And on Friday, just as planned, I found myself on stage, the noon Los Angeles sun beating down on my neck, beads of sweat dripping beneath my collar, preparing to read a letter written to me from the White House. Over 400 people standing upon sweltering black asphalt are quietly looking up at me, waiting for me to read the letter. The tension was thicker than the Los Angeles smog in 1990.

And that's saying something!

My knees trembled. My hands shook. When I began to speak into the microphone, my voice broke, weak and insecure. Reading the first lines, I kept my head down and tried to motor through as quickly as I could.

"We can't hear you!" I heard, as if in unison, from the back of the crowd.

Mrs. Wilkins patted me on the back and whispered, "Speak up Ray."

I tried to be a little louder, with my mouth practically suckling the microphone. I skipped a word. I mispronounced another. The single page extended beneath my fingers and I felt as if I could see text sprawling out over a never ending scroll that could be rolled out miles and miles before reaching its conclusion.

I was still on the first sentence.

I coughed, letting off a fearful, accidental moan, exposing myself to the antsy mob of hyena children waiting for me to slip up. The microphone fired back with an unwelcoming screech. The kids, like vultures, could smell that something was slowly dying, and I knew it was me.

I cringed and looked up, hoping that maybe, just maybe, everyone had been distracted by something and left. But I was disappointed. They were all still there, smirking, judging, trying to hold back the thought that this was about to turn into the funniest thing they'd ever seen.

And right about then, it did. The microphone shorted out.

Mrs. Wilkins tried fiddling with it a bit, but as the crowd grew restless, she simply asked that I speak up very loudly. She instructed me to begin where I left off, which was the second sentence.

Squealing as loudly as I could from the stage, entirely devoid of confidence, and presumably oxygen, I could tell that nobody was listening. When my voice came to life, the students shouted, "We can't hear you."

Oh god. I hate my life. Somebody get me out of here.

Doing my best to continue, I began to hear noises. The students had realized that in such a big crowd it was hard to be reprimanded. So they started shouting things.

"Loser."

I tried to ignore them but everyone knew that I heard.

"Nice suspenders, fatty!"

Dozens of kids were sent into wild fits of laughter at the insults being thrown my way. I put my head down and endured, racing through the text to the best of my abilities. The sky was closing down on me as I grew smaller and smaller.

"He sounds like a girl!"

Throughout the letter I sputtered. I missed entire sentences. Nobody could hear me anyway.

At long last, after what felt like eternity, there was nothing else to read. And I skipped back behind some people where I could hide from the public view.

My principal congratulated me and demanded that the students give me a round of applause. She condemned the kids who lashed out at me and scolded the others who laughed, but it was no use. They had done exactly what they intended to do.

I was the butt of the joke. I was completely alone.

At home that night, I replayed the scene in my head over and over again. Lying in bed, I could hear the kids taunting me.

Fatty! You sound like a girl! Loser!

There was nothing I could do about it. Now, every kid in the whole school knows me as the fat kid who sucks at reading. That's not even true! I was one of the best readers in my class, but for some reason my anxieties about reading aloud made me sound like a deaf kid with Down Syndrome.

The following Monday, after failing to sleep for even fifteen minutes that night, I was terrified to go to school. With shades of blue and yellow light painting the wall across from my bed, I started coming up with a plan. How can I avoid going to school today?

After an hour of contemplating my options and rehearsing the lines that I would deliver to Mom, she walked in to wake us up.

"Good morning Mijos. Time to get up for school. Let's go!"

As my brothers slogged out of bed and began taking cycles in the bathroom, I covered myself to hide, and forced an agonizing look onto my face. By the time she had noticed my inaction, I was fully prepared.

"Why aren't you up Ray? You're going to be late!" she said.

"Mom, my ear hurts. I couldn't sleep all night it hurts so bad."

At least I wasn't totally lying.

After some inspections on the part of Mom, and some feigned cries and whimpers from me, she absolved me of my responsibilities. I had earned myself a much needed sick day to keep my distance from the other kids and rebuild my confidence. For the rest of the day I would progressively feel better, spending the whole time watching TV in my parent's room.

Inevitably, however, school ended and I started to hear kids walking down the block, playing and making noise. The anxiety bubbled up again inside of me. And on that day, the first person that I saw running up to the house after school was not one of my brothers.

Since I was in the sixth grade, they all attended schools farther from home. Ruben was now in the seventh grade and Mando was in the ninth grade at Nightingale Junior High, a couple miles down the street. Richard was already in high school, the tenth grade at Franklin High in Highland Park. It took all of them about fifteen minutes longer to get home than it did when we all went to Aragon Elementary, just a couple blocks away.

The kid that I saw running up to the house was Ruben's friend Angel, who was still at Aragon because he got held back a year. Now, I had the great privilege of sharing class with him, and he had the great privilege of ensuring that I knew my place as his inferior.

He knocked on the door.

Annoyed already, I shouted, "Ruben's not here." I made sure that he couldn't see me and hoped that this would make him go away.

"No, Ray. I'm not here for Ruben. I have to tell you something," he shouted eagerly.

Nobody ever came to the house to tell me something, unless it was to kindly let me know how stupid and fat they believed me to be.

Excuse me, aren't you the one who flunked the sixth grade? Yeah, that's what I thought, genius.

However, his Rubenless presence threw me off, and I began getting a little curious. I went over to the door to let him in.

"You won the essay contest!" Angel said, hardly a step in the door and out of breath.

Still distrusting his motives, I begrudgingly replied, "What are you talking about? I didn't even enter an essay contest."

"Yes, we all did for class. Remember the whole thing about oral, uh, oral. You know, keeping your mouth clean. For class?" Angel stammered.

Now it all became clear what he was referring to. I had entered an essay contest. The teachers at Aragon, especially in the older grades, had been trying to figure out ways that the students could get more involved with writing projects. Yet, nothing that they did could get kids to really take their time, do their research, and write on a topic. For the most part, students would just scribble something out five minutes before school, rambling and incoherent, and then turn it in for some fraction of a grade.

Their solution was to create a school wide essay contest with cash prizes for the winners. If grades don't get kids excited, maybe money will—probably a good thought. As a result, every teacher hammered away at preparing their kids to enter the essay contest, also giving extra credit to any students who entered. So I did it. Why not, right? I could earn extra credit and it wouldn't even be that hard. I remember that I didn't really do much research or anything. I just read one article on oral hygiene and then wrote out some ideas that I had, citing information from the article. It was easy and I didn't think much of it. And I definitely didn't think I'd win. I never won anything. I'm the chubby, anti-athletic little brother. What could I possibly win?

Somehow, I placed first in the whole school. My prize was fifty dollars, more money than I'd ever had before.

Okay! I am going to get to win a prize and get fifty bucks.

Somewhat excited by the prospect of winning something, including fifty bucks, I went to school the next day with a new sense of optimism. Would I get a trophy? Or a certificate? Maybe they would take me and the second and third place winners on a field trip or something. That would be groovy.

After checking the winner's announcement on the outside of Mrs. Wilkins' office, I entered to claim my prize. When I walked in, she congratulated me immediately. She went on to explain that she would have my cash prize and a certificate for me after I finished accepting the award.

It was at that point I realized that there was more to winning than I had imagined.

Her sentence did not stop there. She had something else to say. As if in slow motion, I watched every twitch, every motion that her lips made, anticipating what it might be.

With that fateful mood hovering over me, the next thing that came out of her mouth was this: "…and in order to get your prize, I will return your essay to you. And you have you take it around to every sixth grade classroom today and read it aloud! All of your classmates will get to admire the work you did. Congratulations Ray!"

What is wrong with this lady? Every time that I do something good, I'm going to have to humiliate myself in front of everyone in the damn school? If this is what they give to the winners, what do the losers get? God damn it!

Again, speechless by her generous offer to ruin what was left of my self-confidence and autonomy, I acquiesced, stupidly. I couldn't muster the words to appropriately describe how truly pissed off I was and was thus doomed to make another public speaking performance. I felt like throwing up right there in the principal's office.

Yet, there I was again, palms sweating with a piece of paper in my hand, the principal standing next to me, preparing to read something, again, to a crowd of unwitting onlookers. I was paired with a sixth grade girl who won second prize and we were escorted into the first classroom where we would read our essays to the class.

Mrs. Wilkins interrupted, "Hi everyone. Sorry for the interruption, but we have two *very* special students here who are the winners of the essay contest. They have each won cash prizes for their hard work and writing talent, and they are here to read you the winning essays that they wrote. So please give your full and undivided attention to our second place winner, Maria Hernandez."

Feeling my stomach trying to escape my body, I had to observe Maria as she read her essay perfectly, with a smile, to the class that would soon be bearing down on me. When she was finished, the class offered a light applause, at the demand of Mrs. Wilkins.

Now, it was my turn. "And here is your first place winner of the essay contest, Ray Serna."

I stepped quietly to the front of the room, gingerly holding my essay between my fingertips. The class of students, already bored out of their minds from hearing one essay about dental hygiene, was bracing themselves for the crippling boredom that I was about to smack down upon them. What genius tried to get kids invested in writing by choosing *Oral Hygiene* as the hot topic? I resented that person with every fiber of my being.

I began, "What's so compelling about oral hygiene? Well, it is the single most important thing that people can do every day to protect their health. Did you know that poor oral hygiene can lead to chronic diseases that will cost people a lot of money and pain? These problems can even be easily solved, but…" I droned.

I'm making myself bored for god's sake!

Taking a quick survey of the crowd, I knew that nobody was listening. They were just staring at me blankly, judging. My chest started caving in, wondering what they were thinking. Projections in my mind imagined that they were about to shout, "Nice essay fatty! Look how stupid he is! He can't even read! You suck!" Anxiety and fear rippled through my body, as my voice began racing. I stuttered on words and stammered through periods and paragraph breaks. A few kids in the back started to giggle. It was getting worse.

They hate me. I can't do this.

When I finished, I focused my gaze downward at the soiled tiles on the floor. I didn't want to look up to see the expressions on the faces of those children. I knew what they were thinking. I knew I had failed.

The principal again prompted them to provide a mandatory round of applause and they begrudgingly obliged. With my eyes buried upon my feet in front of me, we walked to the next classroom, then to the next, and then to the next. And each time I read, my anxieties grew in intensity.

Each time I read, I felt myself growing smaller and smaller. And each time we moved into another room, I refused to allow my eyes to make contact with another human being.

When it was all over, Mrs. Wilkins handed me fifty dollars and Maria got twenty-five. We each received a certificate commemorating our accomplishment. She told us how well we did and excused us to return to class. And in this moment of apparent victory, I felt as if I had lost everything.

The troubling part was that I enjoyed writing. When I was alone, I would often write out my feelings. It was a way for me to express myself and allow me to make sense of my harrowing thoughts. When I wrote, I felt like I was at peace without being alienated and alone. Yet, every time that I shared my writing with people, they would make me share my work aloud in front of others. So I stopped after that. I didn't want to write if it meant that I had to constantly be on guard, wondering if my work would be exposed—judging eyes beating down upon me with their cruel, immeasurable intentions.

Expression was important to me but I could not handle being the presenter because I knew that every time people looked at me, they saw something I didn't like. They saw a painting of vulnerability. They saw a repulsively formed sculpture dripping with insecurity. And I saw it too.

I saw it every time I looked in the mirror.

Chapter 10

The sequence of embarrassment surrounding my writing accomplishments left me with one medium through which I could relate to people—art.

I didn't want people to look at me. I was pudgy and awkward. My teeth were crooked and I didn't have many friends. I was uncomfortable with myself and my life and my home. Yet, my drawings produced a uniquely intimate connection with people.

They could judge my work without judging me.

My mother loved looking at my art. My brothers enjoyed looking at my art. My friend Sergio enjoyed sharing art with me. And I enjoyed it right along with them.

That feeling inspired me. It made me want to learn. It made me want to get better. I imagined myself creating things more spectacular than I'd ever seen before. The only problem was that I had nobody to teach me how. That is, with one strange and unexpected exception.

Since my dad began distributing unmentionable things, he also befriended many unmentionable characters. Consequently, these characters became as close to me as any of my extended family. They were over at our house at all hours of the day and night partying with my parents.

One such character was my dad's friend Alfred. Contrary to having a name that sounds better suited to a butler, Alfred appeared the kind of guy who you should avoid on the street. He was short, stocky, and overweight like he'd never skipped a meal at Mcdonalds. He smelled worse than the inside of a forgotten gym bag in the attic, and had an unkempt mustache in the styling of a Super Mario Brother. He wasn't much to look at.

And if you were educated to his biography, you'd be even more skeptical. He was born the son of a heroin addict. From the time he was old enough to branch away from home he got hooked on drugs and his habits landed him in prison for significant chunks of his life. The home that he inherited from his mom when she died was the house on the block that all of my neighbors would avoid when travelling past. The lawn was a mangled mess. The porch was collapsing on itself. And on the inside, cobwebs and collected junk gave the impression that someone had died twenty years ago, the day before putting on a thrift sale in their home. He met my dad in the neighborhood and they became friends shortly after he gave my dad some of his furniture in exchange for a cure to his addictive fix.

By all accounts, he was a total mess.

Yet, he had redeeming qualities. Once people got to know him, they usually found him harmless and kind, if tragically doomed by his habits. For me, there was one thing in particular that made me gravitate toward him.

About two years before I was humiliated by sharing my writing with practically everyone at Aragon Elementary School, in the fourth grade, Alfred saw me drawing. He had been out of prison for a while and at our house partying with my dad. He commented that I was pretty good at art for a little kid. My dad overheard and came up with one of his ideas.

"Hey Alfred, you know all about drawing, can you teach Ray something? He loves it."

Alfred, apprehensive at first, explained, "Peanut, I know a little, but I don't think I can help a kid."

"It doesn't matter. Drawing is drawing. What the hell's the difference," my dad said exuberantly.

Alfred agreed to help, even though his professional expertise in art was unorthodox at best.

He had spent the bulk of his illegitimate prison career as a tattoo artist.

Now, I don't mean that he worked in a tattoo parlor and received a paycheck for his services. I mean that he earned himself protection from the prison gangs by penning their tattoos. He was never an active member, but he knew how to do something that the gangs liked.

Let's just say that his artistic expertise was unconventional. Prison tattoos are not created with professional instruments. He had to build his own tattoo machine out of a plethora of smuggled and found items.

In prison, the gangs had high demand for tattoo artists, and Alfred filled that role because he had learned how to work a makeshift tattoo machine from a former cellmate. The machine was comprised of a regular Bic pen, a walkman motor, a guitar string, and a homemade battery. Alfred would drain the plastic tube of the toxic ink from the pen, slip the guitar string through it, secure it with the outside plastic tube of the Bic pen, and coil the guitar string around the Walkman motor. When he turned on the battery that was connected to the motor, the guitar string, which was sharpened at the end, would vibrate up and down like a piston, making a stabbing motion that punctured the skin just enough to inject the ink.

The ink that he made was from the soot of toilet paper. In his cell at night he wrapped a plastic bag loosely around a burning candle with toilet paper propped up above the flame. When he woke up in the morning, he took off the plastic bag and scraped the inside of it off with a playing card. The soot from the burning toilet paper formed a residue on the inside of the plastic bag and he piled it up on top of a newspaper. Then, he poured the soot into a cup and used a Visine bottle filled with liquid soap to add liquid to the soot. After a few drops, achieving the desired consistency, he mixed it together and had a cup with enough ink for a small tattoo.

Alfred brought me a sketch book with all of the tattoo art that he had performed in prison. The designs and pictures that he created with his makeshift tattoo machine were nothing short of amazing. The detail, shading, and clarity of them were of professional quality, even though the materials he used were anything but.

I would stay up, late into the night, trying to mimic the tattoos from Alfred's sketch book. It wasn't easy to decipher the intricate patterns of the tattoos, but after realizing my unusual interest in his art, Alfred offered to have me over to his house regularly so that he could teach me everything he knew.

Much to my surprise, this unsightly heroin addict knew a ton about art. He taught me about shading. He taught me about colors. He showed me how to make images look three-dimensional and how to mix different components to improvise art materials. Every week, I would spend three or four hours with him, two or three times per week, either at his house or at ours.

And as I worked with him more and more, I realized that he was kind of a genius when it came to that type of stuff. The longer he sat with me, showing me how to do things, the more he realized he had to teach, and I soaked it in like a sponge. Yet, in those teaching moments, I could sense the tragedy behind Alfred. He knew all of these things and had all of these talents, but he lived in a disgusting home by himself. He was addicted to drugs, had few friends, and, growing up in Cypress Park, there was no one to teach him.

There was no demand for his type of talent in the neighborhood. However, after all those years, he found the one kid who shared his passion—me.

He didn't want me to turn out like him.

By the time sixth grade was winding to a close, I had been taking lessons with Alfred for almost three full years. I was becoming a master at drawing things typically inked onto gang members like big-breasted women, clowns with tears rolling down their faces, skeletons wearing fedoras, spider webs, and gothic calligraphy—items not typically prized by the professional art community.

Local gang members, however, found them inspirational beyond their wildest dreams.

During my last month at Aragon, in the weeks leading up to my highly anticipated graduation, I received an opportunity to show off all of my hard work. Right before the bell rang, my teacher passed around flyers for a design contest. She explained to everyone that all sixth grade students are encouraged to submit a picture that can be featured on the cover of our graduation commencement pamphlet.

Thinking back to the writing contest, I questioned whether I should ever enter another contest again in my life. However, in the end I couldn't resist. It's not like I had anything else to do. At least I'd be drawing something that was assigned by school instead of ignorantly drawing gang symbols.

Right when I got home, I started working on my submission for the contest. Our school mascot was an eagle so I decided to draw an eagle with a graduation cap on, with a scroll unraveling out from his wing to the floor. I added detail to the feathers and practiced the shading techniques that Alfred and I often worked on.

As it turned out my picture came out pretty well, and, as I filed into my row of chairs next to my classmates at graduation, I was handed a booklet with the picture I drew printed on the front. Sitting down in my seat, I stroked my finger gently across the page and admired the art I had created. Looking back for a moment, I saw all of the parents in rows. They too were enjoying it. And all of the students, the same ones who had laughed me off stage after reading a letter from the president, peered down at their booklets, apparently granting me approval.

Right beneath my drawing these words appeared:

Artwork created by: Ray Serna, 1991 Aragon graduate.

For once, I could show off my creation without being the object of people's scorn and judgment. For once, I could be on stage without being featured. For once, people could learn of me without seeing me.

And I smiled, but only on the inside.

Chapter 11

Feeling good was getting a whole lot harder around my house. Everyone was getting older and my parents had less and less money since Dad's most stable source of income was coming from the sale of non-taxable items. It seems that the family had drifted apart in the time between sixth and seventh grade. Richard was going into the eleventh grade and spent most of his time at his girlfriend's house. Mando was entering the tenth grade and spent most of his time at his weird friend's house reading comic books and so on. And Ruben was totally falling apart, walking around with a shaved head and Dickies pants with the neighborhood dopes that spent the bulk of their time looking for trouble.

It made me think back to the last time everyone seemed to do everything together. It made me think of Christmas, 1987. I was in third grade. Richard was still in sixth at Aragon Elementary. For all the years of my life, it was our tradition to wake up early on the twenty-fifth of December, get dressed up, and walk five houses up to grandma and grandpa's house. We were all lined up neatly in a row, following no more than two steps behind Mom and Dad, and everyone was filled with the excitement of young children on Christmas.

As I mentioned earlier, Grandma and Grandpa's house was like a museum. Everything was perfect and all for show—neatly packaged and tidied up like the inside of a catholic church on Sunday. When we walked in the door, the living room looked exactly like it always had. The bright red shag carpet was spotless, the old oak coffee table was without a scratch, and the gigantic saltwater fish tank was shined and glistening from the sun beaming through the windows, with tightly pressed curtains tied up with a golden tasseled rope.

Yet, one thing was very different on Christmas, and it was something that all of us waited for all year long. Grandpa was jovial, wearing a furry red and white Santa hat, with a black hefty bag slung across his back that was bursting at the seams with presents for his grandkids. Grandpa always loved Christmas, and we knew that for one day, even if we wouldn't see it again for another year, his eye had a sparkle that made him careless and light-hearted. It was as if for one day he could forget about the hardships of his life and the atrocities he had seen in war and be a child with us again.

On that day, we played as a family, laughed as a family, and enjoyed every moment of it. I unwrapped the art supplies that I was given and drew pictures on the coffee table while grandpa knelt on bended knee showing Ruben how to put together his toy train. Mom smiled while talking to Grandma, a rarity in itself, and Dad was clearheaded and fun, helping Mando pick up the mangled piles of wrapping paper.

It was a magical family day. And it would turn out to be the last.

The next summer, Grandpa was behaving strangely. He was experiencing tunnel vision and taking days off of work—something that he had never done in the past. Grandpa was always known as an excessively hard and reliable worker, the kind of guy who wouldn't take a day off work if his right arm got chopped off.

On his days off, he went to church.

Soon after, he was diagnosed with a massive brain tumor.

In the days leading up to the surgery to remove the tumor, Ruben went to church with him. They would sit together in the pews, Ruben dressed like a fine young gentlemen, praying and praying, over and over. Grandpa always told Ruben that *if you pray enough, God will fix anything.*

Grandpa was an extremely tough man, and ever since Ruben was old enough to walk, they shared a special bond. They both loved toys and assembling them, like toy trains and model cars. Ruben would go over alone to see him on a pretty regular basis, something my other brothers and I never did.

So Ruben was particularly affected when Grandpa's health was deteriorating.

For whatever reason, my dad, who deeply cared about Grandpa even though it was against custom for two men in my family to ever say it, never really took the brain tumor seriously. I think he just assumed that Grandpa would pull through because it was part of his character to never give up.

However, despite all of the prayer, Grandpa went in for surgery and when he came back he never looked the same. His speech was jumbled and hard to understand and his skin was pale, his muscles weak. Every time that we came over, hoping that he would show some signs of improvement, it became more and more obvious that he was drifting away.

On Thanksgiving of 1988, all of my family came up to Grandpa's house to drop off a cheesecake and check on him. When we all went in to say hello, it was clear that his condition was worsening. His voice was barely audible and he groaned frequently in pain.

My dad, who had been avoiding the prospect of visiting, because he was still in denial of the seriousness of his father's condition, went in alone to see how he was doing. He knelt down by the bed and tried to speak with Grandpa.

Grandpa, signaling my dad to come closer, opened his trembling mouth and whispered, "I, I would like. Ahem. I would like some cheese-cake."

Dad nodded and left the room, walking into the kitchen to dish up a piece of cheesecake for his ailing father. As he began walking back to give it to him, my grandmother stopped him.

"What are you doing Peanut? Where are you going with that cheesecake?"

He stopped, and stammered back, "Dad. He asked me. He told me that he wanted some cheesecake."

My grandmother, tight lipped with laser-like eyes snapped back, "You will not take that cheesecake to your father. He is in no condition to eat unhealthy food like that."

Flabbergasted, my dad raised his voice abruptly, "He is lying in there suffering. Who gives a shit if he has a piece of cheesecake?"

With complete certainty, she responded, "This is my house and I will not allow you to bring him that cheesecake. It's not good for him."

Enraged, my dad grabbed a coffee cup from the counter and whipped it into the sink, shattering it into tiny jagged pieces that deflected into the air and all over the windowsill and floor.

"How the fuck do you know what's good for him!?!" he shouted.

Dad paused and looked around, biting his tongue, before bolting from the kitchen and slamming the front door behind him. Out the window I could see him running towards home, flailing his arms in emotion. My mom quickly gathered me and the boys and hurried home without saying another word.

When we tried to enter our house from the back door, both the kitchen door and the sliding door to my parent's bedroom were locked. Through the screen windows, we heard my dad wailing in sorrow. He sobbed feverishly, his booming voice rippling through the alley and out into the neighborhood. It was the only time in my life that I have ever seen or heard him cry.

A little less than a month later, my grandfather was dead. That night was the last time that I or my dad saw him alive. Ruben, as he had been doing for months, had continued going over to pray with him, but, in the end, they went unanswered.

And, for he and my dad, a gaping wound was opened that would never fully heal.

At the funeral, my dad sat silently, unresponsive as did Richard. Ruben cried uncontrollably. I didn't know how to feel, but I observed everyone very carefully, in search of meaning.

Walking up to the casket to pay my respects, I approached my grandmother. With clear, tough eyes, she looked at me and opened her arms.

It was the only single time in my life that she hugged me—ever. To this day.

When we returned home, my dad started drinking tequila, lit up a joint, and inhaled plenty of other stuff in the process. He took painkillers and sat alone in his room carelessly consuming all night long. Unlike most nights, he didn't have friends over and there was no boisterous laughter. It was just quiet. The whole house was put on edge.

Later, when my mom entered the room to check on him, he was lying on the ground, convulsing and unresponsive. She screamed from the top of her lungs, "Peanut! Peanut! Wake up!"

Without any luck, she shouted for Richard to come in to help, and I followed closely behind. Mom was smacking Dad across the face, "Open your eyes! Can you hear me? Wake up!"

She took a glass of water from the dresser next to their bed and splashed him in the face. "Get up! Open your eyes!" He made muffled sounds, but no words. His eyes remained shut.

She told Richard to help her drag Dad into the bathroom. I scurried out of the way as they corralled his cumbersome body and drug him along the floor. Mom pulled from his back and Richard from the legs, and they were able to slide him over the edge of the tub and flop him down inside. Mom turned on the shower, cold water descending on his pathetic mass of a body.

Our family never called an ambulance or went to the hospital. None of us had insurance, and there was too much risk that Mom and Dad might get in trouble for the drugs.

So all we could do was wait and watch. Mom signaled him again to revive.

In minutes his eyes opened, pupils rolled deeply back into his brow. Mom slapped him some more and kept talking to him. With time passing by and by, he showed more signs of life, as incoherent and ridiculous as it were. Mom dried him off, and she and Richard hoisted him again to bring him back to bed. All night long, Mom lay with him to make sure that he wouldn't fall back asleep. She knew that if he did drift away once more, he may never return.

Dad lived. He made it through. He continued to exist.

Yet, something in him changed that night. You could see it in his eyes. You could hear it in his voice. And every time he turned back to substances, any slight tendency toward moderation was gone. You could tell that he no longer cared. For whatever reason, even though he and his dad didn't spend much quality time together, the death of Grandpa somehow signaled a death within him.

We never talked about the death with Dad. It would remain as obvious as the changing tides of the seas, but Dad would never venture back out to reflect on what Grandpa meant to him with other people. Expressing emotions had no place in his life. Instead, he kept them bottled up inside and tried to smother them away with consumables that would help him transcend his time and space. And every time he crashed back down, we all knew it wouldn't be long before he travelled again.

Ruben too continued to exist. After all of the prayer and all of the hope, the eleven year old boy was left without his grandpa. From that day forth, what was there for him to believe? What was the point of having faith?

These unanswered questions dripped and dripped, day after day, until Ruben's heart became filled with anger. After all that Grandpa had taught him about prayer, Ruben thought that God had failed him.

I reflect on Grandpa's death in this way because it became a turning point moment for my family. We never went back to Grandma's house on Christmas anymore. Richard and Mando were in middle school and we were no longer all little children together.

And my dad would change, from a somewhat enigmatic man that was hard for us to understand to a distant father—one who lived in our house but wasn't really there.

Chapter 12

If you live in Cypress Park and make it through Aragon Elementary, they send you to a place called Nightingale Junior High. It's one of those places where the pronunciation is very different from the spelling. Go ask a Cypress Park or Highland Park local and they will tell you that the junior high is referred to as "Night-in-jail." The name is apt because, from the second I walked into that place, I knew I was trapped, imprisoned, stuck.

Just walking up to the building gives you a feeling of emptiness. The imposing two story structure is merely a front for a system perpetuated by insecurity, torment, and fear. Inside, narrow hallways lead you through a series of buildings with lockers and classrooms—prison cells for the young.

In the center is the prison yard, an expansive blacktop surrounded by fencing, walls, and distant supervision.

The prisoners were all between twelve and fifteen years old, awkwardly placating their peers and dripping misunderstood hormones out of each one of their seeping, conflicted pores. My only advantage in this environment was that I had been in my awkward phase ever since the first grade. I was resigned to it and believed whole-heartedly that I would never grow out the unfortunate physical condition. These people, I could tell right away, were still deeply entrenched in the denial stage of awkward development.

Each person had fled from their terrifying sense of individuality, instead resorting to the warm and cushy comforts of misdirected solidarity. In this northeast Los Angeles middle school, you were nothing if it weren't for your group, and they could destroy you as fast as they could build you up.

The first clique that I came into contact with in my inaugural trip through the prison gates was the jocks. The jocks were mostly white. As a seventh grader I stood six feet tall and weighed about 225 pounds. Thus, the jocks found it necessary to pretend like an earthquake was striking as I approached. Since earthquakes were common in Los Angeles, the joke really hit a chord. They rolled around laughing and slapping each other's backs like a bunch of monkeys. They wore polo's and khakis. They enjoyed sports almost as much as picking on me. So I guess I was supposed to feel privileged to be the brunt of their scorn.

I, not finding them so amusing, rolled my eyes and shed another invisible tear in my heart. These tears had a hardening effect on my psyche, driving my state of mind into an unrelenting cynicism that came to expect such cruelty from total strangers. I avoided eye contact and moved on.

I clearly didn't fit in with them.

I entered my first class trying to forget the idiots who had been picking on me, and as I sat down my mind began to wander. I thought about my family, which had grown increasingly desperate over the summer. My dad was totally out of work, staying home selling bags of items in demand to the neighbors whenever he could. The problem here was that he emptied about as many bags by himself as he sold to his customers. Typically, this is a poor business practice.

You don't see the local owner of Taco Bell scarfing four dozen tacos every day.

This left us totally reliant on the welfare checks, which only went so far in a six person family. My mom asked us just about every month what service we would rather have, electricity or hot water. Sure, showering in cold water wasn't fun, but it beat not having a refrigerator or a fan in the hot California summer.

As a peripheral consequence of our deep economic failures, my wardrobe was never able to keep up with my weight gain. So my fashion options entering the seventh grade were this: one pair of stretchy grey sweatpants and two plain white t-shirts.

Those grey sweatpants would be the only pants I'd wear all year. Unless there was a *sweatpants clique* at "Night-in-jail," then I could reasonably expect to go without both hot water and friends.

I was already disappointed by my social situation because the one friend that I actually enjoyed hanging out with at Aragon, Sergio, was not attending "Night-in-jail" like me.

One day, I was out in front of my house sitting in the grass when we heard a helicopter flying into our neighborhood. It kept circling around and around the few blocks in closest proximity to our house, when I heard a voice screeching through a loudspeaker.

"Sergio Diaz. Come out with your hands up. It isn't worth it. Turn yourself in."

The chopper continued its apparent search.

Did I hear what I think I just heard? Could they really be hunting the same Sergio Diaz that used to get bullied with me? The twelve year old Sergio Diaz?

Apparently, they were. Rumors swirled around all summer about what had happened with Sergio. I would soon find out that the reason they were looking for him was even more serious than it sounded.

The story went something like this.

He was in his house on a summer afternoon playing with his best friend, when they got into his dad's dresser drawer. Inside, they found a box of condoms, a Hustler magazine, and a nine millimeter pistol. Pulling it out to inspect the impressive piece, Sergio held it up in his hand. His friend, amazed by the first handgun he had ever seen in such close proximity, began examining the front barrel of the gun. Then, in a fateful moment of curiosity, Sergio placed his hand on the gun to show it off, as his friend was still staring down the barrel. The gun accidentally discharged, catapulting a three-quarter inch long piece of metal through his friend's face and killing him instantly.

In a moment of panic, Sergio ran from his home and found a hiding place in a neighbor's garage. When his parents returned home to find a dead child in their bedroom, they immediately called the police, informing them that their friend's son was dead and that Sergio was nowhere to be found. A neighbor had also called reporting that they heard the gunshots and witnessed Sergio frantically sprinting from the home where the shots were fired. The police correctly suspected that Sergio had fired the gun, and, after a short helicopter search, he came out to accept his impending arrest.

He would end up spending all of junior high in juvie. My only reliable friend would not be at "Night-in-jail" to experience the torment with me—though he would have similar academic accommodations after accidentally murdering somebody.

Anyway, these were the things plaguing my mind on my first day of junior high. I knew clearly that I was a poor, friendless, fat kid wearing dirty grey sweatpants. When those are your circumstances, it is hard to even think about advancing your social life. It's more about survival.

Recess at "Nigh-in-jail" was a madhouse of fervent neo-pubescent activity. In every corner of the vast, unforgiving blacktop was a lingering social group of one kind or another. In the center, children ran and pushed and played ballgames while supervisors blew whistles and attempted futilely to organize the maniacal hordes of lawless teens.

The cultural divisions presented everyone with a very bleak set of questions to answer. Where should I sit? Where should I stand? Should I try to play sports? Who should I talk to? How can I impress people?

For me, the question went more like this: *Oh no, where do I hide?*

At the top of the stairs leading out of the lunch room I looked to my right to see the gang members, or the Cholos and Cholas. Cholos were the gangster boys and Cholas were the gangster girls.

"Night-in-jail" was a particularly dangerous school because of its population. The school was home to two neighborhoods with increasing street gang activity, Cypress Park and Highland Park. In my neighborhood, Cypress Park, the CP Boys patrolled every night to secure its dominance. In Highland Park, and frankly on many streets in Cypress Park, the Avenues, or Los Avenitas ruled the neighborhoods. Ever since the 1960's, these gangs have run underground operations in the area and have been rivals for drug territory.

The street gangs held our communities in terror during the night with gangbangers roaming around tagging and banging in rival turf. With more and more kids living in poverty or in single parent homes, and an increase in demand for elicit drugs, these gangs were getting larger by the day—though gang killings would help regulate the population size.

At my first day of middle school, I could see the gang divisions in cold, hard reality. The CP Boys tended to have shaved heads and a lighter complexion, while the Avenues tended to have slicked back dark hair and a darker complexion. They stood on opposite sides of the schoolyard, but they spent most of their time plotting how they could assert their dominance to the other.

My brother Ruben rolled with the CP Boys now.

Things had been changing around the house in the summer before I entered seventh grade. Ruben would stay out into the night, often not coming home until five and six in the morning. When he did, he stunk of weed and booze. He lashed out at people who asked him questions, and was totally unreachable. With his eyes glazed over, he was becoming a blank blob that could deal only with his immediate needs. He was now fully entrenched in the gang culture. And he was only thirteen years old.

I avoided the gangs at school. If pushed in a certain way, I knew that gang members would not just beat kids up, or call them fat, or steal their lunch money. They might stab somebody, and there was no way that I could defend myself from animosity like that.

Not surprisingly, I turned to the other side of the 'prison yard,' where I found a cluster of rocker kids, decked out with excessive piercings and eccentric hair styles. They wore t-shirts with their choice bands on the front with an open flannel shirt and scuffed up blue jeans. The look can be best described as grunge. It was a deconstructed, haphazard way of dressing that made it look like they cared even less than they showered.

The Rockers reminded me of my brother Richard, who was now in high school. Since his last description in the book, he had gotten piercings all up and down both of his ears and donned punk rock t-shirts of bands like Rancid and the Misfits. As I walked by, the rocker kids never even looked in my direction. And though I appreciated being ignored, I knew I would never fit in with them either.

Looking out across the yard, noisy and littered with over a thousand kids, I noticed another crowd congregated against the far wall. They were clad in vintage clothes and looked like a gang from the movie Grease. Their hair was done up and slicked back. The girls wore classic-looking dresses and the boys wore leather and boots. These were the Rockabillies.

I looked down at my grey sweatpants and kept walking.

"You're fat!" someone yelled. I didn't know who or why, but I trudged away with my head down, making it seem like I hadn't heard them.

Like old times, I was in search of a location deplete of judging eyes, where I could find some serenity and peace. And in weaving around behind the music building, I thought that I had found the perfect place. Tucked in the corner was a sparsely populated set of bleachers surrounded by a smattering of misfit types—unattractive without style or purpose.

Maybe I can camp out here until I am allowed to go back into a classroom.

I sat down on the bleachers and took my backpack off. My hope was to get out a notebook so that I could practice my sketching. Then, suddenly, a pungent waft of stench startled my senses and I felt heat bearing down quickly on the back of my head. I swept my hand through my hair, hearing a short sizzle, and felt that it was singed. Turning around to see what had happened, I saw a large Mexican girl, a *torta*, as they would have said in my neighborhood, glaring at me with a sinister look. Her makeup was wildly overdone and I could feel the angst projecting from her eyelids.

She had used a lighter to burn the hair off the back of my head. What a freak!

I couldn't even reach a peaceful agreement with the misfits that nobody liked anyway. Not even my Asian friends, who let me play jump rope with them in elementary school, would hang out with me anymore! What kind of cruel and unusual hellhole is this?

Discouraged by my own appearance and the strange Twilight Zone episode that I had time travelled into, I wandered into a corner alone to just bide my time. After a while, a bell rang and an announcement came on over the PA.

"All eighth and ninth graders please report to class at this time. Seventh graders now must gather and take a seat in the courtyard across from the gymnasium for your official Nightingale orientation."

The crowds scurried steadily away to their next location, leaving behind the space which we had all shared for an exhilarating forty-five minutes of agony and destitution. I tramped over to the courtyard, where hundreds of seventh graders were already seated. The black asphalt was torrid from the glaring sun, and many of the students sat on their Trapper Keepers and backpacks to prop themselves up from the scalding surface.

When the full congregation of students had arrived, the teachers surrounded us with their arms crossed, as if attempting to scare us away from misbehaving at this important moment. The principal, holding a megaphone, traipsed up onto a platform walkway that acted as her stage for this gathering. Staring down at us like a commander would at a squadron of soldiers she began to enlighten us to the nature of this peculiar institution called junior high.

Hello everyone and welcome to Nightingale.

(This greeting was followed by a sigh and a deep breath, as if being welcomed were so overwhelmingly disingenuous that the chemistry of her body wouldn't allow her to say it without rebuke).

I'm sure that you've heard many things from your friends and family about how things work around here, but I want to make the rules very clear to you on your first day. Our goal is to keep you safe and make sure that you have the best chance possible to get a good education. Here's what you need to know.

You are not to leave school property at any time. You are not, under any circumstances, to bring weapons or drugs with you to school. Doing so will result in immediate expulsion. You are not to touch anybody or their property without their consent. You are not to use inappropriate or disrespectful language while on school grounds. You are not to follow people around in packs or groups. You are not to wear blue or red, except for during physical education class. You are not to wear headbands or hats of any kind. You may not bring any paraphernalia to school that is in any way gang related. Your belt must not be any more than four inches longer than your waist.

Your pants may not be baggy or hang below your waist. You may not wear an A-shirt without another shirt overtop of it. All shirts must be buttoned all the way down or all the way open with a shirt underneath. You may not wear dark glasses or athletic sneakers, except during gym class.

Any violations of these rules will result in disciplinary action. Each one of you will have a folder and repeat offenders will be expelled from school. This is an educational environment, which means that the only reason you are here is to learn. Bringing any activity onto these premises that break the law will result in police intervention. There have been many students in the past who have been arrested for the actions that they chose to take at school. I hope that none of you plan to be one of them. We take discipline very seriously here at Nightingale.

Everybody is now excused to their fifth period class.

A riveting speech, I know. It gives you the real sense that you're important and can be anything you want to be when you grow up! I got the distinct sense that I had a better chance of getting arrested than I did of graduating.

The only thing I could do was just move on. I strapped my burgundy backpack to my shoulders, which looked tiny because of how huge I was, and made my way towards class. Burgundy, for whatever reason, made it obvious that I was out of place. In my neighborhood, colors really mattered. All of the cool kids had black backpacks, and mine being burgundy signaled that I was not only clueless but poor.

"You're fat!" another kid contributed as I walked through the hallway—as if I didn't already know.

"Night-in-jail" was very stressful in terms of getting to class. The school was a huge maze, with five main buildings where classes were. We had to loop around and travel hundreds of yards between rooms in just five minutes. I had an assigned locker, but I never went to it because there never seemed to be enough time. I always kept my belongings on me—five books, my Trapper Keeper, and a drawing notebook.

If you listened closely, you could hear a faint screaming sound coming from the backpack, as if it were saying, "Please, no more. I can't take it!" It was so heavy that it left welts on my armpits. By the later part of the day, I just started dragging it on the ground behind me like a dead body. I had seven classes in total, so it seemed like I spent most of the day wandering through the hallways. I was a fat sweaty mess, and kids made sure to remind me of that on a regular basis.

My next class was physical education, and I arrived five minutes late, which awarded me with ten mandatory pushups. I plopped my backpack down and dropped to the floor. Securing my hands to the blacktop, I strained and squealed, arms shaking. My eyes felt like they were about to burst from my face.

"Uggh!" I exclaimed, falling to the ground in despair.

The kids laughed feverishly. "The fat ass can't even do a pushup!"

My teacher looked at me, a whistle dangling from his neck, and shook his head in disappointment.

"Alright, get in line," he yelled, while pointing his finger authoritatively.

He then started us off with our first assignment. "Run a mile in circles around the courtyard. I'll be timing you so that you can improve over the course of the year. Go!"

Without gym clothes, I started jogging in my sweatpants and dirty white t-shirt. My body jiggled and my legs strained beneath the increased pressure from my upper half. Not one minute into the exercise, I found myself trailing badly behind the rest of the class. Soon, some sprightly, skinny kid lapped past me and then another and then another and then another, in a descending order growing less sprightly and less skinny with each passerby, until the whole class had lapped me. Many did so twice as I chugged along slothfully. When the first kids were finished with their four laps around the humongous track, I was still working on my second go-around.

Wheezing and hacking my way along, the kids started pointing and laughing. I felt like I was breathing through mud and a wet sock. My eyes started welling up with tears because of my lack of breath. I wanted to keep going, as if there were still some chance I could avoid embarrassment.

Eventually, after what felt like 100 years of solitude, I was the last one to cross the finish line in just a shade under sixteen minutes. Even the girls who walked the whole time to avoid getting their hair all sweaty had made it in fourteen.

My chest looked like I had been doused by a hose.

The only benefit of my unbearable sloth was that the kids had all gotten bored of making fun of me by the time I was finished. Now, they looked on in disappointment and pity.

My teacher's last words to us when we left were, "Tomorrow, and every day after that, you have to change in the locker room before class. No more street clothes."

Now I have to change in public? Oh, hell no.

When I arrived home, Mom asked, "How did your first day at school go, my love?"

She knew just by looking at me that she should brace herself for my response.

I looked up at her, memories painting every corner of my brain with emotions I didn't want to revisit. I thought of some words but none quite fit so I just rolled my eyes and lumbered distraughtly into my room.

My first day at "Night-in-jail," was wrought with fear and uncertainty and embarrassment. Disappointment abounded within me as I learned that all the time I had spent in elementary school earning just the slightest bit of mutual respect from the people I shared class with had dissipated in an instant. Junior high was a whole new ball of wax, and, for whatever reason, I had missed the memo. On that first day I felt like the distant observer. I watched on as kids that I had known for years put on a show for the people they were trying to impress. Everyone was playing a role, like life had entered into the first act in some elaborate three year play.

I was just, me.

It was a role that nobody liked on the surface, and when people looked at me it was as if they weren't seeing me as a person, but as the role that they hoped they themselves wouldn't have to play.

Nobody wanted to be the fat kid in grey sweatpants.

And since middle schoolers were nothing without their group, the only thing that anyone could do to avoid playing my role—to avoid being the fat kid in grey sweatpants—was to publicly shame me in front of others. And what was I supposed to do about that?

My thoughts, feelings, expressions of self were irrelevant. And this left me with a choice. Do I try to secure a better part in the play? Do I act along with others and behave as people want me to behave? Do I become their clown? Or do I just keep acting like I always have?

This may be the quintessential choice of middle school, those awkward years when the only thing people know about themselves and life is that things are changing and it's scary, when the only thing that makes people feel good is gaining the approval of the group. Yet, in order to satisfy these needs kids have to step away from themselves, abandon the child who they had always been to reach for the adult that they hope they will become. And somewhere in that process, they lose the character that they actually are.

This was my choice.

That night, I went home and painted a picture of a pink flower on a blank, white sheet of paper. And when I woke up in the morning, I strapped on my grey sweatpants with a dirty white t-shirt to go back for my second day at "Night-in-jail."

And so it went for an entire school year.

For those who sought the approval of the group in my neighborhood, who did put forth an effort to be popular and fit in, life got pretty real, really fast. The people who joined the gangs were judged based on how gangster they could be, which meant how many people they could beat up, how far into another gang's turf they could tag, or how tough they could talk. Not surprisingly, this culture of proving your worth to the gang led to violence, pain, and oftentimes death.

On one normal school day toward the end of my seventh grade year, I was sitting in social studies class when I heard three loud pops. The students all ran to the window to see what had transpired. By the time I got over to get a glimpse of the street outside, I just barely caught a glimpse of a black Monte Carlo spinning its tires and peeling away.

On the sidewalk leading into the school lay a boy with a shaved head, no older than my brother Ruben, lying face down, bleeding out into the grass. Nobody in the classroom knew why he had been shot. Nobody in the classroom knew who it was. But we could all tell by the clothes he wore and by the way the car had screeched off, that it was gang related.

The principal came onto the loud speaker and informed us that we were on lockdown. He demanded that all teachers close and latch the doors and nobody would be permitted in the hallways or outside of the building until further notice was given.

As the kids in the classroom speculated about who had been shot and why, I grew increasingly worried about my brother Ruben. Earlier that day, I had written a note excusing him from school. One of the great benefits to all the art practice that I was getting was that I had better hand writing than most adults. My mom let me write notes excusing myself from class because I wasn't a trouble maker and she trusted my judgment.

For Ruben, who was always involved in one thing or another, my handwriting was his way out. I would write him a note and he would ditch with his gang buddies.

On this day, I doubted my actions. What if my note had gotten him killed?

Peering out the window in anticipation, I felt a rush of adrenaline. Outside the door, onlookers were standing around investigating the situation as a paramedic attempted to treat the wound. From the window I couldn't see anything that would tell me who had been shot. He was loaded into the back of the ambulance and it sped off, sirens blaring.

My fear of school had always been palpable, but in this moment I realized how truly dangerous the neighborhood was becoming. Gangs and poverty, bullies and teenage angst, all added up to create a volatile environment which was endangering human life.

When the lockdown ended, I entered into the hallway and overheard a group of people chatting about the shooting.

"It was Caesar. The Avenues shot him in the ass. Fuckin' idiot!" I overheard someone say.

It wasn't Ruben.

I had seen Caesar before. He was a member of the CP Boys, my brother's gang. He used to get in people's faces a lot at recess, whether it was using a knife to pop somebody's Air Jordan's or tripping people as they walked by, he had been known as the type of guy that got on people's nerves. On that afternoon, he paid the price of *fitting in*.

He was lucky to still be alive.

After a lonely, unnerving one mile walk home I told my parents about the shooting at school. I told them it was a gang member, one of Ruben's friends.

This was troublesome because Ruben hadn't come home yet. Gang shootings often led to retaliation and there was still concern that Ruben might get involved. Mom went to the phone to call Ruben's pager, and I sat on the bed next to my dad.

He offered me some advice about the fickle lifespan of a Cypress Park gang member.

"Man, these gangs will eat each other up Ray. Take a look around at most of the people that you go to school with. They won't be around by the time you graduate from high school," Dad said somberly.

A shiver ran through my spine. "What do you mean?" I asked.

"Most of the people you go to school with are in a gang and most of the gang members get killed. They will be lucky if they live to twenty, and really lucky to live to thirty. That's the way of it, and the more you look like a gang member, the more likely you are to get shot. Just watch Ray, you'll see."

I lived in a neighborhood patrolled by street gangs. And the choice was to join and earn respect or to stand on the sidelines and hope that you don't get caught in the crossfire.

My advantage?

The fat kid in grey sweatpants was clearly not a gangbanger.

My disadvantage?

Nobody respected the fat kid in grey sweatpants.

I was stuck in a stretchy, torturous grey area that I couldn't escape.

As dusk enveloped the neighborhood, the shades of light darkened through the panes separating us from the uncertainty outside. And it kept getting deeper and deeper until I could no longer make out colors. Behind my squinting lashes, all I could see were hues of black and grey.

"Mom, what happened to the lights?"

"Oh, Mijo, we didn't have the money to pay for electric this month. Until he pays the bill we won't have any lights."

The earth revolved, the sun fell beneath our view, and I lay in my bed to wonder if this cycle of isolation and poverty was ever going to end.

Chapter 13

When it grew dark outside, we lit up our living room with an oil lamp. Everywhere we went at night, we lugged the lamp along to light the path.

I was learning that making it in life was all about money. If you had it, the food was better, the lights were on, and you could afford having more than one pair of pants that fit. On the heels of a tormenting year at "Night-in-jail," these were precisely the things that I craved.

Money had to be my way out.

Unfortunately, it wasn't very easy to come by as a thirteen year old boy. Previously, the only place I had earned any money in the past was from my grandpa and aunts and uncles. Every once in a while, I would wash their car and they would give me five bucks. After a bag of pork rinds and a soda, I wasn't left with much.

One afternoon, an opportunity presented itself. As I was sitting in the living room drawing a hibiscus flower, my dad's friend Jay walked in. Everybody called him by his gang name, 'Jaybird.' At thirty-five years old, he was elderly within his culture. Gang members in L.A. died off like turkeys on Thanksgiving.

After trading items with my dad, Jaybird strode past me and into the kitchen where my mother was preparing one of her Mexican delicacies, *menudo*. It was a soup that was made with *tripe* (the stomach lining of a cow), hominy, and chili broth. *Menudo* was basically corn and guts soup. It smelled like a hot steaming pot of pee, but amazingly my mom made it taste pretty good. She was an excellent cook, especially when it came to such Mexican favorites.

Passing by my mother at the stove, Jaybird let out a groan of approval.

"Ooh, is that your famous *menudo*?" he asked.

"Yeah, would you like some?" Mom responded.

"Of course. I would never pass up a taste of your cooking."

Typically, gang members were very stern and distant, especially toward women, but Jaybird and my mom had developed a really close relationship. He sat down at our dining room table, which, by the way, was in the living room and barely fit between the couch and the wall. Slurping and scarfing the soup, my mother asked Jaybird what he'd been doing lately.

He told her that the Los Angeles Department of Parks and Recreation had put a bunch of money into beautifying the neighborhoods, and he was helping a friend put together the summer jobs program.

I immediately perked up and put down my pencil. "What do I have to do to get a summer job?" I asked audaciously.

Probably a little shocked by my sudden interruption, Jaybird taunted me, "Oh, Ray wants to be my *burro* all summer, huh?"

"Yeah. I need money," I responded as a matter of fact.

"Well, if you're serious you have to go down to the school to get a work permit approved by the superintendent. After that, I will tell my guy to put you at the top of the list, but you have to have your work permit by next week. If you don't, then there's no job for you. Are you sure you want to do this?" Jaybird asked.

"Does a bear shit in the woods?" I quipped rhetorically.

"Raymond, you watch your language," my mom said with obligation.

Jaybird laughed and promised that if I bring the work permit into the Cypress Park Recreational office on Monday, I would be able to start working. He finished his bowl of *menudo*, thanked my mother, and told me that he would drop off a work permit form soon before exiting through the back door.

My mind grew focused like a laser on the idea of making money. I knew that I had to make enough over the summer that I could buy myself some new clothes. I would do whatever it took to make sure that I never had to be the fat kid in grey sweatpants ever again.

The very next day I went up to 'Night-in-jail' to get the work permit signed. They had to make sure that I was at least twelve years old and in good standing at the school before they could approve it. Since I met the requirements, they returned my form to me in the mail, and I was ready to start the following week.

The Sunday prior to my first day of work, I was reawakened to the fragility of life in our neighborhood. That morning, Jaybird had stopped by to talk to my dad and make sure that I was all set with my permit and exchange some items, again. We shared some casual thoughts and I thanked him for going out of his way to help. My mom sent him home with more food.

She was like the gangster whisperer. Her secret was nurture and Mexican food, and they all cooed like baby kittens every time she gave them the treatment. Then they would go out and cap some bitches and suck down PCP like a scuba diver puffing on an oxygen tank. It made absolutely no sense!

Anyway, we all hunkered down together that night in my parent's room to watch our favorite family show—The Three Stooges. I should say, it was Dad's favorite show and we didn't mind watching it with him because he laughed and actually treated us well when it was on. Grandpa had loved The Three Stooges and it probably reminded my dad of some good times they had together. Grandpa used to call it 'Los Tres Pendejos.' It always sounded funnier to me in Spanish.

By this time, our electricity was back on because the welfare checks had come through. These checks would be my family's most stable income throughout my childhood. Most times this money would pay for our electric bills, but the timing would periodically go awry, probably from my dad using the money for unmentionable things, and we would have to go a few days or a couple weeks again without power.

We definitely didn't have cable anymore. We watched 'Los Tres Pendejos,' on VHS tapes that my grandpa left for my dad after his death. Every time we wanted to watch one of the tapes, we had to press 'Stop' then 'Rewind' and wait for five to ten minutes before the film on the inside of a small plastic compartment had spun all the way back to the beginning. After pressing 'Play,' the blank blue screen gave way to a fuzzy old black and white picture portraying Larry, Curly, and Moe. It was a far cry from the HD TV and Blu-Rays that I enjoy today.

As the show progressed, my dad frequently burst out into inappropriately noisy laughter. And I looked over at my mom and noticed a glowing sense of unease spreading across her face.

"Mom, are you okay?" I asked.

"Yes, Mijo. I'll be fine. I just have the chills," she responded quietly without making eye contact.

I could tell by her reaction that some emotion had overcome her, and an eerie feeling crept upon me. My mom was always very keen to recognize and respect her instincts, and she was clearly distraught by something.

She patted me on the back and walked out of the bedroom. Minutes later, she came back in then roamed back out. She paced back and forth like this for about half of an hour, growing increasingly restless.

We finished watching the show with Dad, then transitioned back to network television.

Mando and I watched TV late into the summer night. When we wanted to change the channel, we had to fiddle with the bunny ear antennas on top of our tiny little TV until the black and white static subsided and a color picture faintly emerged.

It was at this point, my brother and I lying on our stomachs with our eyes fixated on late night television programming, that we heard a flurry of bangs popping and echoing through our ears. Mando told me to turn the volume down so I jumped from the bed and turned the quarter-sized knob on the TV until all I could hear was the beating of my heart.

A series of shots banged out again, confirming for sure that it was gunfire. An uncertain silence drifted over us. It wasn't unusual to hear gunshots in the neighborhood. Every week or two, shots could be heard, caroming an echo off of Mount Washington and into the Los Angeles night sky. However, most of the shots usually came from several blocks away, usually on the outskirts of Cypress Park. This time, the shots were close and furious.

"That sounded really close," I said to Mando anxiously.

Mando, in his typically lackadaisical manner, said, "Ah, whatever. I'm sure it's fine."

He turned the volume back up on the TV.

Mom bolted into our room to make sure we were okay. We assured her that we were.

"Alright, Mijo," she said despondently, as she slowly moved out of the room.

It was obvious that she was uneasy about those particular shots.

After fifteen minutes or so, the routine sounds around the house—my mom clanking dishes in the kitchen, the TV reverberating from the bedroom, and the breeze lightly colliding with the screens of our windows—the phone rang out loudly.

Mom scurried across the kitchen to answer. It was Jaybird's fiancée Viola.

She was hysterical, and, as I walked out from the bedroom to see who it was, I could hear her voice through the phone from all the way across the room.

"It's Jay!" she shouted. "They're taking him to the hospital. He's in critical condition. He was just shot on Thorpe Street! Oh God!"

Mom, trying to make sense of the situation, asked, "Are those the gunshots from just a few minutes ago?"

"Yeah. He was just shot. I don't know if he's going to make it. It was so bloody. They had to put rubber pants on him just to keep his body together. What am I going to do?"

Trembling with emotion, Mom told her, "Stay calm sweetie. I'll come right up and we can go to the hospital together. Okay?"

Viola agreed and they abruptly hung up the phone.

We couldn't believe what we were hearing. Jaybird had just been in our house a few short hours ago and now he was in the hospital with gunshot wounds.

Mom raced out the door to accompany Jaybird's fiancée to the hospital.

But, by the time they arrived, he was already dead. His wounds were so devastating that he had bled out in the ambulance.

Apparently, Jaybird had been at a neighborhood home that night getting high with some of his fellow gang members. As it got late, he left, and as he walked up the sidewalk, he was confronted by a car filled with Avenues, his rival gang. When he saw the car, Jaybird tried to flee up the street. The problem was that he was so dusted, or high on angel dust, that he was about as agile as a one-legged buffalo. He staggered and stumbled until he approached a driveway two blocks away from our house and one block away from his. In desperation, knowing that he couldn't go much farther, he decided to lie down to hide underneath a parked car.

The Avenues watched the whole thing unfold and pulled their unlit car in front of his poorly formulated hiding spot and got out of the car, well clad with semi-automatic rifles and nine millimeters. Then, the four gang members laid their guns down on the ground to get a good angle at Jaybird and pulled their triggers, releasing a flurry of bullets into their target. When the ambulance arrived, they found Jay, nearly shot in half at his midsection, with over a dozen gunshot wounds.

We had lost a close family friend that day, someone who treated us like family—someone we could always count on. My mother in particular had really grown to like him because of how respectful he was, particularly for a gang member. And he went out of his way to get me a job—one that I would begin the day after his murder.

To my everlasting dismay, I was assigned to work out of the Cypress Park Recreational Center. This was the park that my parents and teachers had always taught me to stay away from. Countless horrifying news reports of drug deals, assaults, rapes, and murders cited the Cypress Park Recreational Center as the location for the crime.

Hooray, now I work there. Great news for me!

My first day was unbearably hot and muggy. It felt as if the smog were at ground level, and with just a few short strides I could feel myself sweating through my dirty white t-shirt. On the way, I made a decision to take a shortcut to the park through the alley across the street. My parents always advised me to avoid alleys because there is no way out of them, but since I was in junior high and getting ready to start working in *the hood* I thought I might as well chance it. I mean, could things really get worse?

As I traversed the four short blocks of alleyway, I was disgusted at the scene. There was trash everywhere and weeds growing up out of the pavement. It stunk of chemicals and human waste.

Gross. Somebody should really clean this place up.

There was an irony to this thought that I would realize momentarily.

Right before I approached Cypress Park, I thought about Jay. I couldn't believe he was gone. It made this day all that much harder because I was comfortable working for him. I knew that he would make sure that I was safe during this job, but with Jay out of the picture, I was left with a feeling of uncertainty. And it would get no better when I saw my coworkers.

Outside of the main office for the park stood a crowd of Cholos and Cholas that looked like my worst nightmare. Jay had made a conscious effort to hire the at-risk teens of the neighborhood to help them get some money and learn a little discipline. They were the kids and little brothers and sisters of the CP Boys gang.

And there was me, the artsy fat kid still wearing those ridiculous grey sweatpants.

I avoided them by going into the main office, where I met the director of the summer jobs program. He was a towering, fat gang member named Armando with a diamond stud earring in his left ear. He told me gruffly to fill out the necessary paperwork, which was simply a timecard with my name on it, and to get outside with the others.

When I was forced to integrate with my new coworkers, I approached with extreme caution. They were all congregated in a grassy, shaded area near the daycare center. There were a couple of benches and a swing set nearby, and everyone was standing around in a loose and disorganized circle bantering back and forth.

I felt like I was part of a scene from an L.A. gangster movie.

It was hilarious to watch all of these thugs at work. They were all told not to dress up like gang members, but they didn't know how to look any other way. The boys wore jeans instead of the typical Dickies, but they still had shaved heads and they stood with their chests puffed up and their hands partially in their pockets, their heads cocked deliberately to the side with their chins high in the air.

It was like a gang member Halloween party, in which they all dressed up like normal people. The girls all had crispy, crunchy hair, like they wasted two bottles of hairspray on their head that morning, and painted acrylic nails that clicked together every time their fingers came within three inches of their thumbs. Their makeup was all dark and overdone, like Mexican raggedy Ann dolls with black lipstick, and they overemphasized all of the vowels in their slang ridden concept of the English language.

I remember that when I converged upon the group, the first thing some Cholo said to me was, "What the hell are you wearing?"

And I, with fear and trepidation on the inside, sarcastically replied, "Uh. Clothes."

Using sarcasm with gangsters is not the right tone.

The guy took a step toward me and interrogated, "What's that supposed to mean? You disrespect'n me homes?"

Keeping my eyes focused downward, I replied adamantly, "No. I just am wearing clothes. I don't know."

Just then, Armando, the boss, came over with a trash bag filled with brooms and rakes and shovels and trash bags, and he set it down to confront the kid who was questioning me.

"What's the problem here Stretch?"

Stretch was his gang name, because he was skinny and a little bit taller than normal.

"I'm cool, but this kid's getting an attitude with me," Stretch replied.

"Just shut the fuck up. That's Peanut's kid," Armando responded with authority.

For whatever reason, the kid's eyes got big, and he said, "Seriously? You're kidding me."

"No. He's Peanut's kid."

At that moment, all of the male gang members relaxed their shoulders and took a step back like cats that had just been squirted with a spray bottle. It seemed like this connection had shouted at them in their perverse world to, "Stay back! This fat geek is a protected fat geek under the order of Peanut. Don't kill or harass. Leave alone."

They were like retarded robots that ran on PCP and crappy Mexican food.

Then, one of them, after a solid minute of processing the concept of family, through that squishy reaction center that he passed off as a brain, blurted out, "Wait. So does that mean you're Ruben's brother?"

Way to go genius. Yep, my dad's other son is my brother. Good job. Big win.

Totally blown away, either by the information, or his ability to process a useful thought, he let out a blow of sound indicating his deep emotional experience, "Dammmn."

And another kid on the other side of the circle smacked the stomach of the person next to him with the back of his hand, and said, "He's Ruben's brother," as if he needed to translate for the group.

Then, because apparently they did need a translator, the group let out a collective groan, "Oh!" nodding their heads as if they had just realized why two multiplied by three equals six, rather than five.

Ruben was known widely throughout the gang as a suave, good looking badass. So it was totally shocking to them that some fat, pimply kid in grey jogging pants could be his little brother. They were super impressed by that odd circumstance of facts, which seemed dumb to me. But hey, at least I wasn't worried that they'd string me up to the flagpole anymore.

After getting a telling look into the intellectual quality of his staff, our boss Armando began explaining to us what our responsibilities were.

"Ok, first of all everybody needs to keep themselves in line and work together. This is a job. So you have to be professional, show up on time, and work hard. The workday will begin when I tell you and end when I tell you. If you are messing around or not pulling your weight then you can find a job somewhere else."

He went on to tell us that our job was to clean the streets, alleys, sidewalks, and parks of Cypress Park, and we would do it all together, one street at a time until we finished. Then, we would start all over again.

Perfect! Now I get to scrub off the putrid, disgusting, repulsive, alleyway that I just walked through. And for four dollars and fifty cents per hour? Lovely!

I put on some rubber gloves to protect me from the germs and diseases that permeated the defiled streets. Armando told me to push a wheelbarrow into the opening of the alley and start pulling weeds from the fractures in the pavement. My goal in all of this was to avoid confrontation and get out of there alive with enough money to buy myself some new clothes before school started again. Consequently, I worked in silence, and spoke only when I was asked a question. I figured it was better to seem like the creepy quiet kid than say something I might regret later.

As I yanked weeds loose from the alley and loaded them into the wheelbarrow, I looked over to see the Chola girls leaning on their brooms chatting with each other—chewing gum and clicking their fingernails. It was amazing how much overgrowth and brush there was in this one alley. It was like nobody had ever cleaned the damned place.

When I asked if they were going to help, one of them said, "Those weeds'll bust up my nails, 'n stuff."

"'N stuff," was how kids in my neighborhood filled time at the end of a sentence that they didn't know how to finish. It sounded more like this: "enn stuuuuff."

The other girl scowled with downturned lips and added, "Yeah, and it's all nasty."

"Whatever," I thought to myself, as I went back to clearing the foliage.

In front of me, one of the sweepers shouted, "Eh! Armando, get over here."

Armando, standing at the end of the street checking on our progress came over to see what was happening.

"Look at that pile of shit! Is that from a dog?"

Armando examined it and quickly replied, "No, human."

"Aw, gross. How do you know?" the sweeper exclaimed.

With startling logic, Armando responded, "Do you know any dogs that eat corn?"

"Oh, shit. Good point. So what should I do?" the gang member asked.

"Pick it up and toss it into the bag."

At least for the first day I had a better job than that guy. Throughout the day we found all kinds of disgusting stuff, from human crap to used condoms and syringes—all the more reasons to make Cypress Park in L.A. your next holiday destination!

We all got a half an hour respite around noon, and lunch was provided by the city. Every day it was peanut butter and jelly sandwiches that had been roasting for five hours in the summer sun.

Yeah, rather not.

Instead of eating, I grabbed a bottle of water and slinked away to sit on the swings—as far as possible from my half-baked coworkers before they start making fun of me again. Just sitting there on the swing set, minding my own business a group of the guys came over to me.

"Yeah. What do you want?" I asked, not knowing what to make of them.

Awkwardly, one of them blurted out, "Hey, we heard you are Ruben's brother."

God, what the hell does everyone know Ruben for? Ok, I'm Ruben's brother. What is he, the fucking mayor? Leave me alone about Ruben.

What I actually said was this: "Yeah. So, what?"

"Nothing," the kid replied. "We think that's cool. What do you do?"

I wasn't sure how to answer that question. I said, "Well, I'm not in a gang or anything if that's what you mean."

"No. Like what do *you* like to do?" he asked.

It felt like it took minutes for me to answer. I stammered and stumbled and all I could come up with was, "I like to draw."

Nobody outside of my family had ever asked me, "What do *you* like to do?" before.

My response was acceptable enough for them to continue the conversation. We talked back and forth for a couple of minutes about how school sucks and our job sucks, you know, normal teenager stuff. Yet, the whole time I couldn't stop thinking about that question: what do *you* like to do?

Nobody cared. Nobody had ever wanted to know more about me. What a fascinating concept!

When one of kids said, "I can't wait 'til we're done with "Night-in-jail," I was inspired by a thought and uncharacteristically just blurted it out.

"I can't wait to get out of high school."

"What do you mean, high school?" somebody asked.

"You know, graduate. I want to get done with high school and move someplace really cool—like New York City," I said.

Shocked at the prospect of leaving the neighborhood—almost no one left the Cypress Park after spending their childhood there—one of the boys asked, "Why would you want to leave?"

I said, "I don't know. I want to live someplace else. I want to live in New York and make 100,000 dollars every year by the time I'm twenty-five."

One of them laughed and another chuckled while exclaiming, "Yeah, right."

When they saw that I was totally serious, they slowed their laughter and uncomfortably swayed back and forth—another scratched his head and looked down at the ground.

In that moment, not one of them had anything to say, and sensing that the conversation had gotten weird the kid that originally started up our conversation suggested, "Well maybe we should get back and see if it's time to get working again."

The others agreed and we all wandered over to the crowd, picked up a broom, and went back to our respective duties.

I've always remembered that moment.

I knew that, number one, they all thought I was crazy for saying that I would make 100,000 dollars by the time I was twenty-five. That lit a fire under me because I hated people telling me that I couldn't do something.

But secondly, it made me sad. It made me sad because, even though I had thought about moving away from Cypress Park hundreds of times, not one of them had ever considered getting out. I mean, who would *want* to live like that forever? They had all totally bought into the culture of tough guys and neighborhood loyalty. Their highest aspiration was to have lots of drugs and souped-up cars.

For me, these things were all empty promises—facades for the ambitiousless fools who were too scared to admit that there's a whole world out there that they know nothing about. I hoped to one day explore that world, but those CP Boys couldn't relate. The neighborhood was all that they knew. To them, *getting out* simply meant not having to go to school anymore.

To me, it meant starting a new life. And, at least for the moment, a new life started at four dollars and fifty cents an hour for picking up shit.

Chapter 14

By the end of the summer, I had made just a little less than 1,000 dollars—over 200 hours of stripping the streets of all the waste that the people in my neighborhood left behind.

I had earned enough to buy my way out of being the fat kid in grey sweatpants—at least the sweatpants part—for a second consecutive year of junior high. The previous year had been horrific for me. As alienated as I was from all the other kids, I was willing to do just about anything to reach the unattainable peace that I had been craving—blending in. I hoped to be invisible. I needed to be present but unassuming, a chameleon in the Cypress Park jungle.

That's why, on the day that I went out to go shopping for new clothes, I shaved my head down to a buzz cut, leaving only a small patch in the back as a memento of the full head of hair I once had. Over the summer, I learned that the gang members I worked with never seriously picked on one another. They all had the same basic fashion and mannerisms and it made each of them almost indistinguishable from one another, and, for that, they were respected and left alone. That, is exactly what I needed.

A shaved head indicated that you were a boy from Cypress Park. Now, all I needed were the clothes to fit the part. I had heard from some of my coworkers that they liked to shop at a place called The Swap Mall in Highland Park. In order to get there, I walked to "Night-in-jail" and caught a bus from there to the store.

Highland Park was even worse than Cypress Park as far as gang violence and being a feared neighborhood. Just saying the word Highland Park induced thoughts of the Avenues, the massive and entrenched street gang that was notorious for random violence and banging.

Walking into The Swap Mall, I felt like a fish out of water. Not only was I out of my neighborhood alone, but this whole operation felt daring and out of character. It must have been similar to how a man might feel buying a mask that he would use to rob a liquor store. I knew it was illegitimate. I knew that whatever I bought would only serve to facilitate the masquerade that I hoped to pull over the heads of my schoolmates, but it had to be done.

Picking through the clothes rack, I asked myself this question: *Does this piece of clothing look like something that most of the kids at my school would wear?*

It didn't matter whether I liked it or whether it looked good on me. My only concern was to put together an ensemble that others would recognize as part of the culture. The clothes had to simply avoid igniting the fury of the freaks and bullies who got a charge out of making outliers miserable.

When I checked out at the counter, I had accumulated a collection of apparel befitting of a real life gangster. I bought five XXL wife beaters and two Pendleton jackets. The jackets were plaid, thin flannel that buttoned down the middle and had pockets on the breasts. To this day, I have no idea why L.A. gangsters loved them so much. It was hot all year round and they made you sweat all day, but whatever. I bought them anyhow. Then I capped off my order by purchasing two pairs of baggy, Dickies work pants, one black and one khaki. My waist size was a whopping fifty inches, and I was lucky to find two pair in my size.

With a full bag in each arm, I left the store with my mission accomplished. I thought that for all of my hard work, I would never again have to be that disgraceful fat kid in grey sweatpants, who I hated so much.

Right when I got home I strapped into some of the clothes, and to my everlasting satisfaction they fit. It felt pretty good to wear some pants with an actual waist for once, and when I snuck across the hall, not wanting anyone to see me yet, I looked into the mirror and imagined the new Ray.

On my first day of school, I was overcome by some strange fusion of anxiety and excitement. I'd never looked forward to going back to school before, but I was curious to see if my fashion experiment was going to work. Walking up the steps and through those large metal doors to the entrance of "Night-in-jail," my heart skipped. Turning the corner and walking down the hall, it seemed that I wasn't attracting any attention. Up the stairs and around to my classroom, everything seemed to be going to plan. I sat down, opened up my book bag, and plopped a notebook down on a desk. Not one person stared, or pretended that I was causing an earthquake, or impulsively shouted, "You're fat!"

For that entire day, I kept my mouth shut, pretending like I wasn't there, and nobody hassled me. It was great. I could actually pay attention to what the teacher was saying for once.

I am Ray the chameleon. I can pretend. I can blend in. I can keep my mouth shut and make you think that I'm just like you. I can be whoever you want me to be.

In the first two months of school, my little gangster masquerade was working like a charm. Of course, whenever I opened my mouth, my timid, squeaky prepubescent voice informed people that I was no gangster. And simple eye contact with someone exposed my soft, caring eyes. But I had something else on my side that stopped them from harassing me.

I was Ruben's little brother.

During the previous school year, Ruben had been expelled for the final two months for fighting. Then, over the summer, in late June and July, he got sent away to Juvie for getting caught with drugs. By this time, everybody in school had learned that I was his little brother, and they all thought he was a total badass, like he would kill you for messing with me. And that might have been true. Ever since Grandpa died, he had been spiraling into an abyss of anger and acrimony. In response, he made it clear to people that there would be consequences for crossing him, and his solidarity in gang life gave him a reputation that nobody wanted to put to the test.

This connection had eased some of the pressure I was feeling at school, and now that I looked like a gang member too, I think it made people think that I had the full support of the gang—which was false, but who cares? At least I was getting some respect.

However, this disguise—this chameleon existence—that I was donning was incidentally bringing me closer to a life that was not my own. Ever since I had been old enough to judge people, I had thought that the gang members were a bunch of illiterate half-wits.

Right when I shaved my head, my mother said, "Ray, what are you doing? This is not you."

I heard her but did not listen.

On the first morning that I put on the Pendleton jacket and Dickies, Mando laughed. "Look at this! Ray's a Cholo now!"

I laughed too but did not truly understand why he was laughing.

One Saturday morning, probably three weeks into school, my choices were put into a new light.

It had become routine for Ruben's gang buddies to hang out at our house. They always had to be together, like a neo-pubescent couple in puppy love. My mom, hating the idea that Ruben would be out running the streets all day and night, had embraced the idea that if he and the gang stayed at home then she would be able to keep him safe. So when I got up in the morning, my lawn was strewn with a bunch of ninth grade thugs sitting in a semi-circle, periodically sneaking behind the shrubs to take a drag off of a pipe.

As I looked out of our front door at them, I received a strange impulse to join them. I was wearing the same clothes. Why not?

So I did.

I strutted out the door, grabbed a lawn chair, and leaned back with one arm hanging over the back of the seat.

I said, "What's up?" and the guys all nodded, acknowledging me without being overly welcoming. It was cool, just getting to hang out with a group like that. I felt all grown up. That is, until my brother walked out and saw me chilling with his homeboys.

"What the fuck are you doing out here? Go inside," he demanded condescendingly (even though there is no way he could ever spell *condescendingly*).

For the last two years, he had treated me like a little punk. Every time he was around his friends he would pick on me. He called me a pussy and pushed me around, and I knew he did it to show off. I never did anything to him, but for whatever reason he found it necessary to humiliate me. And on this particular morning I was feeling a little defiant toward his bullying.

So I didn't go inside. I just sat there and looked away from him, my hands crossed over my chest.

"What the fuck is your problem?" he asked, this time raising his voice.

"You're an idiot. That's my problem. You're just pissed off because you're a loser, you gangster drug addict."

My face flushed. A silence ensued that I could feel was about to end.

Ruben slowly walked over to where I was sitting. His presence grew over me like the tide over a rocky shore. And when I felt him standing right over top of me, I turned to look his way. He looked down at me and time stood still. My eyeball twitched and my toes curled, anticipating what might happen next.

In a swift instant, Ruben raised his left hand high above his head, and, with red-eyed fury, backhanded me across the face, knocking me clean out of my chair and onto the chilly grass lawn. I lay there with my forehead pressed against the soil for a moment gathering my anger, and then suddenly sprung up.

In a fit of rage I charged Ruben with my gargantuan body, lifted him and sent him flailing chest first into the ground. Ruben never anticipated that I might actually fight back. I'd never fought before.

He clawed himself from the ground and jumped on my back, pulling his forearms tightly across my neck. I swung my body to the left and then to the right to pry him loose and then I bucked forward, tossing Ruben over my back and down to the lawn again.

Mom heard the commotion from the bedroom and came rushing out. She got in between us and shouted, "Stop it! Right now! You are brothers."

She put her hand lightly on the back of my neck and looked at me. Blood was streaming from my lips because Ruben had whipped me so hard that my cheek was torn open by my teeth. Ruben looked up at Mom and grew calmer, realizing that the fight was over.

An overwhelming wave of emotion came over me. My chin trembled, and I ran inside. I slammed the door to the bathroom and locked myself in. The blood permeated through my mouth, spreading the taste of iron and salt water into the back of my throat and into my nostrils. With my arms straddling the sink in the bathroom, I spit and watched blood coalesce on the porcelain before sliding like a flash down the drain. Tears quickly followed, dropping steadily from my stinging red cheek.

Ruben chased after me, trying desperately to apologize for hitting me so hard. He was like Jekyll and Hyde, instantaneously flipping his emotions like a switch. He banged on the door and demanded that I come out. But I didn't want to come out. I didn't want to show him what he had done to me.

When I gathered my thoughts, and my tears slowed, I raised my head to look in the mirror.

And when I did, I once again saw a familiarly pathetic face. With puffy eyes and flaring nostrils, the fat kid in grey sweatpants looked back at me with a shaved head, wearing a flannel jacket and a wife beater underneath.

During the next month of school, I kept wearing the same ridiculous gangster clothes, just as I would for most of the eighth grade. Yet, I couldn't look at myself in all of those clothes and see *the new Ray* anymore. All I saw was a fake—somebody who had given up his individuality to avoid the scorn of others. And, again, I wasn't happy with myself. Sure, I didn't have to deal with bullying like I had the year before, but it felt like I was still keeping a long held secret. It felt like I was hiding from myself.

All the while, the neighborhood was continually getting scarier. Ruben's gang was getting bigger and more active. My dad's elicit business deals were increasing, and, as we got older and older, we peered deeper and deeper into our vulnerable lifestyle.

One Halloween night, Richard, Mando, and I were at my Uncle Ray's house passing out candy to all the neighborhood kids. Uncle Ray lived about five houses down from us, right behind my grandmother's house. He was out at an adult Halloween party, and he asked us to come down and take over the candy duties for him. So we had the house to ourselves, and whenever somebody knocked at the door, we would open the door and the kids would say, "Trick or treat!"

Yeah, whatever, here's your candy you little twerp.

Meanwhile, Richard had this great idea to watch The Texas Chainsaw Massacre. For whatever reason, I thought it was a good idea too. And I was horribly wrong. It was absolutely terrifying. We stayed up at my uncle's place in total darkness watching, all completely freaked out and alone, at night, in Cypress Park.

When the movie ended, we had to walk down Maceo Street, the road that runs directly in front of our house, in darkness because there weren't any street lights at the time. In silence, we crept back, turning to check behind us every five seconds because it was in our heads that some creepy psycho would pop out of the bushes and gash us to bits with a chainsaw.

Yeah, not fun.

Anyway, we made it home safely, but were still all on edge. I made a bee line straight for my parent's room, where they were congregated, because I knew that my new favorite show, the Simpsons, was on. The house was totally dark except for the faint glow of the TV. On Halloween my parents wanted it to be spooky so they kept all the lights off.

After watching the show for maybe ten minutes, a blast rang loudly in the street, rippling another harrowing echo off of the embankment of Mount Washington.

Frightened by the bang, I impulsively shouted, "What was that?"

"It was a gunshot. Get down on the ground! Everybody, down on the ground," Mom insisted.

My brothers and I did as we were told.

My dad scoffed. "They've already shot whoever they're going to shoot—no point in just laying on the floor," he said mockingly.

I stayed on the ground anyway, waiting, listening, wondering what might happen next. Of course, I thought of the Texas Chainsaw Massacre, which makes no sense because it was a gun, but hey. It's hard to control your fears when gunshots are being fired right outside your house.

In moments we heard scurrying feet coming up the driveway and a desperate pounding at the front door. "Peanut! Are you there? Squiggie just got shot!"

My dad walked over to the window to talk to the man. His name was Flaco. He and Squiggie were friends of Dad. They had grown up together and enjoyed sitting around with one another, periodically lighting little cocoons of paper on fire together. So I knew them well. Dad signaled to him to come over to his bedroom window to talk.

"Where is he?" Dad asked.

"He's lying out by his car on Loosemore."

"Alright, drag Squiggie into our driveway so he'll be away from the street and we'll call an ambulance," Dad commanded.

He opened up the screen door to the bedroom and hurried outside to investigate. My mom went into the living room to call the ambulance and grab an old first aid kit that was a relic of the Vietnam War.

With the door open, I could feel the wind pressing through the doorway and onto my chest. I gazed out, still lying flat on the ground, and wondered whether I should try to help. After enduring many frozen minutes of crippling fear, my curiosity finally impelled me to enter out into the night, and I slowly, as if sneaking around on creaky wooden floors, crept outside.

Looking over to my left as I cleared the doorway, I could see a crowd of five or six adults standing around Squiggie. A steady streak of blood traced his path behind him, and the adults knelt over him, trying to comfort him and place pressure on the wound. I will never forget that moment for as long as I live. My mother, who was inadvertently blocking my view, got up to get a towel for the wound, and my eyes were set at just the right angle to give me a close up view of the gunshot wound.

A motion sensored light shone perfectly from my neighbor's roof and onto the victim's body, making him appear vividly, as if under a spotlight. Blood was pooling steadily on the cement, creating a glowing deep red. As his arm was lifted by a neighbor, I could see that the bullet had blown off about three inches of his elbow, exposing the white bone and tendons covered lightly in flowing blood to my eyes.

Right then, Squiggie began convulsing uncontrollably in pain and shock. Seeing carnage like that in real life, up close and personal as it was, I gagged and lumbered urgently back into the house.

I went straight to my room, slammed the door, and dove onto my bed, where I sat upright with my legs folded up into my chest. Wrapping my arms tightly around my shins, I began rocking back and forth anxiously, trying desperately to make myself forget. Red glowing light from the alarm clock lightly painted the room, as I heard the ambulance screeching its sirens behind the house.

This place is a nightmare. I can't be myself. I don't feel safe. Nobody cares about anything meaningful. It's all about the street and the drugs, but what about us? What about the people who can't protect themselves? What about the people who don't like it here? What about the people who can't choose?

Tears began rolling down each side of my face. My jaw froze in place, haunting thoughts infecting my brain. Anxiety and anger and fear pressed the walls and ceilings down upon me until I knew that I couldn't get up if I tried. I looked at the clock and wondered how long it was going to take. How long would I have to sit here—stuck, frozen—forsaken by the world?

And the thoughts wouldn't go away.

I don't belong here. I am completely alone. It's never going to end.

I don't belong here. I am completely alone. It's never going to end.

It's never going to end. It's never going to end.

In my recurring nightmare, I was running away from this place through an alley. At the end was nothing but waste. And every time I tried to run, I was caught by ugliness and pinned down and told that it wasn't going to end.

When I woke up, I could rationalize that it was only a dream. I could tell myself that it was a fiction ginned up in my mind. But on nights like this, I knew that there was nothing fake about it. My life in fact existed in an alleyway and at the end, all that anyone would ever end up with was a heap of wasted things and people and time.

The path down which I ran ended before I ever get out. And I hated it. I hated it so much. All I wanted was to have a chance—one single chance—that would allow me to see a different way.

In total darkness, with the ambulance now gone, my brother Mando came into our room to find me—still rocking back and forth with my arms wrapped tightly around my legs. He sat beside me and placed his arm around my back.

"Everything's going to be okay, Ray. Everything's going to be okay."

Mando was my buddy—the only one of my brothers who tried to comfort me when I was scared. He read to me when I was young, and made me laugh when I was down. I appreciate everything that he ever did to make me feel better.

But on that night, I knew he was wrong. In my mind I knew that it was real. We were running down a dark alley together, and the difference between Mando and I was that I knew where it was going to end. I knew where this neighborhood would lead.

And that, was something I would never be willing to accept.

Chapter 15

A sudden roar shouted out and I leaned my head back into my seat. I closed my eyes, trying desperately to send the fearful, fatalistic thoughts to the back of my mind. Pressure begins building in my ears, the beating of my heart pulsing firmly through the veins near my temple. A bright white light from above leaves a resonant glow in the tops of my eyelids as I toss my head back and forth in search of comfort. A sharp, cool burst of air presses against my skin. A faint, high-pitched whistle stings my ears alongside the powerful sucking sound of a vacuum. A baby begins to moan and then cry somewhere in the background, and I squeeze my eyelids more tightly together, my eyeballs jutting back and forth rapidly beneath my lashes. A slow, droning conversation begins to develop outside of me, sparking off a series of mundane interactions. A bell rings twice in descending tone and a succession of clicks spark off. My feet wiggle, sensing that the ground beneath me is not real. And the deep droning roar and faint high-pitched whistle never stops.

I feel someone tapping me on the shoulder.

"Excuse me sir. May I use the bathroom?"

I open my eyes to see an innocent five year old boy looking over at me, his mother sitting directly to his right. He is wearing finely pressed khaki pants with a polo sweater. His hair is neatly combed, so that he looks like a miniature 1970's game show host.

I am thirty-two years old. I live in New York, and I'm on an airplane headed to Hong Kong.

Every time the designs for my collection are approved by the company, and I have drawn all of the final sketches with detailed measurements and material specifications, it is my job to go directly to the factory to fine tune and perfect prototypes for each of the shoes that I designed. The factory in China manufactures the prototypes based strictly on my sketches and I make adjustments to ensure that the vision for the shoe has been met. The process takes about two weeks and is very meticulous.

That is why I always dread the plane ride over. I don't hate going to China. It's actually one of the pretty great parts of my job, but I absolutely hate the flight over. It lasts twenty hours and I know that on the other end I will be greeted by a flurry of work and socialization that will have me worn down to a nub by the time it reaches a conclusion. The one thing that I love is flying business class so I don't have to sit in back with the peasants.

The flight itself becomes a battle between me and consciousness. If I can just find a way to sleep for a whole day, everything will be fine, but it is devastatingly hard to achieve. I think back to when I was a child and I would listen through the wall, holding my breath, to hear why my dad was yelling at my mom. I remember fretting about how I would avoid bullies at school the next day. The bright red light from my alarm clock was my only company and time would crystallize, leaving me to wait anxiously for something to happen.

Little has changed in that regard. A palpable fear still resides powerfully in the frontal lobe of my brain, forcing me to think through every possible scenario of pain and rejection when I lay down to sleep. What if the prototypes look nothing like my sketches? What if I can't get things done on time? What happens if the factory doesn't have the materials I need to make adjustments?

When you grow up in fear, it doesn't just go away.

My remedy for this dilemma is five strong drinks and two Ambien. My doctor has told me that I have insomnia and anxiety and there are pills for that. There are pills for everything now. In my neighborhood growing up, there were medications too. My dad was the pharmacist of sorts, but he never asked for an insurance card. Medication makes the questions go away. They help me to stop worrying, and, without the questions fluttering about, my eyes can begin to close, and I drift steadily away into slumber.

I can never sleep through the whole flight, even though I ingest enough medication to tranquilize a horse. I flip on my Ipod, stare off into nothingness, and let the music guide my thoughts.

The five year old boy next to me is playing a Nintendo DS and seems like he's really happy. That's good for him, but I don't like being around kids. They make me feel uncomfortable—always have.

The flight goes on and on and on until it doesn't anymore, when the pit of my stomach drops. The tires screech as they slam down onto the runway. My ears pop, and I breathe a sigh of relief. My once transient, fleeting state of mind begins transitioning toward the responsibilities that I now have.

Don't forget your bag. Don't leave your sunglasses in the pocket in front of you. Make sure you have your passport.

Once I have everything collected and begin walking through the aisle of the plane, I start to worry again about possible complications with my job.

After I walk the incline of the jetway and pass into the terminal of the Hong Kong airport, the sound of chatter and chaos explode into my formerly serene experience. It's really quite a culture shock just being in the Hong Kong airport. Everything is modern and spectacular, like you would expect to see in a new American airport, but the shops and restaurants are way different. There are Japanese toy stores and places that sell dried abalone, a Chinese delicacy that is basically a dehydrated sea snail. Even at typical western restaurants, like McDonalds, they offer uncommon food choices, like corn milkshakes and wasabi sauce for chicken nuggets. Despite being modern, walking through the Hong Kong airport is a lot like being at an outdoor street market, where things appear raw and stink a little.

Once I have been cleared by customs and collect my baggage, I exit through automatic sliding glass doors. When they swing open, a wave of humid heat collides with my chest and encompasses my body. I begin sweating almost immediately. A waft of mold strikes hard at my senses and I remember one of the most striking things about my travels to China. From the people to the animals, to the food and the buildings, everything smells moldy and stale, like the nation as a whole hasn't showered in months. When I get into the cab, it too stinks of must.

After careful consideration, I have decided that I would like to nominate mold as the national flower of China. Its pungent aroma pretty much sums up the spirit of the country—billions of people toiling every day without shower or body spray.

However, beyond the unpleasant fragrance, the people of China are incredibly welcoming. Like Manhattan, the people of China are ant-like, scurrying around with purpose through massive crowds. But very unlike Manhattan, people are all very cognizant of their manners, and treat people with reverence and honor. Courtesy and etiquette are a part of daily public life in China, whereas, in Manhattan, a person could reliably expect to be verbally assaulted for stopping to ask for directions.

Driving into the city from the airport, I cross over the majestic Tsing Ma Bridge. A thick smog hovers above, blocking the view of lush green mountaintops on the north side of the Ma Wan Channel. The taxi driver takes me to Kowloon, which is a city on the south side of Hong Kong, where I stay at the Sheraton. The hotel is a destination in itself. There are shops and restaurants and it is right across from Victoria Harbor, a beautiful inlet off of the Pacific Ocean.

When I get out of the taxi, a bellhop is there to greet me and take my bags. From the time I walk in to the time I leave, I am treated like a king. It is about this time that I recognize how different I am from the people around me. I'm six feet three inches tall, which would qualify me as a basketball prospect in China, considering how short almost everyone is—little do they know how terrible and uncoordinated I am at sports. My light-skinned Latino complexion is completely unique and my fashion provides a stark contrast. In China, everyone is so interested to know who I am, and it always takes me off guard, even when I know it's coming.

I'm not used to being the center of attention.

My whole life I have felt like an outlier, a misfit, but in China there is a genuine curiosity in people about those who are different. And I think it's weird, like they are trying to trick me or something. But, at the same time, it is kind of nice—like wearing a tuxedo for the very first time.

After my evening of choosing what I do and where I eat, relaxing happily in the hotel room, I know that work starts in the morning. A car will be out front at seven in the morning to pick me up and take me to mainland China. None of the factories that produce my shoes are in Hong Kong. They are all in Donguan, a city in the Guangdong Province. The names of all these cities are so foreign that it's still difficult to get them straight.

Once I see the car pull up in front of the hotel, the driver gets out, happily greets me, and takes my luggage to the car. It is just about a two hour drive from Hong Kong to Donguan. It is interesting because Hong Kong is so different from mainland China. Before 1997, the British had maintained control of Hong Kong, beginning in 1842. Now, Hong Kong is ruled by China, but it is still very western.

It has neon signs lighting up the street at night, big chain restaurants, and towering steel and glass skyscrapers. However, it is also grungy and old-fashioned, adorned with street carts, mules, and makeshift market stands. Animals are sold alive for people to slaughter at their own homes. These classical and modern features fuse together to create a strange dichotomy of old and new world culture in Hong Kong.

In mainland China, things get very different. It is highly industrial and the smog is much worse. The sky is always grey and even yellow from all of the pollution. The smell of mold and waste is even more pronounced than in Hong Kong. The buildings are tile on the outside, and given their location and environment, remind me of a dirty bathroom floor. The towns and cities aren't unkempt, just smoggy and polluted.

The geography is fascinating. Rolling slopes and valleys lie on all sides of dense green mountains. However, the land also appears depleted and worn. Some of the mountains have been mined away so badly that they are now skinny little mountains that look like giant apple cores with a single desolate tree on top.

The natural resources in China are incredible, but it is evident that it is overpopulated and they have been diminished over the years. Nobody turns on their lights and they conserve electricity as much as possible during the day because of the energy crisis that they face. On the drive through, I see clothes and sheets hung up outside of the neighborhoods because only the wealthy use electric washers and dryers. The farther you travel inland, the less modern life seems.

In the town of Donguan, industry is everywhere. This is the town in which my company and hundreds of other American companies choose to manufacture their products. The cost of labor is extremely low and the factory workers essentially live on site, making them very reliable and consistent employees. The minimum wage in Donguan has increased over the years. When I first travelling here, the minimum wage equated to a little less than one dollar per hour. Now, it is ten and a half Yuan per hour, approximately one dollar and sixty cents.

At first, when I came into these factories and had the chance to speak with the workers, I was very apologetic—imagining that they must be unsatisfied with such low pay—but I came to learn that they are very noble and hard-working people who are appreciative of their jobs, even for a low wage. Since housing is covered, their take home pay is relatively high compared to competing options as a worker in China. The best alternative for most would be laboring in rice paddy fields and living in a shack with their extended family. That's why I don't openly sympathize with them anymore. They claim to be generally happy with the economic progress in their lifetime.

When I arrive at the first factory on my trip at around nine in the morning, I am greeted by the factory manager and three workers, who all shake my hand and welcome me. They treat me like a god for the entire time I'm there.

Once inside of the factory, they lead me to a big room that has been prepared for my arrival. Inside, lined up neatly on a large table, are forty prototypes of the shoes that I designed. This is always a very surreal moment, seeing all of the ideas that I once conceptualized on a blank sheet of white paper in solid form. Looking at them all at once, my heart flutters and I smile—but only on the inside, of course.

Unfortunately, when I start examining them, flashes of panic begin setting in and I can no longer appreciate the incredible progress that has already been made.

The manager has a worker bring me some water and tea and they leave me with the prototypes of my shoes, a foot model, and copies of the sketches and forms that I sent to them with specifications for the shoes. The factory manager and an assistant often sit in with me and watch. The room is filled with racks of shoes organized along the wall. The shoes are from other companies, Chinese and American, who produce out of this factory.

The Chinese people think that all Americans love candy and Coca-Cola. So there is enough on the table to satisfy a small army of stereotypical Americans whom they hope to please. Of course, I don't eat any of it.

I stay in the room for nine hours—as long as it takes. If the work is not done, then I cannot leave. I examine the shoes, both on the table and on the foot model, and check the shoe for balance and pattern, looking to make sure that it is visually appealing. Then, I check the proportions of the design and accessories to make sure they look the way I envisioned them.

For example, I drew up a strap for a particular shoe on paper that seemed as if it would complement the design, but upon seeing it in person I realize that it is too broad. Since the correction needs to be made, I take the actual prototype and cut the strap to my desired width with a razor. I have a supply bag with me that has all the necessary materials for making shoe edits, such as markers, scissors, measuring tape, and pencils. When I make the change, I check with the factory manager's assistant to ensure that he took proper notes so that he can show the workers how to reproduce it.

All day long, I meticulously inspect all forty shoes that were produced at this factory, adjusting the most minute details imaginable from the inside lining to the sole design and everything in between. Every single feature of the shoe has to be correct to within a half of a millimeter. While I am here, the factory manager will have the corrections made and a new prototype will be produced by the workers on the spot. Oftentimes, I have to correct four or five different prototypes of the same shoe because when one correction is made, other changes become necessary.

This process repeats itself for between ten and fifteen days, depending on the deadlines I have to meet for the company. The pressure is incredible because if I don't meet a deadline, the shoes can't be sold.

One particular story from this trip accentuates the point I'm trying to make.

A boot design that I created for the fall collection had gone through several prototypes and corrections, and every time it came back to me, I had to return it because of something else that didn't look right. On the fifth correction, I instructed a change that had to be made and was informed by the factory manager that they had run out of rabbit fur I needed to produce another prototype. Upon insisting that the prototype needed fur in order to be complete, he sent someone to check on the inventory to see what they could find.

When the worker came back, he handed a sample of fur to the manager who told me, "Here. We have this fur, which is very nice. You can use this."

I grabbed a hold of it, stroking it to find that it was very soft and fluffy, exactly the kind of fur that I needed to fulfill the vision for the boot. "It's soft. It feels like a golden retriever. What is it?" I asked with curiosity.

The manager stammered. "Um. Well. The fur is very good quality."

"What is it?" I repeated.

With apprehension he conceded his answer. "It is dog. Yes, it is golden retriever fur."

"Oh, no," I exclaimed in shame, a look of disgust painted all over my face. "Are you sure that this is all you have?"

"Yes, sir. This is the only fur that we have."

With only another day to work at this factory before moving on to another, I knew that the only way I could complete the project was to confirm the dog fur. Filled with shame, it was the only way that I could do my job in this foreign land.

More than a few American companies made an order of boots based upon a sample made from dog fur. Yeah, I know. It's awful. But don't worry. No customers who purchased one of my shoes actually got one of the golden retriever boots. They were only for the wholesale samples.

At the end of the workday in the factory, all of the floor employees, who are all very young, between sixteen and twenty years old, retire to their dormitories, which are located on-site. The managers and office employees, however, don't turn in so early. It is Chinese custom to entertain your business associates with lavish food and nightlife. Even though I am tired and just want to go back to the hotel to rest and be alone, it is considered very rude in China to simply leave work and go home when you've been asked to go out for dinner. My coworkers are like my surrogate family while I'm there, whether I like it or not.

That means, despite my fits of inner protest, I go to dinner with the factory manager I worked with on a particular day on most nights that I spend in China. It's like a ritual, and our nights on the town usually take a minimum of three hours.

First of all, real Chinese restaurants aren't even similar to the typical American-Chinese cuisine. The Donguan establishment that the manager and his coworkers drag me to is enormous, looking more like an office building than a restaurant. On the outside of the entrance, caged animals, such as chickens, goats, turtles, snakes, ducks, and fish, are featured to show you who you will be eating before you walk in.

That's how you know it's good!

As we walk into the restaurant, it smells more like a pet store. The host at the inside of the door takes us to the dining room. In a typical American restaurant dining room, it's just a big room with tables organized on the inside. It's not like that in actual Chinese restaurants.

Typically, we are taken upstairs through a corridor that looks like an ancient palace. The stairway is adorned with golden rails. Crystal chandeliers hang above our heads. The host takes us upstairs to a private dining room with a massive oval table that appears suited for royalty. On the inside of the door, a women waits faithfully with her hands folded politely in front of her, waiting to serve us at our beckoning call. The restaurant host takes our orders on a handheld electronic ordering pad, and he has a headset on that relays the orders instantly to the kitchen. Everything is written in Chinese and I have no idea what's going on.

I always order something with mushrooms because they are the most normal thing to eat. It is a never-ending battle for me to find something decent. The chicken is all bloody, chewy, and pink, and they serve it with the freaking head still on it—gross. Everything you order seems like a total mystery. You're never sure what's in it and if you ask too many questions it may come across as impolite. So I usually just go with mushrooms, fish, or a bowl of rice.

A common misconception is that rice is served with everything at all Chinese restaurants. In China, you have to specifically ask for rice to come with your meal. It doesn't automatically come as a side, like in America. Also, if you order brown rice, they look at you like a crazy person because it's widely known in southern China that brown rice is what poor people eat. At a business meeting it sends the totally wrong message.

In any case, I order as plainly as I can because being adventurous with authentic Chinese food is not fun. Just swallow something that's identifiable so you don't accidentally eat something with dog or rooster testicles in it.

If I run into the situation that I can't explain what I want to one of my coworkers or the host, I have a sketch pad with me at all times and I use it to draw a picture of what I want. It works great. I'll draw a mushroom and the host will nod his head feverishly to show me that he understands.

Art is a universal language.

Once the food comes and I gradually choke down a necessary portion, the businessmen talk with one another and attempt to politely involve me in the conversation. Again, they are all very curious about me. They want to know everything, which generally makes me uncomfortable, but I sense that they are genuine. Most people at the table speak at least some English so I can follow the conversation most times. And it goes on and on, laughing and talking and entertaining, until I almost can't take it anymore.

Our private waiter brings us a bowl of fresh fruit at the end, which I love. They never serve American desserts, like cake or ice cream, just fruit. This signals that the engagement is winding to a close, which gives me a thrill of excitement—thinking that I might be able to just retire to my hotel room alone.

Then, suddenly, the factory manager begins excitedly motioning to the people around him, who smile and nod their heads.

"What is happening?" I ask.

"We all go to karaoke now. You come with?" he responds.

"Ah, no I'm very tired. I don't think I should."

"No, you come with. You must come. It will be very good time."

Crap.

On the first night that I spend with my coworkers in China, I always end up getting dragged to the karaoke club. I don't get it. Those guys can just work all day long and then it seems like every night they go out to the club and drink like fish. It is unbelievable, and it always sets up a very awkward evening for me.

You see, these karaoke clubs are not like the places you'll find in America. It's not one stage in the middle of a bar with one semi-talented karaoke host calling the names of the people who signed up—forcing everyone to listen to some miserable singer regurgitate the same crappy songs. Don't get me wrong. There are a wealth of crappy singers and crappy songs in China, but it doesn't work like that.

Out in front of the karaoke club, there is an incredibly beautiful fountain. Suspended high in the center is a gigantic bronze marble, which probably weighs a literal ton, and the water spouting out from beneath jets out with such power that it has enough force to spin the massive bronze marble. The club is like nothing I've seen. It is as large as a hotel with the aura of a palace.

When we walk in, a madam is there to greet us upon arrival. Young women, clad with cheap prom-style dresses, line every wall of the entrance. The club is dimly lit with lights and colors gyrating about in the back. Stained glass and mirrors are located all around, reflecting the colors and lights fantastically throughout the entryway. The madam leads us up two flights of stairs and into a private karaoke room with a table, an enormous wrapped sofa, leather chairs, and a TV with microphones attached. Bottles of cognac and fine scotch are placed with glasses on the bar in back of the room.

Once we have all taken a seat, and my coworkers have fired up the karaoke machine, the madam leads a lineup of girls, wearing tacky plastic dresses, into the room and the men begin to applaud and smile. I sit there meekly with my head focused squarely downward. One of the men points his finger to a girl and she skips over to take a seat next to him. Then another man does the same and a girl leans back on the couch and puts her arm around him.

Finally, after all the others carefully make their selections, it's my turn. I'm sitting toward the corner of the room hoping that they have forgotten about me when I look up to find observing eyes watching me intently. I lift my arm and reluctantly point at a girl standing at the end of the line who I believe has the prettiest hair and makeup presentation, and, as she saunters over to me, I avoid making eye contact in hope that she isn't expecting much. Then, the factory manager, laughing ecstatically, pointed to another and sent her over to me.

Great, now I have two call girls.

With all of us satisfactorily paired with beautiful young women, the madam leaves and the girls pour us all a shot. Knowing that I will need plenty more than one shot to make this situation comfortable, I guzzle it enthusiastically.

Then, one of my girls pours me another and giggles, flirtatiously placing her hand on my shoulder. I roll my eyes in humiliation—if she only knew.

These girls have quite a life. They're in a private karaoke room flirting and being groped by creepy old Chinese factory managers for money.

I feel dirty.

And one of my girls pours me another shot.

"Why not," I rhetorically signal to myself as the cognac burns its way through the back of my throat.

Everybody is living it up, having a great time while I sit blank faced, sandwiched between two prostitutes. I look to my right to see the factory manager getting jerked off through his pants while one of his employees sings a monotone rendition of *Thriller*, by Michael Jackson A couple others are escorted upstairs by their girls to receive enhanced services.

Woo hoo. Time of my life.

Feeling too awkward to just keep sitting there, I turn to the girl next to me and ask if she likes to have her hair braided. She smiles and giggles, having no idea what the hell I just asked, thinking that I was hitting on her.

"No," I say, shaking my head and waving my hands. My eyes closed, trying to block the mental images from disgusting my mind. I turn her sideways in on the couch. "Here." I begin sorting her hair into three neat strands and wrapping them around.

Realizing what I'm doing, she motions to the other girl and points back with a big smile on her face. For thirty minutes, while the other men did their thing, I sat there with my two Chinese escorts and braided their hair.

Now, that's my idea of guy's night out.

By the time we are all too drunk to read the words off of the karaoke screen anymore, the men signal that it's time to leave. The madam orders car service for me out front and I get in, finally able to go home and get some rest.

After stumbling into my lavish hotel room and plopping down on the bed, still fully-clothed, I try to think about how I got here. The ceiling spins over my head, the tacky wallpaper melding together with the smooth white ceiling and wavering back and forth in long incongruent semi-circles.

I'm half a world away from home, by myself, being treated to meals and parties that would satisfy a corrupt Middle Eastern dictator. To everyone else, I'm this big important American businessman, but I'm not so sure.

I think about my mother. I imagine her sitting in the same bedroom that she's slept in for thirty-five years. Next to her is a husband who still doesn't have a job. She is living in the same impoverished state as she was when I left. I think of her beautiful face, worn slightly by the years that have passed her by. I dream of her being here with me in this fine hotel room being treated to exotic meals and seeing the sights of a country a world apart. And I remember the world in which she lives—the one that I had so desperately hoped to escape.

A tear slides down my cheek as I think through all of those images that I wish I had never seen. Even though I am gone, my mind has not left.

Why was it me that made it out? Why was I the one?

Even new memories of wealth and luxurious accommodation cannot erase the things that I feel, the things that I know, the thing that I am. A heavy stream of sorrow swells my chest full, holding me tightly against the bed, as my numb, liquor-filled head passes out of consciousness, catapulting me headlong into a pitch black world of chaotic reflection.

When I wake up in the morning, my head is foggy. I look around and wonder why I'm still wearing shoes. I have to be ready in thirty minutes to meet the car that will be taking me to a new factory for another day of corrections. So I slovenly slide out of bed, a frown clearly displayed by every inch of my face.

"Damn Chinese businessmen and their damned karaoke night," I say lightly under my breath as I rub the side of my face with the palm of my hand and stumble to the bathroom.

As I get into the shower, I remember something about the water in China. Up until this point it had all been bottled or filtered water, but now I'm getting a taste of the real thing. It is a pale yellow color and it smells like, not to be stereotypical or anything—it's not my fault—steamed rice.

I trudge out of the shower, trying my best to wipe that funky smell off of my body, get dressed in my finest, and take two deep breaths before I step outside.

I know that when I get in that car, it starts all over again—the corrections, the new prototypes, and when I'm done, the three hour dinner followed by a potential karaoke binge. I'm exhausted already.

For the next ten days, this is my life. I live high on the hog, get treated like royalty, and work myself down to a pathetic little nub. Part of me doesn't like this experience because it's so odd to me that I'm the center of attention and everyone is going out of their way to please me. If I had my way, I could just quietly do my job and then slip behind the scenes and let the shoes speak for themselves.

Yet, another part of me feels differently about these trips to China. As much as I can't stand being waited on and forced into socialization and given female escorts to keep me company—I can't even tell them that I'm gay because there is "no such thing" in China—I feel comfortable with myself. I know what my job is. I know what people expect from me. And I can have the satisfaction of being appreciated by others for something that I appreciate in myself.

They appreciate my expertise in art and design. The factory managers and employees in China could be given a drawing with specifications and produce any apparel in the world. They can do it efficiently. They can do it affordably, and they do everything the right way. For that, it is a remarkable group of people with skill and dedication. Yet, if you gave any of the people that I work with a blank sheet of white paper and said, "Make a shoe," they wouldn't have the slightest idea of where to start.

That's why I matter in China. I can do something that nobody else is trained to do. And in America, I am similarly important in my industry. Sure, there are plenty of artists. There are plenty of graphic designers. But there are very few people that can independently do the research, draw the sketches, create designs that conform to and progress the company's image, organize the materials and specifications, meet all the deadlines, and then go to China and show the factory how to make them look great.

Within my profession, I have an identity. It took years of practice and failure. It took years of education. And it took a lot of luck—the whims of the universe falling into place at the right time, in the right place to allow me to see a different path to travel. Through it all, I have established a role for myself in the world.

I am thirty two years old. I live in New York. And I'm a women's shoe designer.

This sense of identity is what makes me love my trips to China. By the time my business trip winds to a close, I have visited five different factories, edited 120 unique prototypes of my own design, and officially created a multi-million dollar collection of shoes that is ready to be presented to retailers around the world. It came with a lot of stress, a compulsive attention to minute details, and an excessive amount of bizarre food and flagrantly below-average karaoke.

On the very last day, after all of the work and long nights out, I get to enjoy thirty-six hours of true bliss. A car with my own private driver takes me on the two hour journey through the lush green mountains and overpopulated industrial towns of Southeast China, back to westernized Hong Kong. The lights and the buildings and the people, the general motions of daily life, suddenly seem more routine, more like home. And the best part about it is that when the driver drops me off, I will be all alone. Nobody will be taking me out to show me a good time or choosing restaurants for me.

It will just be me.

When I get into the hotel and pick up my room key, I go straight upstairs to put down my stuff and just sit. The silence, the stillness of being in my little cookie-cutter hotel room by myself expands the walls around me and I feel, for the faintest of moments, free.

When shades of grey begin painting the walls across from me, I get the urge to spend one night out on the town, alone, doing exactly what I want to do. I rummage through my suitcase and find the perfect outfit to represent my liberty on this night, spread some makeup across my cheeks, and walk straight out the door without a thought or care in the world. Exiting the large automatic sliding glass doors at the front of the hotel, I remove a pair of dark sunglasses from my shirt pocket, slip them on, and march alone down the streets of Hong Kong.

The swarms of people, even at night, are impressive. The thick night air, with its constantly effervescent stench of mold, never seemed more inspirational. As I stride about the streets, I can see the people looking at me curiously, but they can't tell I'm looking at them.

I am unique, yet anonymous. They see me as I want them to. They can admire the design of my exterior, but they don't have to know what I was before.

It's ironic, I think, that I feel more safe, more comfortable, and more at home walking the streets of Hong Kong than I did on the streets of Cypress Park. There is an exhilarating freedom here, where it seems that my history is being written in the present. I've always looked differently than the people around me. I've always felt different.

But here, I can confidently hold my head high and be somewhat proud of what I have accomplished. I know that I have been useful to somebody. I know that I have created something of value. I can think back on the people who infected my childhood with waste and hate and reassure myself that, "at least I have produced something lasting."

I have made shoes, something that other people can use to project more lovely images of themselves to the world. And I can identify with that.

Chapter 16

An identity is no simple thing to devise.

In the seventh grade, I had endured the experience of being an outcast because other people looked at me and couldn't find anything they could relate to. For that, I didn't like them or respect them, but I learned how hard life can be when it is devoid of shared experience—connections of solidarity that help a person find a place in their environment. When nobody at all likes you, it is very hard to like yourself.

In the eighth grade, I shifted my tune by creating an image that blended with those around me. I was the chameleon of Cypress Park. I wore a costume that made me appear alike to the masses at "Night-in-jail" Junior High. Yet, when I looked in the mirror at myself, I came to see the same ugly misfit that I had seen the year before. My image had changed, but my identity was still the same. I was afraid everywhere I went, fearful of isolation and persecution.

To say that I lacked confidence would be the understatement of the millennium. I didn't like who I was. I didn't like the way I looked. I didn't like where I lived. I hated the path I was travelling. The images being drawn on the blank, white sheet of paper that was my life were pictures that I never wanted. Yet, it was all that I could see when I looked in the mirror. It was all that I had ever known.

And as much as I hated what I saw, there was a little section, a tiny little area that was being printed onto the canvass of my life that I wanted to expand upon. It had started in elementary school and became a passion that swelled within me until visible to the outside.

Every time I looked in the mirror, if I looked past my disgraceful skin and awkward physique and emotional scars, I could see a pale fire in the dark of my eyes. When I moved my lips, I would look squarely into that tiny pale fire and tell myself something like this:

You can do it Ray. Get yourself out of here. Make it end.

All summer long, in the months leading up to my ninth grade year, I worked again with the crew of gangsters, cleaning the streets of Cypress Park. Over and over again, day after day, I kept scooping up used condoms and pulling weeds and sweeping streets, only to see them soiled again by my neighbors. Every few nights another gunshot would ring out across the neighborhood and every few nights an ambulance would come screeching in to take another person to the hospital. It was a cycle that I could see and feel and smell and hear, and all I could do was keep sweeping. All I could do was earn every hour's worth of my check—four dollars and fifty cents at a time.

And one thought kept perpetuating through my mind: *You can do it Ray. Get yourself out of here. Make it end.*

Looking back, this thought was ridiculous. How naïve was I? I had no plan. I didn't know how I was going to get myself out of my neighborhood or make the pain and fear go away. I was completely ignorant. The only thing that I really knew was that I meant it.

Get yourself out of here. Make it end.

And so, the fire spread.

It helped that I had earned enough money to buy a Walkman. As I swept the streets in that summer before ninth grade, I listened over and over to the new Janet Jackson album. In particular, the song *Again*, meant something to me. She explained that, "I come from a place that hurts, and God knows how I've cried. And I never want to return—never fall again."

The music blasted through my bulky black headphones time and time again, and the hours went by and by—the money I earned gradually adding up to more. I thought about how I could possibly stop myself from falling into the same old patterns of being bullied and tormented without sacrificing who I really was.

I would rewind and play the song again.

How can I be me without being hurt?

The first, obvious problem for me was the same as every thirteen year old. I didn't really know what it meant to be me. I had clues. I knew what I didn't like. I didn't like the gangsters. I didn't like the way they looked. I didn't like the way they talked. I didn't like the way they smelled. And I especially didn't like their music. I swear, if I have to listen to Ice-T say *Original Gangster* one more time I'm seriously going to lose it.

Those ridiculous, barely pubescent, teens got on my nerves like no other. They were always hanging around in my living room, talking about absolutely nothing. Combined, they had the intelligence of a flea. It was just constant verbal diarrhea about people "disrespectin'" them and never-ending hypothetical scenarios about how they are going to "pop those mothafuckas."

Please.

And by this point, there was absolutely no avoiding them because my brother Ruben was like the gang superstar. He always had everybody over to our house, hanging out on the front lawn, sitting on our couch, smoking illicits, and eating my mom's food.

She wanted to protect Ruben and felt that as long as he and the gang were around the house she could keep an eye on them.

For me, they were a nuisance. Ever since Ruben and I got into a fight over me hanging out with his friends, we stopped talking to each other. I was still mad at him for smacking me and treating me like trash, and I knew that I wasn't welcome around the gang.

I guess trying to form an identity requires role models, and Ruben was clearly not an option. Maybe I could have looked to my dad for guidance?

Not so much.

That summer, after another day of working like crazy on the streets of Cypress Park, I had collected a reasonable amount of money. I was saving it up to buy new clothes again, maybe even some art supplies and a couple CD's. However, I had to pay my dad too, so that we could pay our electric, hot water, and cable bills.

And, despite fulfilling that obligation to my family, it still wasn't enough for him.

One night, lying awake in bed as usual, Dad crept into my room and started looking through my drawers with a mini flashlight. Out of curiosity, perhaps meekness, I kept quiet, wanting to see what he was doing. Watching him dig around, my vision partially blocked by the blanket wrapped over my right shoulder, I was able to see him open the lid of my money jar before sticking his fat hands inside to make a grab.

My stomach sank. Whatever childlike hopes that I had left about my father washed away in an instant.

In the morning, I woke to discover that 200 of my hard earned dollars were missing. The smell of skunk wafted throughout the house in delicate clouds of white smoke.

Role models were scarce for me. Of course, I had women to look up to—my mom, Janet Jackson, and Madonna—but if I showed up at school for the ninth grade wearing a low-cut black blouse, red heels, and a cone bra, I sense that the consequences would have been even more severe than a blubbery physique in grey sweatpants.

In my quest for self-discovery, an honest identity that allowed me to keep my head up was difficult to find, partly because I didn't even know what I was looking for. All that I could say for sure was that I had a deep craving to express myself.

And one afternoon, about a week before my return to "Night-in-jail," I ran into an unexpected role model who had been there all along.

My oldest brother Richard was entering into his senior year at Franklin High School. Richard had been pretty absent during the previous three years. He was always good at getting along on his own. Most of his time was spent hanging out with his girlfriend and driving around Los Angeles, fraternizing with friends and going to punk rock concerts.

He had piercings and tattoos that would impress the most hardcore bikers and prison inmates. His hair was unpredictable, constantly changing shape and size and color. Richard was fascinating to me because he was able to be popular with the gang without joining and somehow live independently from our home and the neighborhood. He never seemed to be trapped at home, like I was. He could move freely in his own way without being alienated.

When our paths crossed one afternoon, he was in the bathroom dying his hair with streaks of red and spiking it up into an impressive long mohawk. I stood at the doorway staring at him.

Growing annoyed, he asked, "What?"

In a spontaneous moment, I replied, "I want my hair bleached. Will you help me?"

Richard laughed for a moment, stroking his crispy hair lightly with his fingertips, his eyes still fixed on the mirror. I stood there silently, awaiting reply, and when he looked over to inspect my demeanor, he could tell that I was dead serious—my gaze set squarely into his with a blank expression.

He looked back at the mirror, as if pretending for a moment that he hadn't noticed me.

And hesitantly, like he was still contemplating his words as he said them, Richard said, "Alright. I don't care. I'll help you dye your hair."

My haircut at the time was misguided. At the front of my head, hair jutted out past my brow. The sides were shaved to a buzz, and in the back—oh in the back—was a ponytail that began in the center of the back of my skull and extended down to my shoulders. It looked like a baby badger had dropped dead, fell from a tree, and was permanently transfixed by the top of my brain.

When Richard got done sculpting his hair, he grabbed his solution and began working on mine. I asked him to only dye my ponytail, leaving the top black. After about thirty minutes, my ponytail was bleached blonde. Excitement coursed through my veins. I couldn't put words on why at the time, but now I know that the prospect of change kindled my imagination.

"So, what color do you want it," Richard blurted out, recapturing my attention from my secret thoughts of transformation.

Without having put much thought into it, I quickly came to a decision. "Let's do green."

Like many important decisions in life, this one came in an instant. I could have chosen any color on Earth and, for whatever reason, green just felt right.

Richard brushed the green hair dye through my newly bleached rat's nest with a tiny brush for a few minutes, and after a few minutes it was bright apple green.

"There ya go, little bro," Richard said. Then he gathered up his things from the bathroom and walked away.

I turned my head to the side and checked out my new look. My eye sparkled as I looked in the mirror. It was radical. It was different. It felt like, well, me. At that specific time, in that unique moment, my hair seemed to represent something that I'd been trying to express for a very long time.

Mom walked by the bathroom and saw my new hair and turned to Richard, "What did you do to Ray, Mijo?"

"He said he wanted his hair green. So I dyed it green."

She shrugged her shoulders and muttered, "Oh Christ," before meandering back into her room.

I think she just didn't want to fight it. She had endured so much with the gang being around and shootings in the neighborhood that fighting green hair just didn't seem to make much sense.

With only a couple days until school started back up, Richard also took me to a shopping center called the Glendale Galleria to get some new clothes for the upcoming year. Richard and his friend Roach were going to the mall anyway, and, at the order of my mother, I got to tag along.

Searching through the stores, I ran into my typical problem. Almost nothing in the store fit over my unseemly frame. I looked everywhere, in every store, high and low, and thought that I would never find any shirts that actually fit. It was so depressing.

It wasn't too hard for me to find some jeans that worked, and I bought a pair of Georgia Logger Boots, which I loved, but attempting to persuade a normal sized shirt over my chest was like putting a condom on a Winnebago.

And then, right before we had to leave, I found something in the pajama section of a department store that caught my eye. They were night shirts, like a nightgown for men, but they had really unique, kind of weird designs that were interesting. Since they were all so long, they fit over me. The sleeves extended three-quarters of the way up my arm and the bottom extended to the top of my thighs. One had two buttons down the neck and another looked like a jersey, which made them appear sort of fashionable. It was totally out of the ordinary to buy them as street clothes, but they were perfect for me.

After trying them on with my new jeans and the boots and my green hair in the back, I looked in the mirror and whispered to myself, "This looks pretty cool."

It is amazing what fashion can do to help people searching for an identity.

And while supreme confidence inebriated my senses for a few days, the cloud of school drifted over my head until I panicked. I hadn't really thought through the whole green hair thing, and what other people would say. I started to realize that it could get really bad for me. Nobody had green hair. The usual fears entered my mind. What have I done? Am I sure I want to go through with this? What are people going to say to me? Is this too much of a change?

My history forced me to imagine the worst in people and those fears had plagued me for so long. Yet, this year, going into the ninth grade, something definite had changed. I knew what it felt like to be a misfit that nobody wanted to associate with. I knew what it felt like to seek people's approval and try to blend in. And none of it worked. None of it made *me* feel good.

The transformation in my mind went something like this: *I don't care anymore. I'm so sick of caring. I'm tired of taking myself so seriously and trying to gain other people's approval. If they aren't going to like me because of something that I like, then screw them.*

Maybe it was a little odd. Maybe it was funny. Maybe it even looked cool. No matter what, my new look was me. This time, instead of allowing the false categories of others to paint my image for me, I created a category.

I started making my own choices.

And that gave me something real to build upon. Creative fashion gave me something to believe in. As it turned out, it also gave me something to fight for.

On my last first day of school at "Night-in-jail", I was blatantly tardy. None of my brothers attended anymore, since Ruben had been promoted to high school for essentially doing nothing the year prior. He went to Alcerino High School.

Traditionally, people from my neighborhood—including Mom and Dad, Mando, and Richard—went to Franklin High School, but Ruben decided to go to Alcerino because Franklin was in rival gang territory, where the Avenues went to school.

Needless to say, the bar was not set very high for me academically. As long as I didn't literally murder another human being I would be on a better track than my brother, who made it through "Night-in-jail" without ever really attending in his final year because he spent much of it in juvie.

Since I walked into school late, there was basically nobody around, which made me feel somewhat relieved because I wouldn't have to deal with the massive scorn that I was expecting for having green hair. Instead of walking in through the hallways and classrooms where the office was, I slipped into the side entrance, where I thought I could avoid getting caught by a tardy sweep. My plan failed. Just as I got to the top of a stairway and onto the asphalt 'prison yard' at the center of the school, the Vice Principal was standing there with a clipboard and tardy slips.

He approached me immediately and said, "You're late. Here is a tardy slip. You know that if you get five, it means after school detention?"

"Yeah," I said absently.

"What's your name?"

"Raymond Serna."

"Ok, Raymond. Get to class."

As I began moving toward my first class, the Vice Principal stopped me in my tracks.

"Wait a minute," he said. "Why is your hair green?"

"Because I dyed it green," I responded with a hint of ritualistic teenage sarcasm.

He shook his head and fastened his pen to the clipboard. "No way. That's not going to work. You need to go to the Dean's office right away."

"Why?"

"You can't have green hair at school. It's in the dress code. Get to the Dean's office, now."

This was new territory for me already at school, and I hadn't even seen any kids.

"Where is it?" I asked.

"What do you mean? Where's what?"

"The Dean's office. I've never been to the Dean's office before."

Bewildered by my question, expecting that I was another typical trouble maker who had dyed his hair to stir up controversy, he pointed down the stairs and explained how I might find the Dean.

As I approached the office, new sensations came over me. First of all I was mad. Why can't I dye my hair? What does that have to do with school? Second, I was scared. I was not the kid who got sent to the Dean.

I nervously handed my referral slip to the secretary and took a seat, waiting for the Dean to call me in. When the Dean came out, I was surprised to see that she was African-American. The reason I was surprised was because there were almost no black people in the area. The African-American and

Hispanic gangs were notorious for violent conflict at the time and simply being black put you at a very high risk of being shot in a drive-by, even if you weren't the least bit involved in gangs.

She brought me in and told me to sit down.

"So, Raymond, what's with the green hair?" she asked.

Brought back down to Earth a little by the anxiety of speaking to the Dean, I tried to drop the sarcasm. "Well, my brother likes to dye his hair and I asked if he would dye mine. I like it. Is it illegal to have green hair or something?" I asked, failing only slightly to avoid a sarcastic comment.

She pondered the question for a moment. "Well, no. It isn't illegal, but it is a cause for distraction that you may not want. And in this school, we can't have distractions like this."

Sidetracked by the comment about my hair being a distraction that I may not want, I became upset. "Isn't that for me to decide whether it's a distraction for me? How will this affect anybody else?"

The Dean slid back in her chair and said, "You know what? I think I'll just call your mother."

"Ok. Call her. She knows it's green. She saw me dye it," I responded, the bitchiness not so slowly creeping back into my voice.

As she made the phone call, a noticeable lump had formed in my throat. I didn't know what was going to happen. I didn't want to be sent home from school. That's what happened to bad kids, and I certainly didn't think I was bad.

When my mom picked up the phone, the Dean introduced herself and they exchanged some mandatory niceties before getting down to the brass tacks of the matter. The Dean explained the problem and told my mom that having green hair violated school policy.

When told that her son couldn't have green hair, Mom got really pissed off. She snapped back, "You mean to tell me that you took my kid out of class because of his hair?"

Taken off guard by the intensifying controversy, the Dean quickly responded, "Yes. You're not allowed to have green hair at school. It is too much of a distraction."

At this point, I heard my mom's voice start blasting through the phone. "Too much of a distraction?" she asked rhetorically. "Since when are you not allowed to dye your hair? I'll tell you what. When you tell every little chola in that school that they have to dye their hair back to their natural color, then I'll tell my son that he has to lose the green hair."

Suddenly becoming defensive, the Dean said, "You know I can't do that. There's a big difference between girls streaking their hair blonde and having kids all over the place with green and blue and red hair."

"So it's ok for girls, but not for boys?" my mom offered as a retort.

"Ma'am, it's not ok for anyone to have wild colors in their hair. I'll tell you what I'm going to do. I'll create a petition for Ray and let him take it to all of his teachers. If all of them sign, testifying that his hair is not a distraction, then he can keep it. How does that sound?"

My mom agreed. The Dean kept me in her office while she made up a petition for my teachers and gave it to me, explaining that I need to bring it back to her by the end of tomorrow's school day or I will have to get rid of my green hair.

What a productive use of my education!

So I took the petition and I left. The form had a box to check for 'yes, it is a distraction' and 'no, it's not a distraction,' and an area for comments explaining why.

That petition about my hair turned into the spark that would ignite my social life.

When I sat down in my first class, the kid sitting next to me exclaimed, "Holy crap. What'd you do da your hair?"

"I dyed it green, and now the Dean is trying to get me in trouble."

"For what?"

"I don't know. Having green hair. I need to get all of my teachers to sign this petition saying that it's not a distraction or I have to cut it off."

Then, he turned and told the person next to him that the Dean's trying to stop me from having green hair. And that person told the person next to her, and she told the person next to her, and he told the person next to him. In a single day, word had spread throughout the school that my hair was controversial, and everyone stopped me in the hallways to talk about it. They all wanted to know what was going to happen next.

And after every single class, I took the petition to my teachers, and every single time, the teacher got a sort of confused look on their face and said something like this: "Why would that be a distraction?" My homeroom teacher even commented on the petition that my hair was, "refreshing," and she couldn't understand why she had to waste her time signing a petition about a kid's hair.

I'm sure that I benefitted from having been a good kid during my previous years at "Night-in-jail." My teachers always liked me and thought I was very creative, even when I was shunned by my peers for wearing grey sweatpants every day. After all, I never bothered anyone and I had the best handwriting in the whole school. Teachers appreciate that.

When I got the petition completely filled out, and not a single teacher was willing to call my hair a distraction, you would have thought that I was Michael Jackson or something. All of the kids were asking me to see the petition and congratulating me by saying things like, "That's so cool!"

I'd never been called cool before.

Then, the next day, when I returned the petition to the Dean and I got to keep my hair like it was everybody started asking me questions. "How'd you do it?" "Where did you get the hair dye?" "Will you help me do mine?" And the whole time, I was just pretty indifferent to their compliments and their interest because these were the same people who had always made fun of me.

Why should I give them the time of day now?

But, much to my surprise, my indifference only made them more interested in me, which is totally ironic because it used to make them *hate* me. Now, kids wanted to sit with me at lunch and they asked me about my interests. Instantly, overnight, I had all kinds of friends.

At this point, sitting in class and doodling, I remembered something that my mom taught me. "How you present yourself to the world determines what people will think of you."

On that day, it rang truer than ever before.

It's just a little green hair, but, whatever. It's better to be identified by your hair color than having to hate yourself or spend every day hiding from people. When I figured out how to present it correctly, people seemed to like something that I never thought they would.

Me.

Chapter 17

There was a lot less to hate about school once I had friends and didn't feel like I was veiling my true personality. However, becoming popular, while refreshing, wasn't what I was looking for. I was just hoping that I could be myself without being tormented every day. So, yeah, I got lucky. Things worked out. But my goal was to get out of the neighborhood—not become one of its social icons.

And I still didn't know how that might happen. Classes were boring, filled with remedial work and generally uninspiring teachers. Now that I had "friends," one of my favorite things to do in class was crack jokes. I learned that my crass, sarcasms made people laugh. So I spent most of my time in class thinking of clever things to say.

In social studies class, while the teacher lectured about African geography, I waited for opportunities when I could inform classmates that, "Djibouti looks fat."

In science, we learned about the solar system, and my answer for everything that week was, "Ur-anus?"

Sometimes, I got a little carried away.

In crafts class, my first ever formal art class, our teacher had us making sculptures out of pipe cleaners. Yes, we were fourteen years old and making sculptures out of pipe cleaners. I found it less insulting to just sit there and talk instead of doing the childish assignment.

I said something like this: "I know. That new Madonna song is totally awesome," when the teacher passed by and noticed me.

Our teacher was Mrs. Barham. She was a young lady, a kind of typical, dorky looking school teacher. She had big blue metal framed glasses. She wore pantyhose and homely skirts with boring shoes. Her hair was twisted around into a swirling mess of a bun, patched together by dozens of poorly plotted hair clips.

The most relevant complaint about her at this point was that her crafts class seemed like a joke, which to me, after spending years practicing drawing on my own time, it was.

She tapped me on the shoulder and, in a light but critical tone, said, "Ray, are you planning on doing some work today?"

Offended by the interruption, I decided to get a little sassy. I looked up at her and then back down at the table where I was sitting. Blank sheets of construction paper and pipe cleaners were strewn about chaotically. I grabbed three of the pipe cleaners, latched them hurriedly at the top and propped them up on the table haphazardly.

"There you go. It's a pyramid. All done," I said.

I kept my head down as I said it, so as to not be held accountable by eye contact.

She stood there for a moment, and I could hear all of the frustrated thoughts grinding through her head. I waited impatiently, internally begging for some kind of angry response so that I could justify being such an asshole.

Instead, she answered softly. "Ray, please stay after class with me. I'd like to talk to you."

There wasn't the slightest bit of anger or harshness in her voice.

When the students began filing out of the room, I stayed put as requested. Mrs. Barham went on with her business—tidying up the tables, and organizing the projects that were turned in—without acknowledging me. Feeling awkward just sitting there, I walked over to her, hoping that decreasing the distance between us was like the magic button to make her start talking. She just kept on doing her thing.

"So, I'm here. You wanted to talk to me?"

She turned, made glancing eye contact with me, and sat down on the corner of her desk. As she removed her glasses, she said, "Look Ray, I'm your teacher. I want to help you learn and have a good experience in my class. What's stopping you?"

"What do you mean?" I asked.

"Why did you spend the whole hour talking instead of doing your assignment?" she said bluntly.

While my first instinct was to be challenging, because I hated being lectured and told what to do, she had approached me in such an unassuming way that I felt I could be honest with her. "Wa-Well," I stuttered. "It's just so easy."

Then I rambled. "I love art, but your class is like kindergarten. It's boring. No offense. I just don't get much out of making little clay figurines and pipe cleaner collages. I already know how to do this stuff."

She responded quickly. "So, if I were to give you more advanced work, would you do it?"

I paused, not wanting to come across as overeager. "Yeah. Uh, yeah. Yeah. I'd do that."

"Great. I'll tell you what. You create something for me tonight and bring it to me tomorrow so I can see what level you're at. Then, I'll make more advanced, private lessons for you," she said.

My head filled with all kinds of awkward concepts, like, "That was really helpful" and "Wow, you actually care about me."

But, since my eighth grade psyche was uncomfortable with making myself vulnerable by saying nice things, I said, "Okay. That's cool," instead. And I walked out of her room without so much as a *thank you*.

It didn't stop me from thinking though. It didn't stop me from dreaming that this might be a chance for me to do something I'm proud of. That night, I drew a portrait of my brother Richard's friend Roach, and I brought it back to class the next day. In my mind, it felt so good to have a reason to draw something, a reason to create.

When Mrs. Barham saw the portrait the following day, she seemed impressed. Despite the fact that Roach was unusually ugly—he kind of looked like an actual roach—she said, "Ok, this will work out great. You are definitely more advanced than the others."

Pride swept through my nostrils and into my lungs. She made me feel like I was good at something. Even if I you know deep down that you have talent, even if your family tells you that you are good, it means a lot to hear it from someone else because they have no obligation. Mrs. Barham didn't have to do that. She didn't have to give me harder work. She could have just told me to get in line and do what I'm told like the others. But she didn't, and it made me want to try harder.

For the rest of the semester, Mrs. Barham brought in fine art supplies for me to use. She brought charcoal and oil pastels, canvasses and acrylic paint. While everyone else did the standard lesson, I had the freedom to take on more challenging efforts. Mrs. Barham was tougher on me too. My grades weren't just guaranteed because I was more advanced. She took the time to critique my work and challenge me to try new things.

One day, after the bell had rung and the kids had all scurried out the door, Mrs. Barham was putting things away while I tried to finish up the painting that I'd been working on. When I walked by her to set my painting in a safe place to dry, she stopped me.

"Oh, yeah, Ray. I've been wanting to talk to you about something. We are working on putting together the yearbook for the school, and the yearbook committee decided that they want the cover to be a piece of artwork designed by a student. I really think that you should do it."

"I don't really think that anyone would want to see my design for the yearbook," I responded with suggestive insecurity.

Mrs. Barham looked me in the eyes and asked, "Well, how do you know that if you don't try?"

Both stumped and secretly interested in creating a yearbook design, I conceded, "I don't."

Mrs. Barham then just went on explaining the project to me, as if I had already told her that I was going to draw something. "Ok, so the design has to be created on a standard eight and one-half by eleven inch piece of paper. It has to be in black ink and cover the entire page. Have it in to me by next Monday and I'll submit it."

"Ok, Mrs. Barham. I'll try."

I didn't want to let her down because she wasn't willing to let me down.

Over the weekend, I planned to work on the project. I had a stack of blank white paper ready in my room. I had the Janet Jackson CD playing. I was ready to go.

Then, Ruben's irritating friends started to show up.

Once one gang member showed up, the crowd steadily built until the house was unrecognizable. They were like a pack of feral cats descending on a bowl of tuna—leaches that stuck to the furniture and sucked the blood out of our home.

That's why, when I heard a knock at the door, I knew that my night of designing the yearbook cover just got complicated. It was Ruben's friend Ralph. His gang name was Fren because he was nice and personable, like a "friend." When I saw him at the front door, I just walked right by.

He shouted, "Come on Ray. Let me in. Don't be such a dick!"

I ignored him, grabbing a glass of water and walking right past him waiting at the door. As I passed, I muttered, "Go away. Ruben isn't even here."

He didn't care. They were relentless. Despite my staged protest, my mom finally welcomed him in, he had a seat, and waited for the others to show up. Like clockwork, they did. First there were five. Then there were ten, and after a while twenty gang members were stockpiled in our tiny living room. They started drinking beer and ripping on each other, digressing into an unbreakable string of 'Mama Jokes' and racial epithets.

After an hour or so, my Mom paged Ruben to let him know that he needed to get home, since his friends had infested our house. When he returned, the group took turns going outside to smoke PCP and to take drags of a joint. Their gangster rap played through a large, battery-operated boom box that one of them kept by their side at all times.

I turned my Janet Jackson songs up louder in revolt.

One of the gangsters asked my brother, "What's the deal with Ray? Why's he listening to that pussy music?"

Shrugging his shoulders, Ruben insisted, "Man, don't worry about him. He just does his thing and I let him be."

Hotel California, by The Eagles, played on their boom box. I'll never, for the life of me, understand how they thought I was lame because I liked Janet Jackson when they listened to The Eagles. What the hell is that about?

Ruben and I still didn't talk very often since our fight the year before. He bothered me with all of his ridiculous friends and he couldn't stand the sight of me anymore. I never did fully understand why.

Even though I didn't get along with my brother, I wasn't in any danger from the gang. If anyone messed with me, Ruben would hurt them. And they knew it.

But I had to live with their partying and all of the dangers associated with being in the same house with the gang.

I sat alone in my room, drawing the yearbook design and listening to my music. When I drew, the sounds just faded to the background. Like whizzing through time and space, my mind escaped while my pen stroked the paper on my lap. I wasn't in a gang house. I wasn't alone. I just tried to conceptualize the most beautiful, free thing imaginable, and if I could put it down on paper, I too could be beautiful and free.

I never drank or smoked or tried drugs like the rest of them. My escape was the music in my head. My escape was art.

When the sun came up in the morning, I looked over to see my drawing painted by the white light shining in through the window. I had created a peacock perched on a twig. In the foreground, the leaves from the tree surrounded her, and in the background, grandiose mountains were shaded in behind her glorious silhouette. It was the most beautiful thing that I could imagine, and on Monday, I gave it to Mrs. Barham as my design for the yearbook cover.

She absolutely loved it. In fact, she liked it so much that she helped make sure that it would be the winning submission. All of the other students that turned in a design created gangster stuff, like graffiti letters and caricatures. The submission that garnered the most votes was a picture of a clown, with tears rolling down his cheek, like in the prison tattoos I used to sketch. And even though it received one more vote from the students than my peacock drawing, Mrs. Barham vetoed the vote and made me the winner.

In a period of a few short weeks, she earned my trust and we built a rapport unlike any I had with teachers in the past.

And that simple act, that simple role of support, built the foundations of a relationship that would lead me to ask one simple question—one simple question that would forever change the trajectory of my life.

Once Mrs. Barham challenged me for being so apathetic in class and gave me work that was more interesting, crafts class became the highlight of my school day. I liked being special. The other kids would sometimes ask, "Why does Ray get to do different work than us?" and Mrs. Barham would simply explain that we had an arrangement that allowed him to earn his grade in a different way.

It allowed me to feel as if I stood out, that I was remarkable.

More than that, art class provided me with the time and space to create, to imagine, to grow without being judged. At home, when I had a moment alone to think about my day, think about my life, my mind would often gravitate to my work in class. I wondered how good it really was. I wondered why people liked it.

Yet, I knew somehow that it wasn't enough for me. A single crafts class wasn't enough. I wanted to create all day long. In math class, I pretended to take notes by sketching in my notepad. In gym, I just sat to the side and scratched my pen along the surface of paper. I also never passed gym class, by the way. Art became my way of expressing my inner most thoughts, emotions, and memories without subjecting myself to judgment.

But at a certain point, I found myself up against the wall. My expression and creativity was stuck. It was stuck inside of my head, and even while I had a few people to show my work to, I didn't have any way to take my work to the next level. Everyone told me I was great.

"How do you do that?" "Your drawings are awesome," "You should enter an art contest or something," they might say.

What contest? How do you know I'm good? What makes people like art? Are they just being nice?

Despite the recognition, I was skeptical of my talent. I had a hard time believing that I was good at anything. So I wanted a way to prove myself. I needed a goal, an accomplishment that could validate my effort.

Yeah, I can draw pretty pictures that some people like, but so what?

I was treading water. Sketching and doodling when you are bored doesn't make you an artist.

So I figured that that's what I wanted—to be an artist, a real artist. If I were actually an artist, I would have proof that my self-expression was valid. I could prove that it was more than just a passing hobby.

At home, I told my mom. "I want to be an artist. Can you help me get into classes?"

"Oh Mijo!" she exclaimed. "You are so very wonderful and I love your art, but we don't have any money for classes. It's hard enough to pay the bills. Maybe you should ask your art teacher if she knows of any free classes."

I shrugged. "They don't have free art classes for kids like me," I assumed aloud.

"How do you know that until you try Ray?" Mom asked.

My dad was a big, fat wet rag. "Nobody's an artist Ray. That's not a real job," he told me cynically.

I wasn't particularly receptive to his opinions about jobs. Like being a drug dealer was a whole lot better.

My options were limited. My family was poor. We didn't even have a car that worked. We did have the old rickety truck, but it was, like our life as a family, stalled, dormant, complacent, and rotting functionless on the side of the street as the sun rose to the east and fell to the west, day after day after day.

My hopes of becoming an artist hung vulnerably in the recesses of a mind too often preoccupied by more pressing concerns:

Will Dad get arrested? Will Ruben get shot? Will Mom have the money to keep the hot water running and food on the table? Will I lose my newfound popularity at school when people got to know what I'm really like?

Out of all the questions that I had to tend to, just one could actually help me:

How do I become an artist?

And all of my musings on the subject, the imaginations that I created out of thin air, meant nothing without a tangible piece of information, some real evidence, that my hopes were possible. I needed something, some structure that would light a new path for me to travel, a path that was currently littered, a neighborhood and family gone bad—a narrowing path that ended in a life that I was unwilling to bear.

It was one very ordinary day in crafts class. As I was walking out the door, the last one in the room as usual, a nagging thought tormented my brain. With my shoulders squared with the doorway and one foot prepared to move forward, I swear that I could feel a force tugging me back into the room. I sensed my mother's voice in my head. In a heartbeat, I stopped and turned back around.

A tiny voice inside my head shouted, "Don't do it," at precisely the moment when my real voice came to life.

"Mrs. Barham, do you know of any free art classes that I might be able to take?" I asked.

Then I rolled my eyes hopelessly so as to ease the emotional risk.

The fan in the room produced the only interruption to complete and utter silence. Then I heard the word that I had been intentionally convincing myself that I would not hear. "Yes," she said. "I think I know of something that could be just perfect for you."

Chapter 18

Our lives are often defined by the snap choices that we make, the seemingly random and unexpected moments when our circumstances coincide with our will at exactly the right time. Some people call it opportunity.

Most attribute it to the whims of luck or the destiny of fate. When something in your life turns out for the better, people will tell you that you have good fortune or you should thank God for the destiny he has bestowed upon you. Others simplify good things as the result of virtue, talent, ambition, or a strong work ethic.

But those moments of opportunity are so fragile, so fleeting, that they can happen to anyone at any time. The bottom line is that I don't know why those moments happen, and I don't know how people are chosen. In fact, I'm pretty sure that there is no rhyme or reason to opportunity at all.

Our world is as chaotic and irrational as a paper bag floating in the wind.

And, sometimes, one of us gets caught up in it and swept away to a place that we never thought possible. We can try to make sense of it, and surely there's always a reason apparent, but in the end we can never truly know. It just happened. And that's the way of it.

This is my opportunity crisis.

Opportunity presented itself to me when I barely had the will to seek it out. There was an inner conflict that I didn't know how to resolve. One part of me, the part that had been painted onto me by the brush of life, believed that people are not here to help you. People hurt you. And the more you open yourself up to them, the more they will take advantage.

Another part of me, the voice of naïve hope—the soothing melody that fools you into believing that life tends to work out for the better—wanted me to put myself on the line, take a risk. Maybe there is somebody out there who will try to help.

I don't know where that voice came from, I think my mother, but it was there. It was there just when I needed it, and, in a world of cynicism, I never know if it's in there somewhere, waiting for that moment when it can guide me onto a better path.

Yes.

I'm still shocked that Mrs. Barham said that word. It seemed like my first green light in a life packed with red ones.

If she had said, *no* then I'm not sure how long I would have been able to cling to that irrational hope of becoming an artist. Perhaps it would have stuck with me—an inextinguishable, lifelong, passion. Perhaps not.

It's that simple.

On the following day of school, Mrs. Barham delivered me an application. On the top, it read "Los Angeles County High School for the Arts: Admissions Application." I was told that all I had to do was fill it out and begin creating a portfolio of my artwork that I would be required to present to an "Admissions Committee."

It all sounded easy enough.

I followed the instructions and a couple short weeks after sending the application in, I received a letter in the mail that informed me of a time and location for an, "Audition."

It was to be held in December of 1993, about half way through my ninth grade year.

This audition, as I came to understand, would determine whether or not I could take free art classes. And, they were not just free classes. I learned that I was applying to a high school dedicated specifically to an advanced education in fine art. The "Admissions Committee" would decide whether or not I was good enough.

When I received this audition notification, I completely freaked out. My tune changed. The task seemed too. I had no idea what I had gotten myself into. I had no idea how to create a portfolio. I had never presented my artwork to a committee of professional artists. The only things that I knew about fine art, I had learned from an overweight heroin addict who showed me how to sketch prison tattoos. I was way, way out of my league here.

An overwhelming sense of impending doom was sailing in my direction.

I went to Mrs. Barham at school and told her that I didn't belong in a fine arts high school. I didn't even know what a portfolio was. I didn't know what I was going to say to the admissions committee.

Right away, she stopped me and said, "Ray, don't worry about it. I'll help you."

I agreed to superficially calm down. I agreed to listen. I agreed to believe, because, even though I knew on the inside that I didn't have the slightest chance of getting in, I wanted to be accepted so badly. If I could get into a school dedicated to the arts, then I could prove that I really was an artist, and I could get myself away from the neighborhood.

The thinking was that plain.

For weeks leading up to my audition, I stayed after school and worked with Mrs. Barham. She made me rehearse my presentation, taught me what a portfolio actually was, and helped me put together new drawings for it. I kept practicing so that I wouldn't stutter and stammer and sound like an idiot at my audition.

And then, just like any other, my audition day arrived. The sun rose in the east as it always had, painting my bed in shades of blue and yellow light. I was one day older than the day before and it showed because I didn't sleep a wink. I played through the audition in my head over and over again, all night, until morning arrived.

In my mind, I knew that this was the most important day of my life. I mean, if I were to be successful, if I got in, I would be able to go to high school with hundreds of other aspiring artists. I would be taught by art professionals, real artists like I hoped I might become. And, most glaringly, I would no longer go to school in a gang-infested neighborhood where aspiring to finish high school was considered 'academically driven.'

It felt like a make-or-break moment.

My Uncle Ray, who lived up the street, agreed to take me. I asked him because I knew my dad wouldn't help, and Uncle Ray was my closest relative who had a car. When he was a kid, he was also interested in pursuing art, but my grandma scolded him, insisting that art can't be a "respectable career." She would rather see him work in a slaughterhouse or at an auto shop. You know, something respectable. I suppose it was fitting, then, that Uncle Ray was my driver.

The school was located on campus at the University of Cal State Los Angeles, a beautiful college situated on a hilltop overlooking the forgotten corners of East Los Angeles. The facilities were immaculate, featuring state-of-the-art classrooms and cafes and libraries. Students milled around leisurely, seemingly without a care in the world.

As I got out of the car and waved goodbye to my uncle, I was overcome by a nervous panic that was practically debilitating. Walking up a flight of outdoor concrete steps, my knees trembled and my eyelids were frozen wide open, my eyes darting erratically in every direction. I became short of breath, and my brow began dripping with sweat. This was equally due to being fat and nervous.

When I reached the top I paused to collect my thoughts.

I heard a voice that sounded every bit as phenomenal as Whitney Houston coming from inside the music building where auditions were being held, and I further realized how utterly out of place I truly was. My portfolio was made from two pieces of light brown cardboard and the handle was improvised from duct tape. I wore a makeshift suit that I compiled from decades of unfortunate family history. My blue sport coat was old, borrowed from my Uncle Ray. My black dress pants were tattered, taken from my dad's closet, and my brown logger boots, though fashionable with other attire, completed a disappointing and unseemly image. I looked more like a floundering Amway salesman than an artist.

Stumbling up the stony cement walkway lined in brick, it felt as if I were walking through a strange room in the dark.

In the courtyard, white metal tables were sheltered from the sun by large, colorful umbrellas. The people who occupied them were so beautiful, laughing, with light-colored blue jeans and book bags.

Everyone seemed so, happy.

My heart raced. The music building had a sign out front that read, "LACHSA Auditions," and it had an arrow pointing in the appropriate direction. Before opening the door, I paused in my tracks, attempted to reconfigure my hair with a couple of hurried strokes, and gave myself a little reassurance.

Ok, Ray. You can do this.

Inside the building, the hallways were lined with lockers for people who had already been accepted to the school. The long corridors were lightly occupied, the students I saw seemed content and in their element. Despite the swell of new people waiting to audition, there was a noticeable calm, an unusual quiet, that harmonized the school. There were no gangsters. Nobody seemed to be heckling weaker students. It appeared that people approached one another with an attitude that would make you effeminate at "Night-in-jail"—respect.

The hallways smelled of fresh coffee, the product of coffee makers that were stationed at every corner of the building.

I asked someone standing next to a locker why it smelled like coffee, and he responded, "You don't go here yet?"

This is what I thought: *obviously*.

This is what I said: "No."

He looked me in the eye and said, "Well if you get in, you're gonna need it."

Oh God. What does that mean?!?

My stomach collapsed. My mouth felt dry, my hands clammy.

Suddenly, someone tapped me on the shoulder, snapping me out of my disoriented daydream. "Excuse me, what's your name? I need your ticket stub and audition time." It was a female Asian student with a clipboard whose job it apparently was to register everyone and make them feel judged.

She was very good at her job.

"Here," I said, hands trembling noticeably. "I'm Raymond Serna and my audition time is 9:30."

She told me to take a seat in a classroom they had set up as a waiting room. In the classroom sat about thirty other kids. My first impression was that they were surprisingly unkempt for an audition. They looked like they had just rolled out of bed and smelled a little. One wore a Bob Marley t-shirt and had long, messy dreadlocks weighing down his shoulders. Another was wearing all black, with silver jewelry, like she was about to be a guest on the Saturday Night Live sketch, "Goth Talk," with Circe Nightshade.

"Great, now I'm the stiff who wore a suit to get into art school!" I whispered to myself as I sat at one of the desks and opened up my makeshift portfolio to review.

I felt like I was in a doctor's office alone for the first time. There was a palpable nervous tension, and I just knew something weird or quirky was going to happen that I was totally unprepared for, like a shot in the leg with a gigantic needle, or something similarly scary. My foot bounced uncontrollably against the floor as I wiped sweat, again, from my forehead. I thought I was going to throw up all over the room.

One student who had been at the school for a semester already, came in to help calm everyone down. His name was Adon Lopez. He was a super-flamboyant gay guy who might remind you of Jack from Will and Grace.

His message went something like this: "I know it's really nerve-racking right now, but I just want all of you to know that everything is going to be fi-ine." His arms flailed in the air and he smiled constantly. He was so fun that it did calm my nerves a bit. I never really saw anyone like him in Cypress Park.

Then, the judgmental Asian girl came into the room and said, "Raymond Serna."

My stomach sunk and my nerves tingled from the center of my body outward. I couldn't feel my extremities as I walked out of the waiting room and into the audition. A panel was set up, consisting of 5 people, including the Arts Chairman, teachers, and one senior class member at the school. It was like a mid-90's version of American Idol.

The Asian student with the clipboard introduced me. "This is Raymond Serna. He is applying for acceptance to the visual arts department."

I stood in the center of the room, about fifteen feet from the panel. I squashed my left hand together nervously, my right arm grasping my makeshift portfolio.

"Hello Raymond," the Dean began. "Why do you want to be an artist?"

There was no introduction, no outline of how the interview would go, no casual conversation to lighten the mood—just a stark, direct, painfully honest question that made me feel like I had been shot in the gut.

Why do you want to be an artist? Why do you want to be an artist?

As simple as that question seems, it was the most difficult and complicated question that I'd ever been forced to answer. I suppose I knew what I wanted to say. I wanted to describe in vivid detail the complex thoughts and feelings that had defined my life up to this point.

I see it every time I look in the mirror,

I don't belong here; You can do it Ray,

I am completely alone; Get yourself out of here,

It's never going to end; Make it end, Ray.

What is an artist if not a person, with vivid experiences, insecurities, and conflicting messages tangled in a confused self-image? What is an artist if not someone with a deep-seated craving to find an interesting way to express the jumbled vignette in our mind we call memory? What is an artist if not a person mired in cynicism yet conducive to hope?

I could have said anything, anything, as long as it were honest, to explain my answer to a question like: why do you want to be an artist?

Do you know what I actually said?

"I want to go to your school because I like art. It's interesting."

And when I said it, it sounded more like a question. On paper, it would have looked like this: "I like art. It's interesting?"

My face wrinkled at the cheeks in pleading shame.

A litany of questions ensued. "How would you describe your skill level?" "What is your ambition?" "What do you envision yourself doing at this school?" "Who's your favorite artist?" "How much formal training do you have?"

The entire experience turned into one massive blur, a memory blackout in which the only thing I could manage to recall from the question and answer session was that first question. Why do you want to be an artist? And all I could remember about my responses were those utterly pathetic, remedial, unbelievably ignorant and naïve words that I spewed to a question that required a sophisticated, expressive, interesting, and, above all, honest answer.

I like art. It's interesting?

I might as well have said, "I'm this many," before flashing ten fingers, followed by the necessary, yet cumbersome, four fingers that would have informed them of my age. At least that answer would have been precise.

Near the end of the interview, the Dean said, "Well, let us take a look at your portfolio," as if he were saying, "Since you have nothing interesting or unique or intelligent to share with us, we had better just check quickly to confirm that you don't have any talent worth mentioning," before clanging a gong and sending me away to execution.

As they looked at my drawings, I explained to the panel what I had drawn. I said, "This is a picture of a buck. I saw it in a magazine and I thought that it looked beautiful, with the background being so open, it's like the buck is powerful."

All ten of my pictures went something like that. I explained what my drawings were and offered a little, superficial blurb about why I drew them. The common theme that I found, as I heard myself repeat the same mundane, nondescript word over and over again—beautiful.

I called everything beautiful. That's what I thought of it. And that's why I drew it.

At about the time I was ready to show them the final drawing in my portfolio, one of the teachers stopped me and said, "Hold on for just a second. I've seen enough, and I need to tell you something."

"Ok," I responded with trepidation.

"You need to draw from life. Your art needs to mean something. Do you understand what I'm saying?"

"Yes, definitely," I said.

 I didn't understand at all.

"Just because something is beautiful doesn't mean that it's good art," she continued.

After a few more quick comments from the panel, they excused me from the room. I thanked them and shook their hands. On my way out, the Asian girl with the clipboard smiled fictitiously in my direction and moved into the waiting room to call on someone else.

I removed myself from the building and shortly found myself standing outside in the courtyard. As I looked down at the concrete, little stars flashed in my vision. I looked around for a moment to immerse myself in the environment. The collegial feeling was so new, so fresh. I felt as if I were removed from reality and placed into my own sort of heaven, where people were respectful and independent, thoughtful but fun.

I wondered if it were the last time I would ever set foot in this courtyard or merely the first of many, at this school, at this college.

My uncle was waiting in his truck at the bottom of that flight of stairs. With each step, I could feel myself drawing farther and farther away from my dream. Approaching the truck, I felt a faint hope beating in the back of my mind.

Maybe I got in.

Time went on as it always had. My vignette of memory got a few weeks longer until a letter arrived in our mailbox from the Los Angeles County High School for the Arts (LACHSA). I opened it ritualistically, waiting until I was alone in my room and had taken an appropriate number of breaths and made the appropriate number of hopeful prayers.

Maybe I got in. Maybe I got in.

The paper ruptured beneath my fingertips. Gently, I slid my finger along, cracking the bonds that held the message intact. Wistfully, I unfurled the sheet of paper, and, gradually opening my eyes, I learned the news.

I hadn't. I was rejected admission to the Los Angeles County High School for the Arts.

Chapter 19

On the day after receiving my rejection letter, I went back to junior high at "Night-in-jail," and I saw the things that I saw. I heard the things that I heard. I smelled the things that I smelled, and I felt the things that I felt.

The kids were rambunctious, running, pushing, and teasing one another. The classrooms were drab with years old posters strewn randomly over the egg white paint. The expansive asphalt yard in the center of the school had a fence around it. The kids wore wife beaters and baggie Dickies pants.

The bells rang monotonously at timed intervals. The chairs squeaked against the floor uniformly as students were excused to leave. In the next room, the chalk screeched across the blackboard while the teacher droned on in typically condescending notes. A friend whispered something humorous into my ear.

The rooms smelled of chalk and mold, the hallways like bleach and hairspray. Outside, a distant scent of blooming flowers were overcome by humid, hazy, city air that gave the impression of total enclosure.

And I felt just as I had felt before. I felt satisfied that I was popular at school and restless for the exact same reason.

Everything was normal. Everything was the same. Nothing had changed.

And I hated it. I hated it with every fiber of my being because I had learned that nothing in our neighborhood was lasting. Everything was temporary, disposable, meaningless. Every time that we came across some money, it was gone before we knew it. When my parents bought substances, they didn't last. When we went a few months with lights and hot water, they would be shut off for another couple of months. When we got to know people, they too would go away.

Nothing lasted. Money didn't last. Cars didn't last. People didn't last. And good feelings, didn't last.

Somewhere deep down, I felt that my popularity at school was based on the way I looked. I had challenged authority over having green hair, and the kids thought it was fun. They laughed at my jokes and talked to me, but nothing about me, who I was on the inside, had changed in a year. If they liked me for any reason this year, they might hate me for the same reason next year.

Nothing good ever lasts, and beyond all of the superficiality I still went to the same crappy school in the same crappy neighborhood and had to deal with my dad and my brother and all of their crappy friends.

Crap.

Getting rejected by LACHSA illuminated this reality more than ever before.

I had received a taste of a great school, with apparently great teachers, and talented peers. I had seen what school is like on a college campus, the way that people's time and space were given respect just because they were part of the same thing at the same time. I had seen people who knew good art and could help me learn how to produce it.

There was a parallel universe in my mind between what was going on *up* there, and what was going on *down* here.

When I had some extra time, on the weekend or after school, I liked to get away from the house. It was exhausting to be constantly dealing with Ruben and his friends and his issues. My brothers tried to get away from home too. Mando would spend his time over at a friend's house reading comic books and collecting geeky items, like vintage weapons and sci-fi figurines. Richard spent his time at his girlfriend Vanessa's house.

For me, getting out wasn't easy. My best friend Kristina lived in Highland Park, several miles away and not within safe walking distance. I needed a bus pass in order to see her. They cost twenty-five dollars.

My money from cleaning the streets was gone. So I went to my dad to ask if he would help me buy the pass. Despite the fact that he frequently had handfuls of cash, which he reliably made disappear, he rejected my request. Dad wouldn't cough up a dime for any of us for any reason, and it wasn't part of some elaborate moral lesson. He was just selfish.

Then, out of necessity, I went to Mom for help, even though she never had any money, aside from our food stamps and welfare checks. Explaining to her that the money would allow me more freedom to see friends and be happy, she agreed to sneak into my dad's secret hiding place when he wasn't home and take the money I needed.

Mom came through for me the next day and gave me enough to buy a one year bus pass. For a teenager, there was no greater gift, and I never forgot that my mom was the one person who would go out on a limb for me when I needed help, and my dad was the guy who would never cough up a dime unless it was to buy himself drugs or booze.

Going to Kristina's house was a scary proposition. She lived on Latona Avenue, which branched off from 43rd Avenue—home to an infamous and violent sect of The Avenues gang. Since a huge part of the gang mentality was to scare off, beat, or kill people who came onto their turf from other neighborhoods, I could have been targeted just because I lived in Cypress Park.

To get from the bus stop to Kristina's house, I had to walk a half of a mile down 43rd Avenue. Every time, it felt like miles. I crossed over the Pasadena freeway and began climbing up a hill through the neighborhood. On my way, I saw groups of cholos and cholas hanging out on front porches, smoking cigarettes and bantering back and forth. They acted exactly like Ruben and his gang, although they were mortal enemies. A Chevy Caprice with Snoop Dogg in the tape deck rolled by slowly, blasting *Gin and Juice* through the speakers. I kept my head down in fear of attracting the attention of its passengers.

The one thing that I had going for me was fashion. Since I had dyed hair and wore night shirts and logger boots, I looked unique. Gangsters were like professional sports players, or whatever you call them. They wear uniforms to indicate their team. I didn't have a uniform, and this made me less likely to be targeted. If I wore a hoodie with a wife beater and still had a shaved head, I surely would have been harassed.

My fashion choices, being unique, allowed me to pass anonymously.

Yet, I was always relieved to arrive at Kristina's house. With gangs, you never know who will be targeted or why. Innocent people like me were shot regularly as part of initiations. There is no logic, no rule, to keep you safe. That's the point. Gangsters want you to believe that nobody's safe, and because of the culture—the weapons, the hatred of outsiders, the tough talk—they built, nobody was.

It was good having a friend in Kristina, who disliked the gangs as much as me. At first glance, she seemed intimidating, with her hoop lip ring and dyed red hair. The lipstick she wore was wildly overdone and crimson. Her pudgy build made her look tough and a little fiery, but she loved to experiment with fashion. She loved to talk, or at least listen, to me about art.

Our friendship revolved around a cycle of going to the mall and coming home to experiment with our images. I had learned that being the guy with dyed hair also required regular maintenance. So, every few weeks, I dyed it a different color. At Kristina's house I dyed it blue, green and red, and every time I alternated the color, it brought a little new excitement at school. Kristina started doing it too. She also loved piercings, and we began doing amateur piercings for one another while at her house.

We'd take the bus together out to Eagle Rock, where the Eagle Rock Plaza Galleria provided us with plenty of places where we could observe the latest clothes and fashions and things to talk about while we watched the people cycle through the stores, as the Earth rolled steadily around on its axis.

We made plans for what we might buy if we had enough money.

It was a time of great exploration. I was learning how to be confident, that it was okay to be different. It was okay not to like the same things as everyone else. It was okay to have an opinion.

There was at least one other person that liked to share her time with me, and that mattered.

Our friendship endured dozens of new hairstyles and clothing genres, all of the years that span the remainder of this story, but it all started back in junior high as two kids finding a person with whom to feel good about ourselves, someone who would listen to our ideas and our deepest, darkest thoughts without judgment or criticism.

When I came home at night, my dad was never there. Part way through my ninth grade year, he began leaving home to "work" at the bar. Every time he left, he'd shout, "Alright, I'm going to work."

And every time, I'd roll my eyes.

By work, he meant that he was going to the bar, and by going to the bar, I must say that he wasn't a bartender, or a waiter, or a bus boy, and most certainly not an investor. By "work," he meant that he sat at the bar and consumed their products until somebody walked in who wanted to consume his.

I'll leave out the name of the bar for the purposes of our story here. Well, on second thought, I'll call it "Tokies." It seems fitting because that's what lots of its patrons liked to do.

When he came home late at night, he was drunk and had no money, or at least none that we ever found out about.

These facts highlight two very important realities for the purposes of our story. One, it is questionable to say that my dad had a "job," particularly considering he didn't accept checks. Two, if you think that he did have a job, he was unquestionably bad at it. He was a "salesman" who always had product and customers, but never had money.

None of this is provable through documentation or tax records, of course. As with everything in the culture I lived, everything was a waste. There was no proof.

Nothing lasted.

Chapter 20

"You would never follow a person who hasn't worn the shoes you want to own. In my life, nobody owned those shoes."

Sometimes I think back on the things that happened to me when I was very young. I think of Eric, that despicable freak who dragged a five year old version of me into a bathroom to sexually assault. He did whatever he wanted to me. He made me do things to him.

I bring this up because of the way that children look at the world. It's different. When you're a kid, things just happen to you. Life strokes its brush against your canvass and all that you know is that it happened. Then, you have feelings, those repellent, shameful, saddening feelings. In your mind, it's your fault. It happened to you.

A child looks in the mirror at the painting she's become and believes that the marks and scars are because of her. In her mind it's all her fault.

That's how I felt at least. I was ashamed of what happened with Eric. It hurt. It hurt so much that I couldn't tell anyone about it. I couldn't tell anyone because I thought it was my fault. I thought I had done something wrong and didn't want to explain it to anybody.

If I had, I know exactly what people would ask. Why didn't you tell somebody? Why did you let him do that to you? Why didn't you know it was wrong? Why? Why? Why? Why? Why?

I knew that the moment I started asking why, was the moment that I would have to start explaining what happened. I was just a kid. He beat me up. I was scared. I thought that you'd be mad at me. I was just doing what I was told.

I would think again of those nights I laid awake, afraid to go to sleep because somebody might come in to hurt me. I would think of 'The Nightstalker." I would think of the fighting. I would think of Vinnie and how he picked on me because I wasn't good enough. I would think about the sixth grade, when all those kids made fun of me while I read my letter on stage. I would think about the fat kid in grey sweatpants and the phony gangster with the shaved head in order to blend in.

That simple question—why?—would require me to make sense out of all that. It would obligate me to look at the paint that life had splattered and splotched all over my canvass for all those years.

It implied a responsibility far greater than yours here today. By reading this all you have to do is know. And that may be difficult for some of you, but it doesn't even scratch the surface of what it meant for me.

Why? Why? Why?

I already knew about the awful thing that happened to me. I saw it. I felt it. I thought about it.

But I never really owned it. I never honestly looked at myself in the mirror and said, "That troubled little boy huddled helplessly in the bathroom was you. You are the fat kid in grey sweatpants, and no matter what you do, for the rest of your entire life, it always will be you. You can't ever be anyone else."

That admission was the scariest thing on Earth.

Something was happening to me though. I didn't feel like the weakling as I once did. By the end of junior high, I was bigger, bigger than almost anyone else in my school. The lenses that I viewed life through were different than when I was younger. They were shaded by my changing sense of self.

When somebody hurt me now, I didn't blame myself. I understood that the kids who made fun of people were the most insecure, angry, and pathetic losers in the whole place. I had formed some opinions of my own. I didn't have to be exactly like everyone else. I didn't have to listen to people I didn't respect, and, even if I did respect them, it didn't mean they were right.

This new sense of self would be put to the test early on. I was challenged by a series of seemingly isolated events that, when pieced together, presented me with an unexpected moral lesson—a chain of odd lessons that required me to do something that the child in me never had the power to do.

Choose.

Immediately after receiving my rejection letter from the LACHSA, I called the recruiter, Ben Fonseca, to debrief on my experience.

When I called and informed him that I'd been rejected admission, he said, "You got rejected Ray? I'm surprised to hear that."

"Yeah, I didn't know why for sure, but I didn't do as well as I could have I guess," I responded uncertainly.

"Well, we have more auditions coming up Ray. You can audition in June and then we have four auditions per year. So you can apply for admission through the tenth grade if you'd like."

This was great news to hear, I thought. "Oh, okay. How do I apply again? Do I have to fill out another application?" I asked curiously.

In a chipper, hopeful voice, he offered, "Yes, that's how it goes. I can send you another application if you'd like."

"Okay," I responded. "I'd appreciate that."

"Just keep at it. It's not easy to get in. I'm sure you'll get in next time," he concluded in a positive but empty way.

"Thank you Mr. Fonseca."

So long as I chose to, I could apply to LACHSA for another year, another five auditions if need be.

My choice was an interesting one because I knew that I was in way over my head during the first audition, and the rejection letter came as no surprise. Yet, I also didn't feel like I had shown them my best.

The advice that the panel gave me, that, "You need to draw from life. Your art needs to mean something…Just because something is beautiful doesn't make it good art," was more of an inspiration to me than a verdict on my potential. I had never received advice like that, and, frankly, I wanted more. And I believed deeply that I had more to show—more talent, more effort, more expression.

I had no idea if it would ever be good enough for them. If I were totally honest at the time, I'd probably tell you that I knew I would never get in at that school. But, by now, I just wanted to prove that I hadn't wasted all of my time. I wanted to prove that I meant something, somehow.

When I received the second application from Ben Fonseca, I filled it out and sent it back.

"Here goes nothing," I muttered to myself as I licked the envelope.

Back at "Night-in-jail" Junior High, things were going okay for old Ray. My hair color was still distracting enough for people to find me interesting. Crowds of kids that I never thought would accept me seemed to be unbothered by my presence.

The most shocking thing was that I was regularly invited to spend lunch hour in The Nighthawk Nest, a hip hangout exclusive to the 'in-crowd' of ninth graders. In actuality, The Nighthawk Nest was a shabby dirt pit shaded by typical California foliage. It was a narrow corridor that branched out from the asphalt 'prison yard' where the plebeians spent their time. If nothing else, I enjoyed the novelty of it, even though the company was annoying at best. Everybody professed to know the most about music and fashion and all that was "rad."

They knew virtually nothing, about anything.

One afternoon, I was talking to one of my friends that hung out in 'The Nest.' Her name was Diana Gonzalez, and I use the term *friend* very loosely in her case. I don't regret saying it was a loose friendship. And why would I? As the school slut, she never seemed to mind being called loose. Guys passed her around like a joint at a party.

We struck up a conversation about life, and you know, whatever—random stuff that junior high seniors talk about. And in the process, Diana asked me, "What do you think you're going to do after high school?"

I had kept my art school ambitions a total secret to everybody at school, aside from Kristina and my teachers. I didn't want to subject myself to their judgment. But during this conversation I slipped.

I responded, "After high school? What about after junior high?"

Confused by the question, Diana responded, "What do you mean after junior high? Everybody goes to Franklin High after "Night-in-jail.""

I don't know what it was at that moment—the way she worded her comments, the feeling that I had when I saw that she hadn't even considered something other than what *everybody* does—but I couldn't help but speak my mind.

I peered to my left to see if anybody was listening before leaning in to whisper to Diana. "Alright, now don't tell anyone, but I'm trying to get into an arts high school at Cal State-Los Angeles."

I leaned back to examine her response.

Diana was baffled at first, "Is it like a magnet school or something?" she asked.

"Well sort of," I explained. "It's like a very in-depth school for fine art. It's really competitive and it's for people who want to become real artists—dancers, singers, actors, visual artists, you know? It's more than just a magnet school."

Her face puckered up and her eyebrows furrowed. She said, "So what do you, think you, can go for?" heavily emphasizing the word *you* throughout her sentence.

"Visual arts," I said defensively.

Diana jerked her head to the side and lifted up her left shoulder. This is what she said: "You can't compete with that."

You can't compete with that.

It was as if she were saying to me, "Yeah, you're good at drawing. So what? You're not that good."

I was blown away with how brutal she had been, how direct.

As we talked it out, she asked, "So what are you going to do after that? Be some kind of starving artist?"

"No," I demanded, at this point indignant. "I can be an architect or a designer or something. You never know. People make money designing things."

Diana dismissively lifted her chin and peered down at her long, red, acrylic nails. "Nobody I know does that. Plus, you can't even do math. How you gunna be a designer?"

She basically laughed in my face. The frustrating part was that there wasn't much I could say. I didn't know any designers either. I didn't know how I could make a career out of art school. And she was right about one thing for sure. I was terrible at math.

Yet, she gave not even the slightest touch of encouragement, not the faintest sense of support or belief in my ability to do something great.

In that conversation in The Nighthawk Nest, that I realized a harsh truth. I looked around at all the people who had accepted me as "rad" enough to hang out with them, and I couldn't find a single person who truly believed in me. There were a few people with whom I shared a basic, superficial connection, but not one who I knew would be there for me if I really needed them.

There wasn't anybody who wanted to go to an arts high school either.

At the end of that lunch period, when I walked away from 'The Nest,' I told myself that I wouldn't tell anyone else about my dream to become an artist. If there wasn't anybody who really cared what I do, if there wasn't a single person that believed in me, why should I give them the respect of sharing my dreams?

None of them could see that there was a life beyond those walls, beyond the chain-linked fences and asphalt play areas, beyond Cypress Park and the City of Los Angeles. All they knew was that when they graduated from "Night-in-jail," it was time to go to Franklin High. After that, they just assumed that everything would work out. It has to right? Nobody's going to end up just wafting through life without ever taking the time to dream up something better, will they?

The next time some girl asked me what I wanted to do with my life, I responded, "Ah, I don't know. I'll figure something out."

When I said this, I received the following response. She nodded her head, and made a noise that was short, but certain.

"Rad."

In early June, I went back to LACHSA for another audition. This time, when I put together my portfolio, I tried to draw from life. I tried to make it mean something. I experimented with new art supplies, like oil pastels and charcoal. I sat out in my backyard and drew the four towering palm trees that hung over my neighbors home. I drew the black asphalt play area at school. I drew my grandmother's house.

All of my drawings were things that I saw in my life. They were clear and proficient. If you were to look at them, you'd probably say, "Oh I know exactly what that is. It is good."

Coming into audition day, I knew where to sit. I knew how it would work. I knew what I was supposed to say.

When they asked me, "Why do you want to be an artist?" I responded, "I want to draw from life. I want my art to mean something."

I said exactly what I thought they wanted to hear.

With one week left in school, my family and I travelled together to Highland Park, where my oldest brother Richard was graduating from Franklin High. All of the students wore navy blue gowns and mortar board caps. Music was played through an organ. Parents cried as the kids lined up to accept an eight and one-half by eleven inch piece of paper called a "Diploma." By all objective standards, it was a coronation to be remembered.

I was proud of Richard because it seemed like a big deal. My mom had never graduated from high school, nor had Grandma Chance.

When he came back over to us to get a hug and some congratulation, I said, "You graduated. It must feel great right?"

Here's what he said to me: "High school, junior high, elementary school—all of it—gives you the biggest sense of false security that you can ever imagine. I went to all these classes and they gave me this piece of paper, but what am I supposed to do now? It doesn't mean shit."

I'll never forget that. High school graduation seemed like a major accomplishment at the time, something admirable. Yet, all my brother had to say was essentially, "What does high school actually do for you?"

There was something honest in his words that impacted me. Don't get me wrong, I'm not trying to claim that school doesn't matter. It does. It's exceedingly important. But, for Richard, the end of school brought the realization, "Now what?"

Like my dad decades earlier, Richard hadn't spent high school mapping out a career path. He didn't apply to college. He didn't have a vision, or a step-by-step dream that he was living out. So, for people in his situation, people in my situation, going to school became a habit of merely biding your time in a safe environment until you're released into an unsafe world, without prospects.

Is that what I want to do? Is that how I'm going to feel if I graduate from Franklin?

Everyone always tells you that if you play by the rules, do what you're told, and do good in school, everything will be great, and it just isn't true for everybody. I saw it that day. We spend all of our time measuring ourselves against those around us, but what if the people around us are untrustworthy dead beats and ambitionless wastoids? Where do the rules get you when so little is expected from the people around you? Where does the school bureaucracy in my neighborhood lead?

It leads right back onto the streets that I spent my summers sweeping.

What I took from Richard's graduating words is this: *if you want to be proud of yourself for doing something, you have to set your own standards. You have to make your own rules.*

On the final day of ninth grade, my last day at "Night-in-jail" Junior High, the school put on an awards assembly for the graduating class. The students lined up in rows on the asphalt play area in front of a stage adorned with trophies.

I remember walking by one of the awards and remarking at how big it was. "Whoa, who's going to win that one?"

I rolled my eyes.

The Dean began the ceremonies and reading off the various awards and names. "And the Citizenship Award goes to…"

The students responded with hollow applause as the winner took a walk to the stage.

The process repeated itself many times over and I grew distracted.

"The Science Award goes to…"

I clapped overdramatically and started making jokes to my friends about the awards banquet.

"The Math Award goes to…"

"Hooray, I won the "Night-in-Jail" Math Award. I'm famous!" I quipped sarcastically.

"And the Art Award goes to…"

I prepared my next joke, which was "Look at me Ma! I won. Aren't I special?"

"Raymond Serna."

My heart fluttered and my face froze. Did I really just hear that?

One of the people sitting next to me slapped me on the shoulder and said, "That's you dummy. Get up and get your award."

I awkwardly hoisted myself up from the asphalt and began slowly heading for the stage. All the kids looked at me, but, uncharacteristically, I wasn't embarrassed.

The Dean smiled at me and shook my hand before handing me the gargantuan trophy. There was no speech required, no written response. I didn't have to sweat while the kids judged my words. I simply turned around and looked out at them, at the vast sea of people smattered about the Nightingale play area.

And I smiled. But only on the inside.

Upon arriving home, before I could tell Mom about the art award I won, she shouted in to me. "Oh, Mijo. I've been waiting for you to come home all day. You got some mail from LACHSA."

My heart thumped as she handed me the thin, white envelope. I closed my eyes, attempting to avoid the news for a moment. That feeling was profound, meaningful, what it must feel like for a skydiver right before taking the plunge from an airplane. Hope tangled with fear to concoct a fusion of feigned ecstasy.

I took two deep breaths before opening the letter.

My eyes read furiously, bounding left to right and back again. My hands froze to the letterhead, clenching at the top and bottom of the page like it was trying to get away.

The words read something like this:

Dear Ray,

Thank you so much for auditioning for a position in visual arts at LACHSA. We see over a thousand applicants every year and are so impressed by all of the talent that Los Angeles has to offer. Your effort and skill did not go unnoticed and we know that you put forth a phenomenal effort.

We, however, regret to inform you that you have not been granted admission to LACHSA for the upcoming year. We encourage you to keep trying and thank you so much for...

I couldn't translate any farther. Once again, my rejection stung. The bottom of my throat swelled. My arms hung limp at my sides as I slumped down onto the couch. At the same time, on the same day, that Nightingale Junior High presented me with an art award, I was declined the opportunity to spend the tenth grade at LACHSA.

Mom sat down beside me and put her arm around me. "It's okay my love. You're going to be wonderful no matter where you go to school. I love you."

Her sweetness, as always, was never-ending.

How can I make sense of this contradiction? Was I good enough for some, but not enough for others—talented in Cypress Park and underwhelming at LACHSA?

What did all of this mean?

I can't say for sure, but one thing was confirmed. I'd be attending Franklin High in the fall, just like my mother, just like my father and my brothers, just like the rest of the crowd at "Night-in-jail."

"Rad."

Early in the summer, we got the extraordinarily rare opportunity to take a vacation. And it sure came at a convenient time, although not for Grandma Chance. She was having surgery, which was the reason that my mom had been saving up money for us to fly to Arizona.

Back then, the plane ticket from Los Angeles to Phoenix was thirty-nine dollars per ticket, round-trip.

Grandma Chance had moved to Arizona when my Aunt Diane's job was relocated. Aunt Diane was Grandma's main source of income, leaving little choice in the matter. For many years now, Grandma Chance had been separated from my Grandpa Edward. He had repeatedly cheated on her with other women and returned only to cheat again, despite her faithful love and service. As her only source of income, Grandpa Edward's absence created a financial void that had to be filled by my mom's sisters.

Going to Arizona that summer was a real thrill. It was the first time I'd ever flown on an airplane and the first time in many years that I'd gotten to see my mom's side of the family.

It felt good to be back in a warm home environment. My Aunt Diane was doing quite well, providing a state-of-the-art condo in a gated community for the family to share. I enjoyed the luxuries of hot water, cable, electricity, and a backyard pool, without the slightest consideration that it might be gone in an instant.

We spent the first few days looking at pictures and reminiscing about the past. I mostly listened, not remembering any of the tales. Watching them try to recapture the past, there was an unspoken tension that was difficult to place. For split seconds, following a funny story and a fit of uproarious laughter, the room would go silent, my mother's eyes seeking comfort in the corner of her lashes. I don't know exactly what she was thinking in those moments. I don't know what my grandmother and my aunts thought either. I could just tell there was something, a comment floating on the surface of their consciousness beckoning to be drawn into the open.

It smelled like regret.

My cousins Eric and Irisa liked to play in the pool, and I sometimes accompanied them by sitting off to the side, in the hot Arizona sun drawing pictures. I never took my shirt off in front of other people. My cousins were about five at the time and it was fun having them around because they were totally fascinated by my artwork.

Arisa would shout, "How can you do that?" and Eric would demand, "Draw me an elephant!"

It got pretty annoying after a few days, but it was nice to have some admirers. They wanted to emulate me, which made up for the innocent vexations. After a lifetime of being the youngest brother, the little twerp clinging along, trying to matter, it was also rewarding to be the oldest for once.

As the days trudged along, I felt very at home. It was refreshing to be so far away from Cypress Park, my dad, and Ruben—enough so to make me distracted from the trying times I had faced at the conclusion of junior high. My grandma went through her surgery and everything turned out surprisingly well. She was able to come home before we left, appearing resilient and unfazed by the operation.

On our last day in town, I was entrenched in a scenario that I never wanted nor asked for, but one that pressured me into a shocking epiphany.

I was sitting at the dinner table, during the afternoon, talking to my grandmother and aunts while my mom was in the bathroom taking a shower. Suddenly, and without my prompting, the conversation took a turn into my family secrets.

My aunt leaned over toward her sister and whispered, "You know what they do in that house, don't you? Peanut sells. That's all he does to make money."

"And they both just use and live off welfare checks," my other aunt chimed in.

Awkwardly following along, I timidly tried to step in, "That's not. I. There's more to it than that," I muttered.

Nobody made eye contact with me or hesitated. They just kept on as if I weren't in the room.

Grandma Chance sighed. "Oh lord," she said. I watched as she turned toward me, gently placing her tiny, wrinkled hands on the cherry wood table.

"I should have taken you away from your mom when you were born," she said firmly.

She looked me straight in the eye and meant it.

It felt like being pounded in the forehead with a baseball bat. I felt dizzy, emotions rupturing in my legs and throat. Feeling them build on one another and rise, they got the best of me until I suddenly began shouting.

"Who do you think you are?"

My voice reverberated through their eardrums as they sat frozen, shocked that I—polite, reserved little Ray—had the nerve to lash out at them.

"You don't know anything about my life. You left me when I was ten!" I screamed.

I shocked myself. My breathing grew heavy.

My mom heard my outburst and came darting in from the bathroom with her hand tightly pressing a towel to her chest. She violently grabbed me by the arm and towed me into her bedroom.

Mom looked me in the eye, pointed her finger directly into my face, and said, "Don't you ever backtalk to your grandmother ever again!" Her veins pulsed visibly in her neck, her face becoming red.

It was the angriest I had ever seen her.

"If I ever hear another thing like that come out of your mouth, you are in big trouble with me. Do you understand me?" Her teeth clenched tightly after finishing her question and her head tilted authoritatively to the right.

In an attempt to justify myself, I pleaded with her. "Did you hear what she said to me? She said she should have taken me away from you."

Mom leaned back on her heels, lowering her voice as she said, "I heard what she said, but it doesn't matter. You don't ever speak that way to your grandmother because she is the only reason that I'm alive. If you didn't have her, you wouldn't have me." Mom pointed to her own chest. "You understand what I'm telling you Mijo?"

I blinked. I blinked much longer than normal. I trailed off into a reflection on the generations of actions that led up to this point in my life. I thought of my mom at my age. I thought of my grandma at my age.

What did they think when they were fifteen years old? What choices did they make?

I'll never forget that moment. Disrespecting my grandma was the first time that I had outright defied an elder of my family. That simple act allowed me to see myself as a unique piece of a family history.

But my mom reminded me of my place in that history. Grandma Chance created my mother and my mother created me. Yes, my grandma left us when we were very young, but there was nothing that could be done about that now. I couldn't rewrite her history any more than she could. But I also realized that I could assert my individuality, and realized my power to separate myself, while still being a member of the clan.

I realized the difference between respecting my family and acquiescing to continue along the path they'd travelled.

"Yes, Mom. I understand."

I went directly into the dining room to apologize to my grandma and give her a hug.

That night, I laid in bed reliving the intense interactions from earlier in the day. I regretted speaking to my grandma as I had, but at the same time I was proud. I was proud to find my ability to say what I wanted to say. I had the authority to do what I wanted to do. I had the strength to be my own person.

My grandmother's name is Aurora Chance.

My mother's name is Lilia Serna.

My name is Raymond Serna.

When my grandmother was fifteen, she had every bit the authority as I did that day. After graduating from the eighth grade in La Magdalena, Mexico, she moved to West Los Angeles with her father and sixteen cousins. She went to night school until she became certified as a nurse's aid. Just as she was prepared to take her first job, she married Grandpa Edward, and the rest is history.

A. Chance spent her life working tirelessly as a mother and housewife. What was her choice? She traded her career, her chance to make her own way in life, for the promise of a loving husband in Highland Park.

When my mother was fifteen, she had the power that I had at fifteen. She could have done anything with her life.

She was going to Franklin High and met my father during her junior year. When her family moved from Highland Park to Norwalk she was faced with a choice—A. *Chance*—like her mother before.

What was her choice?

Lilia Chance spent her life working tirelessly as a mother and housewife. She too was drawn to the prospect of a loving husband, in Cypress Park. Without a career and without an education, she became dependent on him for money, dependent on his family for a home.

The rest, again, is history.

That night, I repeated again the words that A. Chance, my grandma, spoke to me when she said that, "I should have taken you away from your mom when you were born."

I considered what she actually meant. Did it mean that she didn't trust my mom? Did it mean that she didn't love us?

When I thought it through—why grandma suggested that she should have taken me from my family—I realized what it meant.

It meant that she knew things could have been different for me. It meant that she was aware of the troubling, inappropriate, and oftentimes haunting images that life might paint on my blank, white sheet of paper.

That hurt, but it proved transformative to my thinking.

My life didn't have to be what it was.

If A. Chance thought that taking me away from my parents might have made a difference in my life, it meant that *it wasn't my fault.*

My life could have been different; my destiny was not tied to the choices of my family.

So, what choices will I make? If I ever get A. Chance of my own, which direction will I choose?

That, I now believed, was entirely up to me.

Chapter 21

In the train of my family, I was the caboose.

My entire life through, to the moment I begrudgingly entered into Franklin High School, I was dragged faithfully behind my family, stopping when they stopped, sputtering as they sputtered. And the scenery never changed.

Days and nights, then weeks and months, then years had passed since I knew that I didn't like the path down which I travelled. I wonder if anyone liked it. We never spoke much about it. Life had never been presented to us as a choice. Ideas of life, goals, dreams, they were just too far away on the horizon for my brothers and parents. Sure, I wondered and dreamed and tried to piece a new path together in my head, but, remember, I was the caboose. The iron bolted grip latching me to the cars in front of me made it impossible to see the way forward. It made it impossible for me to chug in a new direction.

They all loved me and I loved them back. They were my family, and if I had learned anything during the trials of my early years, it was the value of love and loyalty to my family. They were all that I had.

But I had trucked along that path too far, and I wanted something new.

I was old enough now to make my own choices, and I had learned that all I needed to do, to free myself from the slavery of that journey, was to reach down and unlatch the bolt that fastened me to them and watch them fade into the distance while I sought my own way.

Yet, there I was on an autumn Los Angeles day, peering up from the base of Franklin High, just as my brother Richard and Mando had during the past few years, and just as my parents had decades before. As flowering teens, their futures began on the inside of these walls, and, now, it was my only

choice.

Wandering into the bleak stone corridor at the entrance of the school made me feel like I was

admitting myself to a medieval prison camp. Two police officers out front had guns securely fastened to

their belts as they eyed the little hoodlums passing into the gates, checking us in through a pair of metal

detectors as we reported for our first day of service. On the inside, hundreds of kids huddled together in

tightly packed cliques, talking at one another at a frenzied pace. The collective sound melded together

to create an unsettling howl that echoed through the cramped open air courtyard. Four levels of

concrete encrusted classrooms formed a horseshoe around the courtyard with steel-barred railings

protecting each mezzanine.

Seeing some kids that I knew from "Nigh-in-jail," I stepped over to say hello.

"Hello," I said.

Their eyes deflected off of mine toward the ground and crawling up my body. They said nothing

in response, playing it cool as if talking to somebody that you knew in junior high might damage their

reputations.

Really? We're going to go through this whole song and dance again? Really?

I rolled my eyes, fastened my backpack more securely to my right shoulder and proceeded to

get my class schedule. The long lines, the thick crowds, and chaotic sounds were unnerving. From the

moment I walked into the building I felt completely alien.

I remembered back to the serene, professional atmosphere at LACHSA, on campus at Cal State-

Los Angeles. The smell of coffee in the sparsely populated hallways, the challenging questions, and the quirky, yet harmless student body felt a world away. Franklin was my new school, and LACHSA was the strange parallel universe that I knew about but couldn't bring into consciousness.

My schedule included seven classes, one of which was art. It was my sixth period and would last fifty-five minutes.

My first period was English class, which I was ten minutes late for because I couldn't find the room. I couldn't find any of my classes. I don't know whether it was actually a complicated facility or if I just didn't want to find places, but nothing came easily for me at Franklin. I felt like I was in a hamster wheel of death, desperately scurrying about only to learn that I had made no progress.

When I finally arrived at English class, only one seat remained available in the far corner of the room by the concrete wall. As I sat, the cheap, hard chair felt like I was sitting on a misshapen rock. My ass stung from its shocking lack of elasticity. Around the room, the students were like drones, eyes fixed in random directions, some at the clock, others at their desk, and some at the door. Nobody was engaged in the content of the class, and it resembled a prospective Twilight Zone episode called, "The Class of the Living Dead."

Above my right shoulder was a tiny plastic window protected by metal bars. The damp, dreary room with the faint rays of sunshine painting the ceiling above reminded me of the bathroom. I felt Eric towering over me, the walls and ceilings closing inward.

I don't belong here.

The desks were relics of the 1960's. I examined the weathered plywood surface to see if I could find Peanut and Lilia sketched into a heart amongst the collage of graffiti that had accumulated since. I felt sure that my parents had sat at these same desks.

I pulled out my notepad and began trying to take notes until I realized that the teacher wasn't saying a whole lot worth noting. Instead, I began sketching a flower. As each pedal flourished into form on my page, I looked around to find it was the only thing in the room that I found lovely. All of the people, the posters on the wall, the old, dingy ceiling fan, reeked of stagnation. It wasn't that everyone was ugly. They just weren't attractive, if you know what I mean.

The environment was polluted with years of cultural toxins that left behind a residue of mediocrity which stacked on top of itself, blanketing everyone and everything in the room. This became my view of Franklin High. Everything was just, *blah*.

Like my first years at Aragon and Nightingale, it was a totally new start socially. In the beginning, everybody stayed within themselves until they found a way to assimilate. Everyone wanted to "fit in" at their new school. Some try to impress the other kids with jokes. Some try to fashion a lifestyle or be sexually attractive. Others played a role, mimicking the people of a particular group.

I was sick and tired of the ridiculous game. I didn't want to impress anybody. I didn't want to assimilate into one of the social groups. I just wanted to feel comfortable being me. I wanted to learn from others.

I wanted to be inspired.

For the first few weeks, I kept getting myself up in the morning, putting on my clothes, getting on the bus, and walking to Franklin High for another day of school. And every day that I did, each step that I took got harder and harder. My feet grew heavier and heavier. The monotonous, desensitizing world of school, the uninteresting topics and idle student loafers in class became a burden of the mind.

I'd spend what felt like an eternity sitting there searching for something to connect with, something to make me think, and before I did, I'd look up at the clock and realize that only ten minutes had passed, each becoming steadily longer than the next. And I wanted my life to end sooner. The minutes just weren't worth it. Being at Franklin was like watching the worst, boring, annoying, uninteresting movie that you've ever seen on repeat and having no way to change the channel.

For whatever reason, the thing that I remember most vividly was the walk each morning from the bus to the school. The bus let off at the bottom of a steep hill, blocking our view of the horizon. As I climbed, I looked over at the surrounding neighborhood. It was a fitting example of the mediocrity that I felt in my heart. The homes were clearly once quite nice, of decent size and interesting design, but worn by time, unrepaired by its residents. The soiled white paint had chipped. The gutters began slanting like the slope of the hill I climbed. The neighborhood and I had something in common. Time was our enemy. The longer we waited, the less hope we had that things might get better.

Every day, I climbed that hill, and every day that I did, I regretted the effort.

What was I gaining for myself by sitting in those classrooms, in that crumbling neighborhood? Where did this climb lead?

During the second month, I received my third rejection letter from LACHSA. I had failed again to meet their standards, and I couldn't put my finger on why. I thought about it, over and over again. My mind bounced around ideas about why my presentation or my drawings weren't good enough for them. All I could do was look inward.

What can I do to get it right? How can I draw from life? How can my art mean something?

I mailed in my fourth application immediately.

And one day, in the midst of it all, I woke up, got in the shower, put my clothes on, and sat down on my bed. I looked around the room, then down at my feet.

I asked myself, "What am I doing?"

When I heard that question in my own mind, I made a choice. "I'm not going to Franklin today," I mouthed to myself.

I didn't want to climb that hill anymore.

After missing a couple days in a row, I decided to go back. I went to class and nobody seemed to notice that I had even been gone. The teachers didn't recognize me or know my name. The students were useless leeches, glaring out into space mindlessly. In the quad during lunch, I looked around and thought I was on a jungle safari watching chimps fling poop at one another. It was so chaotic and lackadaisical that I just walked out. Literally, I decided one moment to stand up, walk to the bus stop, and leave for the day.

The next week I didn't go at all, and, again, nobody cared. It didn't matter one way or the other. My brother Mando did the same thing. He had just stopped going to Franklin too. They held him back a grade, and he'd go once in a while, until the one day when he chose not to anymore. To this day, he doesn't have a high school diploma, and, in the neighborhood, that's fairly common.

During the day, while I skipped school, I would draw and reflect on how I might draw from life. How can I be honest and expressive in what I do?

Then I started asking myself, "Why don't I express emotions in my art?"

And I stopped asking that question immediately because it was terrifying.

My audition day came up again, and I got a ride from my brother Ruben.

The hope I once held walking into the audition room had faded. I had now fully embraced the fact that they were probably never going to admit me to the school, but I still wanted to keep going, keep trying. I was at the point in my life where going to LACHSA was 'Plan A' and there simply wasn't a 'Plan B.'

Art school was the only thing that inspired me.

After I had answered the first few questions, the panel asked me, "What is your ambition?"

I answered, "I want to go to your school. My ambition is to become an artist. I want to create things that are beautiful, that mean something to people."

For the fourth time, they thanked me, shook my hand, and excused me from the room.

I spent thirty minutes walking around campus, leisurely observing the environment that I so admired. The pace and flow of everything was so serene. Everyone was totally anonymous to me, and I to them. I took a long deep breath and pretended that I was a part of it all.

After that fourth audition at LACHSA, I didn't go back to Franklin for the last two weeks of the semester. Mostly, I stayed in my room to draw. Mando had recently found a girlfriend and spent all of his time there, so I had the room all to myself.

Every once in a while, my mom would walk by and notice me lying in bed at eleven in the morning and ask, "Why are you in bed Mijo? Why aren't you at school?"

"I'm not feeling well. I don't want to go to school."

"Okay, but you should really go to school my love." She walked into the kitchen to clean up.

I began staring up at the ceiling and thinking about why I wasn't getting into the art school, why I wasn't able to impress them with the emotion and meaning of my drawing. And the questions began building slowly and steadily, like a cloud that grows darker and heavier as it sponges up tiny little droplets from the sky.

The rain so desperately needed to be free.

Whenever somebody was near, my chest began to swell and my stomach tingled. I closed my eyes and suppressed the urges that I felt. It had to be the right time. I can't just tell them until the time is right.

At some moment, sitting alone in my room on the corner of my bed, I started to cry. Tears flowed from the corner of my eyes incessantly, dripping down onto the grimy carpet beneath my toes.

And it wouldn't stop. I cried and cried for hours. The hours turned into days and I felt like I was crying the entire time. I couldn't move. My head hung lifelessly in my hands in silent repose, teardrops soaking my palms.

During the fits of lament, I considered my chances of finding success. I couldn't get into art school and I couldn't force myself to go back to the forsaken hollows of Franklin.

Should I run away? Should I kill myself? What are my options now? I don't know what comes next.

There are certain things in life that propel you forward. Maybe it's a group or a team or an activity. Perhaps it's a class or a friend or a hobby. Life is made bearable during hard times by some glimmer of light at the end of the tunnel, something that you look forward to when all else feels lost. At that moment in life, in my brain, in my body, in my stagnant home, there was no light at the end. The propeller was broken. My life was stalled and devoid of any reason that I should go on.

I had seen so many serious, real, things in the year prior. My brother's friend Dank had been shot behind a dumpster at the Cypress Park Recreation Center. Ruben now came home almost every night 'stuck on stupid,' the term Richard liked to use for being high on PCP. My dad verbally abused my mom just about every night now when he got home from the bar.

And I was just expected to go to school and pretend like I was learning something real? Something meaningful? It was all just a masquerade, a show to go along with a failing culture without having to honestly confront it for a while.

I was absolutely defeated.

Mom didn't check to see if we had gone to school every morning, but one morning she walked by to find me crying on the bed, and it broke her heart.

She came to sit next to me and asked, "What's the matter Mijo? What are you doing still here?"

Inside, I had this desperate feeling and I didn't know what to say. "I can't go back there Mom," I cried.

"Where?" She asked.

"To Franklin. I can't ever go back. I just don't fit in. I don't learn anything and I just can't go back there, ever," I rambled hysterically.

She said, "Okay darling. Just lie down, collect your thoughts, go to sleep if you have to, and everything will be okay."

She stroked my hair lightly with her hand. My throat swelled closed as my face puckered in anguish, tears beginning to dry up on the side of my chin.

Two days went by and I stayed in bed for most of them. I cried every morning and every night. During the serene moments, while I became momentarily soothed, the thoughts and emotions began piling up in my mind, the deep yearning inside of me to express myself increasing with every minute gone by.

Two more days passed, and I, now in more of a reflective depression, spent most of the time sitting in an old barber shop-style chair in the corner of my parent's room, watching morning talk shows.

My ass hurt from being dragged mercilessly along *rock bottom*.

My mom grew irritated with me in a way that I hadn't seen before. She was frustrated and at a breaking point because, no matter what she did for me, or what she said, I just stayed at home quietly— refusing to go back to school.

I knew she was getting upset, but it didn't bubble over until that one morning when she was talking to me, asking me questions, and I ignored her, staring blankly at the TV.

"What can I do for you Ray? Why do you refuse to go to school? Why, Ray? Why?" Emotion boomed from her voice.

Why? Why? Why?

The Ricki Lake show played quietly in the background. My thoughts grew quiet and my heart pumped faster. I felt that it was time.

"Mom," I said. My voice wobbled when I turned to her with my chin in the air. I made direct eye contact.

She looked back at me, frustration transforming into empathy.

She asked "What?" without speaking a word.

Tears began welling up in my eyes once again, and I closed them, squeezing the tears down onto my face. My voice cracked again when I spoke.

"I was molested at school when I was five."

I couldn't believe that I actually said it.

For ten years, I had thought about how I might tell someone, anyone about what Eric did to me in that bathroom. For ten years, I had kept the most traumatic and emotional experience of my life, a secret that was born when I was five and aged along with me through adolescence, and now, at the age of fifteen, I had finally let it out for good.

It was unplanned. I didn't think I was going to say it. In fact, I had convinced myself that I would never be able to say it.

But I did.

And when it was over, I cried and cried and cried. It had been such a long time coming and I was so scared to learn how people were going to react. I was terrified at what they might think of me.

Mom looked over to me in horror and helplessness. The way her brow furrowed and eyes froze to her upper eyelid, the way her hands fell open as if summoning the lord from the heavens, and the way her mouth hung open, wordless, without answers, made me sink within myself. My eyes stayed closed and I looked away, not wanting her to see me anymore. I curled my neck into my arms to hide.

I could only imagine what she thought of me at that moment, pathetically crouching, a weakling who couldn't take care of himself.

Once the words had sunk in and the emotion on my face fully validated the pain and torment it had caused me, she came to me, sat beside me in the chair, and held me. With my head falling limp on her shoulder, her hair brushed against my neck. I could feel her tears dripping down on my forehead, and I thought to myself, "Thank God it is finally over."

When my brothers got home, I was sitting on the living room couch, still crying.

Mando asked, "What's wrong Ray? Why are you crying?"

I cried even harder. I couldn't look anyone in the eye. I couldn't say it again.

Mom walked me into my room and helped put me in bed. I cowered there alone, wishing that it was all just one elaborate nightmare, knowing for sure that it wasn't.

It was real.

This was me.

And I could never be anyone else.

I lay in bed for three days, only coming out to use the bathroom. Mom brought me food. I ate none of it. I just watched the days go by, seeing the rays of yellow and blue light penetrating the window in the morning and painting different parts of the room with shadows as night fell.

The emotions ran their course in my body. I had asked myself, "why?" And now I had to live with the answers. From this moment on, I knew that, no matter what, I could never make Eric a secret again.

Everybody knew.

I am the kid who got molested. I am the fat kid in grey sweatpants, and He is the reason why. There is a reason that I became what I did.

Those experiences, those harrowing thoughts are the base of the painting that is my life. As much as I want that to change, it can't.

For days, I heard the echoing of voices in the other room.

Ruben shouted, "I'd cut that motherfucker down if I'd known about this."

My dad boomed back, "That fucking son of a bitch."

"Who was it?" Richard asked my mom in a deadpan voice.

She explained, "The person doesn't even live around here anymore. Nobody knows where he is."

They now learned what I had known for too long. I knew they were talking about me, but I was still afraid to be seen.

On the third day, I was finally ready.

I mustered the energy to stand up, open the door, and walk into the living room. I pulled out a chair in the center of the room and sat down. My eyes fixed robotically on the TV screen, which made it look like I was watching, but I had no idea what was even on. The TV just allowed me to avoid eye contact with anyone.

My mom asked me how I was feeling, and if I was okay.

Lethargically, I responded, "Yeah, I'm alright," still staring emptily at the TV.

I didn't know what to do. I didn't know how to handle this type of family situation. For my whole life, emotion was like the giant elephant in the room with the other males. Nobody talked about their feelings or explained the hardships they were going through. They just covered it up with bluster and fronts of masculinity. Whether it was gunshots or fights at school or run-ins with a gangster, the boys of my family never made mention of problems. It all just got drowned out by substances or music or fantasy.

But now, the subject was unavoidable and I didn't know how it would be handled.

Then, my brother Richard—the rocker, the oldest, the badass who never showed that he cared about much of anything—walked over to me and placed both of his hands over the back of the chair and gently around my neck.

He said, in a kind, fatherly tone, "Don't worry about it little brother. We would never let that happen to you again. And we're sorry that we weren't there to protect you."

He had never been warm like that before, and I didn't know what to say.

"Thanks," I muttered.

"Everything's going to be okay, Ray," Richard said. "If there's anything you need, tell me, or one of us, and we'll help you."

I always wish that I could have let him know how much his comfort meant to me, but I didn't. I was too rattled. I simply began sobbing again, regretful that my burden was shared, thankful that my family hadn't rejected me, as I feared.

Chapter 22

The secret I held in my heart for so long was like a personal hiding place. I thought that if I kept the people I knew out of that bathroom, away from knowing the things Eric did to me, I would never have to come out and fully admit myself.

Maybe time will just dissipate the secret, and, after a while, I can emerge on the other side— clean, blank, and innocent once again.

What a lovely thought it was. How nice would it have been for it to be true?

It is a shame. My experience at Franklin High, the stark realization that nobody was going to force me to do anything in life, showed me that, if I were going to figure out a way to remove myself from my neighborhood, I was going to have to take ownership of my life.

I was going to have to show people I didn't know, strangers, who I really was. That was the only way for me to achieve my goals.

For my first semester at Franklin, I avoided that reality. I denied that my performance in high school was important.

When I received my first semester report card that December, it looked like this:

Raymond Serna: 10th Grade

English: F

Math: F

Science: F

Social Studies: F

Spanish: F

Art: F

ROTC: F

I had been absent for a total of forty days during my first four months of high school. Essentially, I was a high school dropout who had failed all of his classes. With this type of performance, graduating from high school was against the odds and getting into the art high school or college, close to impossible.

Even though I had convinced myself that Franklin was not the answer to my problems, there was something devastating about receiving this report card with the name, "Raymond Serna," written on the top.

I wasn't dumb. I wasn't a failure, was I?

I had put everything into the art high school and rejected off-hand the notion that I would have to be successful at Franklin. However, the next audition application had already been sent in, with only slightly better grades. And if I couldn't turn things around, I wouldn't be able to get into art school, regardless of my talents.

A young man like me, who neglected his future by stubbornly refusing to attend high school, required a brilliant stroke of luck to get out such a quagmire. And a brilliant stroke of luck is exactly what I got.

At the beginning of the holiday break, I went back to Highland Park to visit Kristina. It had been a while since we'd been able to hang out. After junior high, we went our separate ways.

Kristina had been bullied by a gang of girls, who beat her up and intimidated her in the neighborhood. Worried about things getting worse if she went to school, she learned of an alternative option.

Her older sister had gotten pregnant in the eleventh grade. Since the pregnancy made it difficult to meet the demands of a normal high school experience, the guidance counselor at the school directed her to apply for an alternative high school program. In Los Angeles Public Schools, there was a policy that, so long as you had a letter of approval from a certified doctor or social worker that you are incapable of performing in-school activities or otherwise at-risk for doing so, you are eligible to enroll in the "Independent Study Program."

Kristina's sister introduced her to the social worker who had guided her through independent study during her pregnancy, and the social worker agreed to do the same for Kristina. As she explained to me, the social worker just gives you a stack of books that are identical to the books you have in class and all of the assignments for the semester. Then, it is your job to do the work and submit everything to the social worker for grading and certification.

When she finished telling me about it, I asked, "Kristina, do you think I can get into this program?"

"I don't see why not," she replied. "But you need to either know a social worker or have a valid reason."

A thought popped into her head, "Hey! I have to go check in with my social worker tomorrow to close out the semester. Why don't you come with me and I'll introduce you."

"That'd be great," I said.

That night I stayed at Kristina's house, and the following day we went together to visit her.

The social worker's office was located in Eagle Rock, and we took a bus from Highland Park to get there. When we arrived at the office, I found the environment to be warm and professional. A receptionist took our name and said hello to Kristina, who she already knew well. A ficus plant sat in the corner, set to the foreground of light blue walls. The waiting room was quiet, with magazines scattered about on a table. Soft, padded wooden chairs were placed in an 'L' shape along the wall.

In minutes, the social worker emerged.

"Hi Kristina! How are you today?" she warmly asked, her well-kept white teeth glistening in the glow of fluorescent lights.

"Good," Kristina said in a friendly but short fashion. "This is my friend Ray. Do you mind if he joins us? I wanted to introduce you two."

"Sure," she said. "Hi Ray, I'm Mrs. Gordon. How are you?"

"Good."

We walked back into her office where Kristina handed her a pile of work that she had completed. Mrs. Gordon thumbed through it, apparently checking to make sure it was all there.

"Everything looks good here Kristina," Mrs. Gordon encouraged. "I'll get you some final grade reports in a couple weeks when you visit again. How is everything going with the independent study?"

Kristina responded, "Oh, everything is fantastic. It makes it a whole lot easier to focus without worrying about those girls heckling me. Thank you."

The room fell silent. Mrs. Gordon looked at Kristina, then back at me, sensing that Kristina was about to add something else.

"Umm," Kristina stammered. "I wanted to introduce you to Ray because he is having similar trouble at school and, well, I thought, maybe I could, maybe you..."

Mrs. Gordon finished her sentence. "You were wondering if I could help him through independent study."

"Yeah," Kristina responded as she exhaled.

"Well, tell me about yourself Ray," Mrs. Gordon offered.

At first I was shy. I kept my eyes focused downward, my hands grasping at one another nervously.

"Ok. I just got done with my first semester at Franklin. I failed out of all of my classes because I missed forty days. I just can't stand it there. I've been trying to get into the Los Angeles County High School for the Arts."

"Oh, LACHSA," Mrs. Gordon interrupted. "That's a great school."

"Yeah," I continued. "But I need to get my grades up if I want to keep auditioning. All I want to do is become an artist and I just don't fit in at Franklin. But they won't let me in at LACHSA. So I don't know what to do. I just need to get my grades up," I repeated.

Mrs. Gordon sat back in her chair. "Well, I'm pretty loaded up with students."

I shuffled in my chair uncomfortably.

"But I can take on one more for the rest of the year. So, why not? I'd be glad to help you Ray."

"Seriously? Thank you so much Mrs. Gordon," I said interrogatively, not fully trusting that she was willing to help me.

She handed me an independent study application and promised to send a letter to Franklin, recommending me for the program and volunteering to be my advisor. After the paperwork went through, I was allowed to continue with high school without having to go back to Franklin. Technically, my circumstances didn't fit into the criteria, but because one nice lady, Mrs. Gordon, was willing to say *yes*, I was given a second chance to get my grades up.

I met with her once every two weeks. She provided me with all the materials I needed and I spent my days at home, actually working.

I was totally amazed at how much easier school was when I wasn't at school with the other kids. I had my books. I had my assignments. And I could function independently, without all of the nonsense associated with going to school in Highland Park—no bus ride, no waiting for the teacher to pass out papers, no interruptions from my ruffian classmates, just focused work.

I was additionally shocked to discover how quickly I could finish entire courses. My health class was complete on my second day of work and it wasn't even lunchtime yet. I also learned that algebra books have written instructions at the beginning of every chapter and, when I actually read them, it wasn't that hard after all. In class, the teacher explained things in such detail, using lots of foreign terms and numbers over fifteen minutes or so, that it made algebra more confusing. When I just read it for myself, it came much faster.

And I was motivated because my next progress report needed to be excellent in order for LACHSA to invite me for another interview.

In just two weeks, I went from straight 'F's' to straight 'A's.' All I needed was some space and some motivation to try.

Then, my first test date arrived. It was a requirement of the independent study program to take a test every month or so to verify that you were actually learning what you were supposed to, and to ensure that somebody wasn't doing the work for you. I took the test in Mrs. Gordon's office. And when the results came back, I aced everything.

Devoid of the putrid environment at Franklin, I began to excel.

When I received a letter from LACHSA at the end of the January, I was thrilled to learn that I was invited to come back for my fifth audition.

The problem was that, in my fevered attempt to get my grades back up, I hadn't updated my portfolio. I scratched together some vaguely interesting drawings and paintings and pieced them together as best I could.

When I arrived to the audition, I was running late because my uncle had slept in. I rushed into the building, just barely making it into the waiting room by the time that my name was called by the condescending Asian girl with the clipboard.

She said, "Raymond Serna."

As I walked by, she asked, "How many times have you been here?"

Hurried and disinterested in her interrogation, I muttered, "This'll be five."

"And you still haven't gotten in?" She asked crassly.

"No, I got in. I just love to haul myself across town to audition so much that I thought I'd keep doing it," I replied with confrontational sarcasm, rolling my eyes as I walked past.

As the panel went along with their usual slew of questions, which I could recite verbatim at this point, they came to the one that I always stumbled upon.

"How much formal training do you have?"

And, as usual, I struggled to come up with the answer that they wanted to hear. "Well, I don't exactly have formal training. I took a crafts class in junior high. I'm self taught though. I have been drawing and learning since I was a little kid."

Two of the panel members looked down, writing something onto their audition forms with a not-so-impressed look.

"Raymond, we see on your high school transcripts that you failed all of your classes during the first semester. Can you explain to us why we should believe that you will be able to succeed at an advanced school like LACHSA?"

I swallowed nervously.

"Well, all I can say is that I'm currently in an independent study program now and I've gotten all 'A's' since entering it. The high school I first attended was not a fit for me. If I get into this school, I promise I will give one hundred percent. I know I won't fail here."

I showed them my newest portfolio, and after a few minutes of explaining my work, the chair of admissions looked at me with a blank expression—the rest of the panel held their hands politely together—and he said, "Thank you Raymond. You will receive a letter soon with our decision."

Again, I walked away and hitched a ride back to Cypress Park.

The letter from LACHSA arrived sooner than usual, giving me cause for hope.

I went through my normal ritual before scratching at the fold on the envelope and inspecting it to learn the outcome. The letter made a crackling sound as it unfolded in my fingers. The breath coming from my nostrils was long and smooth like an ice skater gliding gracefully across a frozen pond.

My heart throbbed. After five auditions and all of the hard work that I put in over a grueling period of two years, I was rejected once more.

And all I had to show for it was five torn up envelopes and five letters of rejection.

Through the tenth grade, I endured some major mistakes and was able to come out relatively intact. Early on, I carried the attitude that the only way for me to make good choices was to follow my own road. However, I learned that this didn't mean doing only what I wanted to do.

I took a huge risk with my life by dropping out of high school, and for whatever reason, perhaps no reason at all, I was saved by the independent study program. I was rescued by luck.

Regardless, letting my grades falter in the first semester at Franklin prevented LACHSA from seriously considering me. I couldn't afford to let it happen again.

During the year, I had come out of hiding, releasing the secret of Eric from my heart. The outpouring of emotion allowed me to accept what had happened. I had come to believe that my only way out was to begin making decisions for myself in life, trying to set out on a journey to find a new life path even though I felt damaged and at the mercy of my troubled past.

If I was going to be successful, if I was going to truly transform my life and allow my emotions to speak through art, I was going to have to look deep inside of myself. I was going to have to work. And I was going to have to come to terms with what it was really going to take to earn admission into LACHSA.

Because, the day after I received another rejection letter, Ben Fonseca from LACHSA sent me one more application. And if this one didn't get me in, my chances of advancing in art would be practically zero.

I had one shot. That's all. One more try to get out of the neighborhood. One more try to prove that I was worth it. One more chance, a single chance, to rewrite a history that was drawn on me before I could choose.

Chapter 23

Pokey plop deep plop deep plop deep dough deep plop

Pokey plop deep dough deep plop

Cook cook shhhhhhhhhhhh cook shhhhhhhhhhhh

Pokey plop deep dough deep plop

Cook cook shhhhhhhhhhhhhhhh cook shhhhhhhhhhhhhhhh

That was the sound of the thunderstorm approaching on the morning of my sixth audition. Droplets of water descended slowly from the gutter on our roof to the coarse, rocky cement that had weathered away over decades beneath our home. The cascades of aqua freefalling from the clouds deflected off the spiny, dying grass on our lawn and permeated the soil, which had transformed in minutes from a dull reddish grey to a deep, healthy brown.

The thunder rattled the air in pulsing, invisible waves that rippled into my gut, sending a shock of adrenaline to my brain.

I was frustrated already.

I was frustrated that, after five applications and five rides arranged to East Los Angeles and five auditions with the same five questions and five rejection letters and five days of feeling like I'm never going to advance myself in the universe, I had to do it all over again.

Ruben promised to drive me that day even though he didn't have a car or a driver's license. He borrowed one from one of his gangster friends—the car, not the driver's license. It was particularly kind of him, considering how his life had transpired over the past few years. We still didn't have a warm relationship, but there was at least a quiet, if begrudging, acceptance that we were brothers who still cared for one another.

We didn't talk a lot on the way there. I just told him how to get there and he abided by my suggested route. Mostly, I listened to the rain pattering down on the windshield of the car and thought about the importance of this audition.

At this point, I had decided without a shadow of a doubt that I would never return to Franklin High. Whether or not the district would continue allowing me to earn my grades through independent study, I did not know. But I did know that I would never go back to that place, even if it meant dropping out of high school and looking for a job.

Then I thought about the type of jobs people from my neighborhood held. Some were construction workers. Others worked in factories. There were plumbers or electricians. Gangsters were unemployed, aside from drug trafficking and theft. And there was the option of retail work. Of course, there were hardly any retail stores in or near the neighborhood. So people who work those jobs had to bus themselves across town.

Something like that would have to pass as my 'Plan B.' In fact, I had specifically thought to myself that I wouldn't even consider a 'Plan B' until Plan 'A' was totally in the toilet because I knew what it would entail. It would mean a life in the neighborhood, a life of meager work for meager pay with meager influence.

The reason I didn't want to consider a 'Plan B' was because I had learned that people always take the easy way out. Everyone I had ever known took their 'Plan B.' Nobody went with 'Plan A.' It was too hard and they didn't know how. They would just go with the flow and end up taking their second, more comfortable, less desirable, plan.

Yet, there I was, on that morning, wearing borrowed clothes, going to the last interview available to me, through the rain, in a gangster's car, with my brother Ruben, who was violating the law for driving without a license.

It was a pretty suitable metaphor for how I got here in the first place.

When Ruben dropped me off, I took two deep breaths and slammed the door behind me—partly indignant that I still hadn't been accepted to LACHSA and partly because of the rain.

I had updated portfolio cases since my last audition. My old art coach Alfred, who was now homeless, found a black pleather portfolio case on the side of the street, while rummaging for cans, and he cleaned it up to give to me. It was an upgrade for sure, though still not the classiest option. It made for a serviceable umbrella that morning, however.

I clip-clopped my way up the cement stairway leading to campus and remember thinking that it felt like a daunting mountain to climb. Yet, down the brick-lined walkway I trounced, and around the corner and into the music building—for the sixth time.

As I opened the door, the condescending Asian girl was waiting there again with a clipboard. Before she asked me a question that might aggravate me further, I said, "Raymond Serna, nine o'clock audition time."

She raised both her eyebrows as if I was being presumptive, but I didn't care anymore.

"Second room on the right, please Raymond," she told me, lowering her voice as she said my name.

"Got it. Thanks," I replied with unveiled, bitchy sarcasm.

In the room, several people waited along with me. It was darker than normal because of the rainclouds, inspiring a notably heavy aura—an ominous ambience of gloom. I looked over to see a grungy looking boy sorting through his portfolio. On the inside, I saw a drawing of Mickey Mouse.

Wow, really? And they're not letting me in?

This wasn't the first time I felt this way. I had secretly analyzed several other portfolios during my term of service at LACHSA auditions, and, practically without exception, thought that they were amateurish compared to mine. But, hey, I'm still here and they're not. I wasn't sure what to make of that information and was more than a little bitter when the spiteful Asian girl called my name for the sixth time.

My clothes temporarily stained dark blue from rainwater, I confronted the panel.

The Chairman of Admissions said, "Hello Raymond. Why do you want to be an artist?"

To this point, at every single audition, I had been asked this question. And every time, I had given them the answer that I thought they were looking for. I rehearsed. I took their advice. And when I said it, for whatever reason, they denied my admission.

Perhaps it was the weather that day. Perhaps it was the string of unsuccessful auditions. Or maybe I had matured on some level after an emotional rollercoaster of a year. Whatever it was, my impatient demeanor dominated my tone, and the answer turned out very different.

"Why do I want to be an artist?" I restated.

When the words exited my mouth, they were entirely unapologetic, almost defiant in tone. "You know what, sir? I don't want to be an artist. I am an artist."

I looked the panel in the eyes from beginning to end of my statement.

After a second of silence, a shocked murmur emanated from the panel. Several of them smiled at the unwavering directness of my answer.

"Okay?" The Chairman of Admissions responded, taken aback by the unexpected brevity of my response. "How would you describe your skill level?"

"On a technical level, I am advanced for my age and training, more advanced that most of the kids I've seen while auditioning here. And the maturity and determination that I have in my art is obvious, I think. I mean, this is my sixth time auditioning for you."

A teacher interrupted. "I'm sorry. How many times did you say you've auditioned?"

"Six. This is my sixth audition."

Their responses indicated that they didn't even know, exposing how precarious the admissions process was. The panel interviewed so many applicants that presentation and style became the prerequisites for being memorable and thus gaining admission to the school. I think I got their attention when I informed them that it was my sixth time.

After rustling around for a moment and gossiping briefly between each other in a whisper, they asked me another question.

"What is your ambition?"

I peered briefly down at the ground and said, "I want to make an impact on the world. I want to change my world and affect others in a way that makes them want to change too. If I can somehow bring light to other people's lives by painting something that makes them happy, then I would feel like a success."

I exhaled and looked at the panel as I finished my answer.

They abruptly began taking notes of what I said and, for the first time in my life, I felt that I had captured the full attention of the room. The walls seemed to expand behind me and I began to feel comfortable. If only for a moment, I was not afraid that people could see who I really was.

The questions kept coming, a genuine interest appearing evident on the faces of the panel.

"What do you envision yourself doing at this school?"

I stopped to think. What do I envision myself doing at this school? As many times as I had heard the question, it still was hard to articulate. This school was all that I wanted in life. It was my dream, a validation that I was good at something and a self-assurance that if I commit myself to something, I, unlike my dad and the family figures of generations past, can follow through on it.

This is what I said: "I'm here to prove myself. I want to be proud. There are so many things in the world that are wasteful. There are so many people who spend their lives doing nothing. I don't want to be one of them. I want to make something, be part of something—something that will actually last."

My legs tingled beneath me. My heart seemed to jump an extra beat. But my face remained stoic. I was proud right then, but I didn't let it show. My smile was only for me.

Then began the questions that had left me rambling in previous interviews, when I felt that my weaknesses were clear and visible before me and everyone on the panel could see through me like a storefront window.

"Raymond, who are your favorite artists?" The Chairman of Admissions asked.

I didn't pause. I wasn't going to keep putting on a show for these people in hopes of accidentally saying the right thing.

"I don't have one."

Again, this aroused a few smiles from the panelists, who were accustomed to hearing canned answers. Nobody was prepared for a visual arts student to say they didn't have a favorite artist.

"Alright Raymond, you don't have any favorite artists. How much formal training do you have?"

My feelings of anger reemerged. My defiant tone of voice, my indignant attitude, couldn't help but seep through. I grew up in a drug house. My family was on welfare. Formal training was a basic impossibility for me and I knew that I couldn't give the panel what they were looking for. And were they going to deny me because I couldn't afford to go to art camp? Because I'd never had a private instructor? Because I didn't come from the suburbs like the rest of their students?

This is what I said: "I have already answered that question five times. And five times, I've told you that I haven't really had any formal training except for my ninth grade crafts class. I've told you that I'm self-taught."

I grasped my hand over my forehead, struggling to believe that I was about to say what was on my mind.

"But if you want the truth, if you really want to know, I'll tell you." My hands now hung sturdily at my side. "My only 'training' came from a middle-aged heroin addict named Alfred. While he was in prison, he used to ink prison tattoos for fellow inmates. For a few years, when I was younger, we'd spend a few hours a week drawing together and he taught me how to shade and draw based on tattoos that he designed for gangsters and violent criminals. I used to draw and redraw his tattoos over and over again so that I could get better at the one thing that made me happy—art. And that's the extent of my art training. That's all there is."

Just before they invited me to show my portfolio, I thought of one more thing I wanted to say. I cleared my throat and reached toward the panel with my hands as I spoke.

"Listen, I don't have many options to advance in this field. And if you don't let me in, that's fine. But I'm still going to come to every audition until you stop me. So you might as well just let me in now and see if I can make it."

I tried to make eye contact with each one of the panelists, hoping to extract their feelings. In my heart, I expected that they would be disappointed at my crude answer, but upon inspection, they didn't seem offended.

I had worked hard on putting together a new portfolio for this final interview. I drew a mixture of still-life drawings and original artwork. I tried to vary the composition of the pieces so that each one looked different in style somehow.

However, to be completely honest, it was pretty similar to my others. It was nothing out of the ordinary, nothing the panel hadn't seen before. Yet, there was a palpable interest when they began looking at my portfolio this time. They were asking me questions and taking notes on my answers.

And when they thanked me and shook my hand to excuse me from the room, one of the teachers cracked a smile. The handshakes were just a touch firmer and lasted a split second longer. And, just like I had five times prior, I opened the door and left.

Before I exited the front door to the art building to walk out into the world, to walk down those daunting cement stairs one more time, to get into the car with Ruben, to go back to Cypress Park, I took two good deep breaths.

At the instant when I put my hand on the doorknob, I felt a hand touch my shoulder. I turned around. It was the Chairman of Admissions.

"Excuse me, Ray. Can I talk to you for a few minutes?"

Panic snuck up on me. My voice cracked and my hands trembled as I said, "Yeah, of course."

He walked me back over to the entrance of the audition room where he had a classroom desk set up. He sat down at the desk, and I waited anxiously to hear what he had to say.

He was a short man with salt and peppery grey hair. His voice was big, and even though I was physically much larger than him, he was intimidating to me.

He said, "You know Ray," pausing for way longer than I wish he had. "I think people in there were very impressed with you today.

In my head, I thought, "Seriously? Wasn't I kind of a dick?"

I actually said, "Oh, wow. Well that's great. I didn't really know how this was going to go because, as you know, I've been here a few times already."

He placed his hand in a fist on the table and smiled. He said, "Yes. I noticed that. You're pretty much at every audition."

I thought, "No. I have been at every audition. And you've rejected me every time."

What I really said was, "Well, I was serious about my last comment. I'm going to be here auditioning until you tell me there is absolutely no chance that I'll ever get in. This school really means a lot to me."

"I believe you," he responded. "I think you've proven that with your persistence."

Sensing a certain level of trust, I said, "Sir, please. If there is anything lacking in my technique, if there are any concerns about my portfolio, I can get better at that. Right now, I just need a chance. I need an opportunity to prove myself because there is absolutely no other way for me to do it."

He dropped his head, as if ashamed or embarrassed. And with a pleading voice he said, "What do you really see yourself doing that makes art such a big deal to you?"

I sighed. The question had so many layers.

I responded, "I can't really pinpoint what it is that I see myself doing. But I know I want it to be big."

Apprehensively, with a tinge of exasperation, he said, "Okay. You know this school is a lot of work?"

"It's been a lot of work already, Sir."

He couldn't hold back a smile. "You'll be getting a letter in the next couple of weeks."

My stomach turned into knots. "Not another letter," I thought to myself, remembering all of the heartache they had caused me so far.

"Thank you, Sir," I said.

As I turned to walk out the door, he said my name. "Ray."

"When you get the letter, I think you'll be pleased with the outcome."

Two weeks never took so long.

When I left that last audition and took a seat in the car Ruben borrowed, he had asked, "How'd it go?"

And all I told him was, "I don't know. We'll see."

My mom asked me about it too when I arrived home, and my reply was, "Okay, I guess. I'm not really sure."

I didn't want to tell anybody about what the Chairman of Admissions had said to me because nothing was official. I didn't want to get my hopes up. I didn't want to get Mom's hopes up. Just as I had faint glimmers of hope after the interviews that I knew did not go well, I now doubted that sense of hope when it crashed over me like a fifteen foot wave.

I didn't want to celebrate anything until the letter made it official. The grueling wait was a sensational jolt that made it impossible to keep still. Every day when I pulled down on the aluminum handle attached to our mailbox and the rusty hinge creaked open, I was disappointed to find it devoid of the letter I so deeply anticipated.

On the day that I peered in to see an envelope addressed to me from the Los Angeles County High School for the Arts, I noticed that it was bulkier than before. I didn't have the nerve to open it by myself. It just meant too much. I ran inside to find my mom and I handed the letter to her.

"Is this it, Mijo?" She asked.

"That's the letter. Open it," I demanded.

"Oh, my love. It's your letter, I can't," she said before I interrupted.

"No, seriously. Open it. I need you to."

Standing in the living room with her, I closed my eyes. I could hear the paper ripping and grinding as she pried the letter loose. Silence came over the room, my eyes furiously trapped shut.

And Mom squealed with piercing efficiency. "Aaayyyyyyyyyyyeee!"

My eyes opened and I looked up at her. Her hands were now raised in the air with the envelope in one hand and the letter in the other.

"You got in! My love, you got in!"

When I heard those words, "You got in. You got in," it felt like the weight of the world was lifted from my shoulders. For two years, this had been my dream, my vehicle for proving to myself, and to the world, that I mattered—that I could do something exceptional. I smiled from ear to ear with a big, child-like grin. My eyes went out of focus and I felt that I could see through the walls and over Mount Washington and Franklin High, out of the neighborhood to a peaceful place far away—a place that I could be me.

Triumph, accomplishment, was mine for a moment, and as good as it felt, it was accompanied by exhaustion. I was emotionally drained. The audition process at LACHSA was the test of my life. It was my way to prove that I could put myself out on a limb, make myself vulnerable, and still come out a winner.

For years, I had searched for a path leading from the urban swamp of my neighborhood to a majestic peak of opportunity, where I could look out at the landscape of life and plot my way to greatness.

I had tried and failed, and tried and failed, and tried and failed, and tried and failed, and tried and failed. And that one time—that one last time—I tried and prevailed. I overcame doubt and insecurity, a troubled history and the trappings of Cypress Park.

I didn't know what would happen next. I never thought that far into it.

But, what began as a simple enduring passion, compelling me to lay awake at night and maintain hope while sweeping the streets of Cypress Park, was actualized into opportunity.

You can do it, Ray. Get yourself out of here. Make it end."

My dreams were not fulfilled that day, far from it. But on that day, opportunity and choice seemed to drift with the same wind and sweep me onto a different, albeit temporary, trail.

I now had *a chance* to make it last.

Chapter 24

I've seen dogs who like to chase cars down the street. For hours, days, it doesn't matter—they're dogs—they will sit on the lawn and wait for a car to drive past. And when one rumbles by, the dog sets off in pursuit. Its mouth waters as it leaps up to grab hold of its main fixation, the car bumper.

When the dog is fully extended in flight and reaches its goal, it will chomp down on the bumper with its teeth and paw at it, ferociously trying to dominate its ill-conceived, inanimate prey. Every time

I've seen this happen, the dog fails. He either keeps chasing until the car fades out of reach or tumbles in the street after one particularly aggressive effort before traveling back to the lawn to wait for another.

Each time, the uninhibited car putters away.

But what if the dog actually succeeded? What if, despite the constant barrage of naysayers chiding it for being a silly, hopeless dog, he captured the bumper and, in some miraculous chain of events, rode off into the sunset on his new chariot? What would happen then?

Dogs never think that far in advance. All the dog knows is that the car is his prize and he wanted it, and that's the entire thought process. He wouldn't have the slightest idea what to do with an unlikely success of that magnitude.

In this brilliant use of metaphor, I am the dog. LACHSA is the car. And, somehow, the dog won.

I had no idea how to proceed once my dream came to fruition. I guess somewhere deep inside I thought that I would always just remain seated on the lawn, waiting for another car to cruise along. But not anymore. Now, I had to actually carry out the naïve plan I ginned up as my holy grail.

The pressure created a new wave of anxiety in my life. Admittedly, it was a different type of anxiety from the trapped, powerless anxiety I was accustomed to. When I was bullied in elementary school or picked on for being the fat kid in grey sweatpants, it was alienation that troubled me. It was feeling as if I didn't belong in my own life, in my own home, that was my burden.

Suddenly, people began placing high expectations on me. I had to either perform or quit.

For some, this might not seem like a big deal, but expectations were new to me. In my family, simply not being a gangster, drug dealer, or high school dropout was reason enough to call me a great son. Nobody pressured me toward academic excellence.

School had never been a challenge, never a zero sum game between success and failure. The lines for me were always blurred, the grey area infinite. At Aragon and Nightingale and Franklin, all I had to do was show up most of the time and turn stuff in once in a while and I managed to pass. In eighth grade at Nightingale, I failed science and physical education and received a D in math with twenty-one total absences. Yet, my path to ninth grade was ensured. There were no questions asked, no conversation about it. The school moved me along, and my family considered me a good boy, no matter what.

I was in for a rude awakening.

Simply getting a ride to East L.A. was complicated. For most of the summer, I had no apparent answers. Nobody in my family had a driver's license or a car, including me, and taking the bus would require two transfers and last two hours. The bus option required me to be on the first bus at five in the morning and have me home by between six and seven in the evening.

A couple weeks before school, things changed because my dad got his first legal job in several years. His brother Bobby offered him work filling pop machines in office buildings during the evening. Along with the job came a clunky, white, windowless, child molester van. Since all he had to do was work for a couple hours, one day per week, he agreed to take the job, and, in an uncharacteristically selfless moment, agreed to drive me to school in the morning.

The ride alone was a comedy to remember. First of all, my dad was completely unaccustomed to mornings. He usually was at the bar late into the night and stayed in his room for much of the day. His good morning pick-me-ups were non-traditional pharmaceuticals.

So, when I entered his room at five-thirty to wake him up, he grumbled and grunted and rolled out of bed, exposing his birthday suit shielded only by a tight pair of white underwear.

I said, "Dad, put some pants on for God's sake."

He mumbled back in response. "Do you, fuckin', want a ride 'er, fuckin,' not?" He used the term "Fuckin'" like most people use, "Um" or "Uh."

I shrugged and walked away in disgust, grabbing all of my things and walking out back to wait for him in the child molester van. Every forty seconds or so, I reached over to the steering wheel to blast the horn.

"Dad!" I shouted. "I'm going to be late for school."

When he finally graced me with his presence, wearing old tattered jeans and a wife beater that barely contained his flabby torso, he rubbed his right eye and slid awkwardly into the driver's seat.

"So, where the hell we going again?" he asked.

"East L.A," I responded.

"Aw, fuck. East L.A. That's far man," he complained.

"Yeah, Dad. You knew that already. Do you remember that college we pass on your way to your friend Robert's place? Cal-State Los Angeles? That's where we're going."

"Oh, okay, I think I know where that's at," he said, slightly soothed by familiarity. He handed me a massive old road atlas that was lying on the backseat. It was approximately the size of our front door.

He said, "Look at this and tell me if I screw up."

Obviously, this event occurred in the pre-GPS, Google Maps era in the same way that dinosaurs existed during the pre-historic era.

"Just go Dad! I have to be there by seven!" I screamed before opening the gargantuan atlas, which blocked my view of the entire world.

And away we went to my fist day of art school. It was a quiet, terrifying ride. Shockwaves of panic and doom reverberated through my stomach.

You'd think that a father would want to talk to me about my first day at a new school or see how I was feeling about it, but, of course, he didn't.

After driving up the hill leading up to campus and stopping the creepy, white van in front of the art building, where everyone was assembled, he simply asked, "So what time do you have to be picked up?"

I told him four o'clock, and he said, "Okay."

I left the car feeling overwhelmed and alone.

What did I get myself into?

The day was unusually clear for Los Angeles. I remember peering out over the valley below and remarking that the perpetual cloud of Los Angeles smog was practically absent, illuminating the city with vibrant colors. Perhaps this is a product of a perceptive memory, but the weather on my first day at LACHSA mirrored my principal emotion at the moment.

It was hopeful.

I saw a crowd of students gathered outside the art building. They seemed about my age with a similarly overwhelming pile of things strewn about beside them. I wandered over to them to find out if that's where I belonged.

A straggler on the outside of the group seemed to be the most welcoming person to confide in at the time.

"What group is this?" I asked.

"Visual Arts at LACHSA," she said.

I was in the right place. Not wanting to integrate into the larger crowd, I meandered to my right and had a seat on the curb. A light breeze cooled the back of my neck as I waited.

What did I get myself into?

I could feel the harsh reality of the new environment setting in. I turned my neck around to scan the assembly of just over 20 students who would become my new classmates. Everyone appeared so unfazed, so comfortable to be there. They carried brand new backpacks on their shoulders. Their clothes and appearances were carefully calculated to project an image. Suffice it to say, I was the only one from Cypress Park.

The orientation began when Joseph Gatto, the Dean of Admissions who I auditioned with, approached the group. Mr. Gatto was a tough looking guy. He had leathery skin, battered by time but not old looking. You could tell that he had been through a lot in his life. From the moment he appeared to the moment that he spoke, it was clear that business was about to begin.

There was no pageantry, no comforting, just a stern welcome that would make an army drill sergeant proudly say, "Now that's how you run an orientation!"

The first thing he did was open a box containing fine, black, leather-bound sketchbooks and begin handing them out to each of us. My first thought was, "Oh crap, I don't have any money," which made me shiver in panic.

The first thing he said was, "This is a sketchbook that has been donated to the school for each of you to use. Never let it leave your sight. This sketchbook must be with you at all times. All of your ideas for paintings, designs, abstracts, anything, will be drawn in this book, and each one of your professors is going to check it on a regular basis to make sure you are always coming up with new ideas for your work. I'm going to check everyone's sketch book at the end of the year and part of your grade will depend on its quality."

In the midst of the instructional moment, one of the kids in the crowd turned to talk to one of his neighbors. Mr. Gatto chided him immediately, reminding him that, "You are currently being oriented into the Los Angeles County High School for the Arts right now, and it's only going to happen once. If this is any indication of how you plan to listen while you're here, you aren't going to last long. Anyone who is here to have fun and take some easygoing art classes is going to be sorely disappointed."

The crowd and I fell eerily silent. I did not want to be one of the kids who got a verbal lashing on the first day, so I kept my mouth shut, hanging intently to his every word.

We were led on a tour of the campus, which was sprawled out over about a quarter-mile long segment of the college campus. Towering palm trees and pines lined the broad walkways that led to a mixture of gorgeous modern buildings and sculptures to classical brick school buildings. It was an overwhelming moment, realizing the distance between classes, the level of discipline, and the planning that would be required to navigate the campus each day.

As incoming juniors, each of us were assigned lockers in the same hallway of the art building. Along the way, he stopped to inform us about our class schedule. He told us that the school day began every day at seven-thirty in the morning and ended at four in the evening. The first four and a half hours of the day would be devoted solely to core academic classes—English, Math, Science, Social Studies, foreign language, and one elective.

Mr. Gatto then explained that *all* of the core classes are college placement level courses.

That was the point when I clutched my neck with my fingernails, eyes widened in shock.

This time last year I failed out of the tenth grade in a normal school. How am I going to pass college placement classes?

He continued his description of the rigorous schedule without skipping a beat or stopping to answer questions. He expected us to hear it once, understand, and figure it out as we go along.

After lunch, the remaining three hours of each school day were devoted entirely to a single subject in visual arts.

In total, we would have eleven classes—six core subjects and five visual arts subjects. On Mondays and Wednesdays we had the same core classes, and on Tuesdays and Thursdays we had the same core classes. Each Friday morning alternated between the Monday-Wednesday schedule and the Tuesday-Thursday schedule. Every day was a different visual arts subject. On Monday afternoon, I had Two-Dimensional Drawing. On Tuesday afternoon, I took Introduction to Painting. On Wednesday, it was Sculpture, on Thursday Figure Drawing. And on Friday afternoon, my class was Ceramics and Pottery.

Eleven classes? Eleven classes. Eleven classes! Eleven classes?!?

Those two words kept repeating in my mind with alternating forms of emotional punctuation.

Additionally, it was made clear that each of the eleven classes assigned homework. The homework would be due each time the class reconvened. Mr. Gatto stressed that it was impossible to pass without completing the necessary homework. In the arts classes, this was particularly the case because each class met only once per week, making outside work critical to the learning process.

At the end of the orientation, Mr. Gatto had us all gathered out in front of the LACHSA main office. The group of students and I had blank stares, realizing the height and depth of the mountain we were all now tasked with scaling.

He said, "Here's the deal guys. This is a sink-or-swim thing. You all auditioned and said that you want to be professionals in the visual arts. You all got in, and now is your chance to prove your worth. Nobody is going to do it for you. Success here is earned, and if you can't find it in you to do the work, you can go to a normal high school. It's all up to you."

When he finished the horrifying speech, he walked directly past me, looked me in the eye, and said, "Welcome back."

Oh no, he remembers me. There's no way I can hide.

He then grabbed a stack of papers from a desk inside the office building and began handing them out. The piece of paper was our schedule for first semester. When we all received it, Mr. Gatto instructed us to report to our third hour class, where our journey would officially begin.

I reported to the building and room number depicted on the schedule after wandering around, lost and aimless, for fifteen minutes with all of my belongings.

It was math class.

When I entered, I took a seat at the back of the room, pushed my book bag underneath the chair and set my art supply case on the floor to my left.

The art supply case was a glaring cause for insecurity.

Over the summer, we were sent a checklist of things we would need on the first day of school. The most important and potentially expensive items on the list were art supplies. The only professional art supplies that I had were graphite sticks, charcoal, and a set of oil pastels that I bought at an art store in Pasadena. My Aunt Lilly was a savior to me because she lived in the suburbs, had a car, and loved me enough to help me purchase some art supplies.

But other than that, I had nothing.

One day, when I casually told my Uncle Ray that I didn't have enough art supplies, he informed me that he had a twenty year old kit sitting in his garage from an art class he once took in college. The ancient kit still contained paintbrushes, watercolors, a calligraphy pen, black ink, and acrylic paint. This relic of the past, plus the few things my Aunt Lilly helped me buy, were all the tools I would be able to accumulate in the days leading up to school.

It was as basic as imaginable for a college placement arts school, but I would have to make due.

And my version of an "art supply case" was like wearing a bright orange t-shirt that read, "I'm poor. Everybody look at the poor kid at art school!"

The week before my first day, I was helping Mom in the kitchen, when I happened to glance over at the washing machine to indentify an industrial-sized Tide detergent box. For whatever reason, it clicked that I could use it as the makeshift art supply case that I couldn't afford.

Since it was just about empty, I asked my mom, "Can I have that detergent box after you do the laundry?"

"Of course, Mijo. What do you want it for?" she asked.

"Nothing really. I just want to see about something." I was too embarrassed to tell her what I was going to use it for.

The cardboard detergent box had a white plastic handle secured on the top. A serrated edge ran across three sides of the box, allowing it to open like a hinge in the back. The only problem was that there was nothing to hold the lid shut. So, when I picked it up by the handle, it would fly open and spill all the contents on the floor.

To remedy the problem, I used some thick, metal wire I found in the cabinet to create a buckle. I pierced the box with the wire at two locations on the top and two on the bottom and duct-taped the wire in place. I bent the wire into a fishing hook shape—facing opposite directions on top and bottom.

Once finished, I latched the hooks together and a jankety, yet functional, art supply case was born.

Sitting in math class on my first day with a gigantic Tide box loitering beside my chair, I instantly regretted my creation. Every single other student had a spiffy, store-bought plastic box with a durable latch and flip-tops and side compartments, that their parents probably bought, to hold their supplies.

Everything was kept nice and neat and had a little special place for every little item to go. Many of the students had several thousand dollars worth of paint, supplies, and stuff that I'd never even heard of.

And I had a Tide box with a twenty year old art kit and some pencils. Every time, I picked up the hollow cardboard cube, the supplies crashed and tumbled over top of one another into a messy heap, like a handful of toothpicks in a bounce house.

I gulped audibly, believing I was way out of my league. I drifted into a minor episode of fear and worry.

What if I can't do this? Where would I go then? I can't go back to Franklin. What do the kids think of me with this ridiculous art box? Am I going to make any friends here?

My vision blurred and my arms grew numb when, suddenly, I heard a voice that I was too distracted to understand.

"I'm sorry, what?" I asked to the girl who had spoken to me, shaking my head and refocusing my vision.

She turned to me and, over-annunciating her words, said, "I love your art box. It's so funny and creative!"

I shook my head. "Seriously?" I asked.

"Yeah, it's totally random."

I chuckled and opened my notebook. Apparently, art students mistake poor for creative.

Just as Mr. Gatto had warned, I was given a homework assignment for every class, beginning on the first day. On the second day, I was given more, and on the third day, I turned in the homework from the first day. When I left class, I was assigned more.

Every class, every hour, my responsibilities piled up. Every day, the expectations were clear: do the work or get out.

Frequently, I was tardy because my ride—ahem, Dad—was slow to get up in the morning. He would often pass off the responsibility to Ruben. Sometimes, the planning was confused and I waited for hours before someone showed up. It was far from perfect, but they got me to and from school nearly every day. If they hadn't found the time in their dysfunctional existence to drive me around, I don't know what I would have done.

Keeping up at LACHSA was a full-time job. The second I passed through the door after school, I went directly into my parent's room to do the homework for my core classes. In the far back corner of the room I reliably sat in a chair, feet propped up on the ottoman, balancing my books on my lap, scratching math problems and English papers and French homework onto a lined sheet of white paper.

For the art subjects, I retreated to my room where I slipped into a pair of cut-off jean shorts and the t-shirt that I once wore with the grey sweatpants in seventh grade.

In our room, my bed was now in the back-right corner and Mando had a mattress that one of our neighbors was going to throw away sitting underneath the window on the floor without sheets or blankets. Mando still stayed at his girlfriend's house every night. So I had free reign to turn our room into my personal art studio.

With my cut-off jeans and old white t-shirt on, I unraveled some cheap paper onto my bed, pulled the paint and paintbrushes from my Tide box of art supplies, and started creating. Unlike all the other kids at my school, I didn't have an easel, which is why I painted face down on the bed. I also only had primary colors of paint, which meant that any other color I wanted to use had to be made from scratch by mixing the primary hues.

It was a unique way to paint because the perspective was unusual. Most painters look directly out at their work and formulate their images from that natural perspective. However, I, like an upside-down Michelangelo, looked down at my creation, periodically standing over top of it with my hands framing it like a pretend cameraman, trying to get just the right shapes and angles.

When I changed colors, I would wipe my brush off on my chest, creating a painting all its own on that old white t-shirt. Straddling the bed or crouching down at its foot, I stroked and wiped clean, created and dried off, all the assignments that were passed my way.

And back at school, I would turn in my visualized conception alongside the idealistic suburbanites that I shared class with.

On a normal night, I stopped working around midnight, and when I had things on my mind, or the workload was particularly heavy, I labored well into the morning. During this time, I stopped eating when I came home, which developed into anorexia.

And, even when I wanted to sleep, I mostly just reclined on my bed staring up at the ceiling, mind filled with the expectations and responsibility that I bore. This, I now know, is called, "insomnia."

From the time I left my house in the morning until the sun set in the west and rose in the east, every single day, this was my life. Essentially, it became my obsession to desperately cling to my prize.

A couple eating disorders and a sleep disorder later, I learned how to succeed in the demanding school.

At home, everything else was completely normal, ordinary in the same vein as a circus clown's routine. Sure, there were elephants and trapeze artists and bearded ladies, but, since the clown works in a circus, it's all perfectly normal to him.

Ruben was in and out of juvenile hall, where his various transgressions were punished by forcing him to spend more time around gangsters—a clearly excellent way to rehabilitate young criminals. While he was out and living back at home, he caused more than his fair share of strife.

Practically every day, he'd tell my mom that he had to run out to the liquor store to get a Coke or meet a friend real quick and leave. Then, every time, he would end up being gone for like five hours.

And every time he returned, he was 'stuck on stupid,' sloshing his way around the living room until clawing into his bedroom where he lay with his hands creeping over his face. I watched him for a second and then got back to work on my painting. When my dad found him on the floor, stinking of mint and brake fluid, he yelled at him.

"What the fuck is wrong with you?"

"Look at you, you piece of shit, just lying on the floor like a bum."

Dad kicked at him, trying to make Ruben respond, but he was so messed up that he didn't care about anything. He just existed, letting whatever sensations he felt from the chemicals run their course while he did his best to find peace.

As Dad yelled at him, Mom came in to try to smooth out the situation.

She leaned down to him and said, "Ruben, my love, what do you need?"

This infuriated Dad even more. "Why are you coddling him? He's just a gangster piece of shit—a big waste of space." His voice boomed through the walls.

"Peanut, stop it," Mom criticized.

I could hear my dad flip like a switch into one of his tantrums. I just kept painting.

"Me stop it? You stop it, you fucking whore! You're the one who made him this way. Why did you let him leave the house, you whore? You never stop him. You're the reason he's like this in the first place, you idiot."

Mom's voice began fading into the background of his senseless ranting. She knew, I knew, everyone knew, that once Dad got started, nothing could discourage him. We just had to wait it out until he finished blaming all of the people in his life for everything that went wrong. I feared for Mom in these moments.

I knew deep inside that she could have done better for herself. I wished she didn't have to live in this awful home. I knew that it wasn't Mom's fault. She had never hurt anyone in her life. She never called people names or spread hate. Mom was always the one who put out the fires that the people around her started.

I loved her, but all I could do was stand in my room, hunched over my bed, and keep painting.

"Fucking whore. Your whole family is a bunch of whores. And your kid is a stupid and fucked up!"

His raving continued late into the night until he either stormed out to the bar or lit up one of his tiny rolled up blank sheets of paper, lit it on fire, and watched the cloud expand across the room.

And when Dad didn't have Ruben or my mom to scream at, he took it out on whoever else was in the room. That's why I did everything in my power to be anonymous. If I weren't near him, he couldn't start berating me.

Richard, who was now twenty-one years old, still lived at home when he didn't stay with his girlfriend Vanessa. Yet, every time he was going out to see a punk show or go to a friend's house, my dad would demand that he stay home.

"You are not leaving this house," my dad shouted to the twenty-one year old man.

Richard simply ignored him. Richard kept his arguments with Dad short and sweet because he didn't put up with any of the nonsense. Later that year, Richard grew tired of dealing with the meaningless demands and rants of our father. So he confronted Dad and told him that he was going to move out, permanently.

My dad responded initially by saying, "You can't move out of the house."

Then, after Richard completely ignored another empty command, Dad changed his tune. He raised his voice and ordered Richard to, "Get out of this house. You're twenty-one years old. So, fuckin'," he paused. "Find your own place to live."

In a matter of moments, Dad transformed from not allowing Richard to move out to requiring that he must. It was his own way of convincing himself that he still had some authority in the family, even though he had squandered it over two decades of general carelessness.

I always resented my dad for the silly fights and the delusions of family that he maintained. It was as if he wanted to be some kind of moral arbiter when something went wrong, and also do whatever he wanted, all the time.

There were no rules at home anymore. Everything had been broken. Every single thing that you could think of that might be a rule to live by, my brothers, or my parents themselves, had completely destroyed.

My parents would fight about Ruben being on drugs, and my dad would tell Richard what to do, while simultaneously selling drugs, and doing them, every day of his life. It's not as if he listened to Mom's advice. How was Ruben or Richard, or anybody, supposed to listen to a word he said? What is there left to believe?

It didn't make any sense.

And that's the point exactly. My house didn't make any sense. For years and years and years, the rules crumbled under the weight of hypocrisy. The structure, the order, the will to be good people slowly dripped and dripped from the holes that were being poked in the base of our home until one day, when it was totally evident to six people over the age of seventeen, nothing was left.

Nothing mattered.

The bar of expectations was so low that it wasn't even worth the effort to try anymore.

In my room, I imaginatively peered down at the blank canvass on my bed, trying feverishly to invent something wonderful that I could show to the world.

Chapter 25

Our imaginations are amazing.

Day in, day out, our minds *can* envision life entirely separate from our own. We wish for things to be better. We reconstruct conversations that we've already had, trying to reinvent the situation and say exactly what we wished we had said the first time. We fantasize about exciting sexual encounters. We hope that good things will happen to us.

It's all imagination. It all exists in the mind, and, unless you can express it perfectly, which nobody can, it is trapped. Our yearning souls—the deep, profound, fascinating parts of us—are all trapped within our minds. We make guesses about each other all the time, but only on the most special of occasion do we ever really know *anything* about one other.

Over time, we shut down the imagination; we keep it forever within us because we are frustrated that nobody really understands.

We revert instead to routine.

We wake up at a certain time and go to a specific place. We wear a calculated selection of clothes to fit the day we expect to have. We exercise at times. We get drunk at others. We visit the same websites and watch the same channels on TV. We think about the same silly little common hobbies and fixations that we enjoy, and revel in how they make us feel.

Our days become defined by routine, our minds structured by it. Some people have very positive, healthy routines. Others have very destructive and unhealthy ones. And most people have a contrived combination of both. We don't know exactly what to do with ourselves. We don't know exactly what we want. So we rely on the patterns and the hobbies and the things that feel normal. We do the things that help get us through the day.

And after a while, our routines become habits, compulsions bred from the repeating rhythms of life. Our minds become so structured by our daily life that we begin to do things without thinking. We act without imagination because we have programmed ourselves to do so.

Nobody but us can understand the depths of our own imagination. But our routines, our habits, are much easier to grasp. They're relatable and easy to describe. So it's our routines and our daily experiences that we usually end up talking about.

How was your day? What happened? What do you want to do now? Do you have any plans tomorrow?

All of these questions inspire totally understandable, completely normal answers. They are the beginning and end of most conversations. And there is nothing wrong with that. After all, we can't always spark up conversations with imaginative ideas like, "I would be more interested in talking to you right now if you were naked."

Some things are best kept to yourself.

All I'm trying to say here is that we become reflections of our routines and habits. People look at me, assess me, and understand me based on my routines and outward appearances. I am known to the world by the things I do, the clothes I wear, the people who I spend time with, and the way I treat others.

The first weeks at LACHSA threw me out of the lulling rhythm of routine and habit. Everything was new, exciting, stressful, and different. The beginning of classes presented me with suddenly high expectations, a battle to find my way around campus, and a marathon of homework like I had never experienced before. It was a complete and total culture shock that required every ounce of energy and focus available.

But, like all things, I began to settle in. After a month or two, I became accustomed to the rigor of the homework. I got used to the flow of the classes. I adapted to the expectations of my professors. In an incredibly short time, things seemed normal again.

And when things became normal, I reverted back to the same old patterns.

During my final year at "Night-in-jail," my unique hair color and image made me marginally popular, but it was also because of an attitude I had developed toward school and authority. I learned that kids enjoyed my crass, rebellious sense of humor. So I used it to make friends. I routinely told teachers that, "This is stupid. When are we going to have to use this in real life?"

I cracked jokes about dirty words and outrageous situations. The other kids loved it because it broke the flow of class and provided something to laugh about. It was fun and totally acceptable in my environment.

However, I unknowingly still housed the same attitude toward school. Getting into LACHSA did not change the fact that I had spent my whole childhood as a fat kid from the ghetto. And the routines of that kid wouldn't be easy to break.

It was about two weeks into school during my figure drawing class that I was confronted with this.

Our professor had us drawing the human form based on a live nude model, a woman who was sitting on a stool at the front of the room. The room was well lit and intimate, a very ordinary classroom environment. And everything was normal, aside from the naked woman sitting in front of us. It was my first experience with a naked person, and all of my classmates were absolutely silent, drawing her figure with diligence and care.

Nothing but the scratching of pencils and the slow droning of a fan could be heard.

It was awkward to me. I was accustomed to classes where people made wise cracks and laughed at each other. Now, everybody was sitting in dead quiet working on their drawing of a real naked person, and I was thinking to myself, "Can't somebody say something? We're all just sitting here like a bunch of zombies."

The moment got the best of me, and, when the time seemed right, I said, "Man, it's cold in here. The model knows what I'm talking about. Somebody get that poor girl a jacket!"

Classy, I know.

The room erupted in laughter. Even the model chuckled and shook her head from the comment. I smiled, and after an unfocused minute of rustling and giggles, the room grew quiet again. The dull scratching of pencils on the brown craft paper again took over the room, and I felt better that I had broken the silence.

When the three hour class arrived at a conclusion, I gathered all of my things and traveled out the door. Down the staircase I treaded, and out to the cool grassy lawn where the student body assembled to hang out and wait for rides home.

I congregated with a small group of classmates who had been in the figure drawing class, and we shared some bland comments about how we enjoyed our school day. As I was standing there, I felt a sharp poke on my right shoulder.

When I turned around, it was Judith Yazni, one of my other classmates. Judith was a short Jewish girl with reddish curly hair. I was surprised that she approached me because we had never talked before, and my only impression was that she was pretentious—a kind of hippie, granola girl.

So I responded with a little snottiness. "Yea-a?" I asked in a long, antagonistic tone.

Immediately, she devolved into an angry rant. "I can't believe how rude you were in there. I mean, making jokes like that in the middle of class with a model as a guest? That is not the impression that we should be leaving when people visit us. I mean, this is a fine arts school. It's not a big joke!"

"What are you talking about?" I asked defensively, shocked by her rage.

She hesitated, looked me squarely in the eye, and said, "Some of us are actually here to learn. Some of us are here to prepare for the art world. And it isn't fair when you make jokes and distract people from the model."

Inside, I felt awful. My stomach dropped as I suddenly turned to others in panic.

"Was I disturbing to any of you guys?" I asked.

They all shook their heads.

"No," a couple replied.

Reassured by their dismissive facial expressions, I turned back to Judith, and right before I tried to make the argument that I hadn't been disruptive, she stopped me.

"You were disruptive to me. That's the point. You ruined that one class period, for me." She pointed her finger at her chest as she glared at me.

Without waiting for response, or conciliating our views in any way, she stomped off. And, in my head, I thought, "What a bitch. Who does she think she is?"

I gossiped about it with the people around me and they all shared my feelings.

It was just a joke.

But on the ride home, removed from the daunting social pressures, I thought about the incident differently.

Who did I think I was? Why was my joke more important to me than my drawing at the time?

It troubled me for days. I didn't know anything about figure drawing. I was totally new to all of the fine art disciplines. I worked so hard to achieve my dream of getting into LACHSA. Yet, now that I felt comfortable and slipped into a routine, I was suddenly okay with going back to my old school habits of cracking petty, crass jokes just to win over some of my classmates? Is that really why I was there?

It took a while for my emotions toward Judith's criticism to cool off, but when they did, and reason took over, I realized that I had been in the wrong.

Sure, she was rude, but I was the one who had allowed my habit of cracking inappropriate jokes in class to get in the way of my imagination. If I were really focused on getting better and becoming the best, not just being mediocre and fitting in, I wouldn't have wasted so much of my time and energy thinking up a joke to soothe my own discomfort with a quiet room and a nude model.

Years later, I called Judith to thank her.

"Thanks for what?" she asked.

"Thanks for making me a better artist?" I responded.

"How did I make you a better artist?"

"You made me a better artist because you confronted me for disrespecting the class. It taught me that I wasn't more important than the task at hand. It taught me that I wasn't as smart as I thought I was, and if I wanted to be great, I would have to change who I was, not just where I went to school."

Judith was a person who I didn't really know, a person who didn't know me. But she made me take a hard look at who I was becoming in the eyes of my classmates, and forced me to consciously decide whether or not that was the person who I wanted to be.

Sometimes it takes a stranger to learn a lesson like that.

The lessons kept coming.

One afternoon in figure drawing class, our professor gave us an assignment. He instructed us to draw another human model.

"Draw this woman as best you can," he said.

And over the course of an hour, the class meticulously sketched and shaded the human form. I mimicked every single curve, fold, and detail on the woman's body until it was complete, and my sketch looked great. It was the best human drawing I had ever made.

"Now hand your drawings in to me," our professor said.

He pinched the papers from us individually, lightly shuffling them into order. Slowly creeping back to the front of the room, he pulled the recycling bin to his feet.

"Crick. Crick. Crick."

It was the sound of our professor ripping each of our drawings in half, one-by-one, and releasing them to waft like butterflies into a growing heap of waste. We sat in our seats, dumbfounded. Some people reacted. Others, like me, sat silently, mouths opened, just watching him tear up our work.

When the treasured artifacts of our talent and labor were completely destroyed, he moved closer to us and took a seat on the corner of a table.

"Do you know how many times I've drawn the human figure?" he asked.

Sensing that the question was rhetorical, nobody raised their hand.

"Thousands of times. Thousands and thousands of times," He repeated. "And do you know how many times my drawings have been perfect?"

The room maintained silence.

"Never."

"No matter how many times you draw something, no matter how good you get, you will never be perfect. You will never get it just right. You can always do better, and you'll never be the best at it. That's why, if you want to be an excellent artist, if you want to create incredible things, you can't get there by trying to be perfect. You have to be capable of letting go—trusting that if you can draw it once, you can do it again, even better the second time."

The professor paused to scan the room.

"The only way to be great is to have style. Every mark, every line, every shade, that you draw should say something about who you are, what you are feeling, what you've been through," he explained.

"Class dismissed," the professor said with a smidgen of drama in his voice.

The day was over, and we had nothing to show for our three hour Figure Drawing class. Our work lay in a purposeless mound at the bottom of the recycling bin. Yet, I'd never gotten more out of a class in my life.

Ever since elementary school, I thought that art was drawing something that looked real, that looked just like something that I had seen before. In essence, I had falsely believed that a good artist was like a copy machine. But in that class, on that day, a man who was amazing at figure drawing, whose work was a spectacular sight to behold, admitted that he has never been perfect. He will never be perfect, and he knows it.

There was liberation in the idea of imperfection to me. If I could admit that I would never be a perfect artist, never create a perfect piece, then what was the true purpose of my art?

Perfection was like an unconscious barrier that I could sense, but couldn't see. It was immaterial. Every time I used paint, every time I worked on a canvass that was unforgiving of mistakes, I tended to draw things that were easier in fear of making errors that I couldn't repair. Every time I imagined an idea for original art, I stalled, hesitant to get caught overwhelmed by a project that I wasn't talented enough to complete.

I was afraid to cross a barrier that was actually as false as a mirage in a wavy, sun-drenched desert—the hope of being perfect.

I was semi-consciously settling for mediocrity. There was no ambition to create something meaningful because my fear of failure outweighed my imagination's craving to be set free.

I had misunderstood the central premise of art.

Between the tongue lashing from Judith and a lesson on imperfection from my figure drawing professor, I was inundated with emotions. I was trying to transform old habits, while admitting that I wasn't, that I would never be, perfect.

Standing over my bed, staring down at a necessarily imperfect painting that I'd produced for another class, I felt the air pulsing against the back of my neck. Memories clipped through me rapidly, and I needed to express what they meant.

At the time, I felt guilty. I knew that much. I felt like I had let myself down. I felt trapped and afraid that I wouldn't be able to escape my flaws, and I had to take a good long look in the mirror. I needed to consider who I truly was as a person.

But instead of looking to the mirror, I decided to paint instead. I took an old painting that I had made for another class and put it on top of the bed in my room.

Then, I began to paint my feelings onto that flawed base—letting my imagination run wild to see what came out. It was the first time that I had seriously attempted to creatively draw from emotion in paint and the first time that I drew a painting on top of a painting. According to my professor, I would never be perfect. So what would happen if I took a picture that was already there, already imperfect, and tried to create something wholly new on top of it? Was it possible to make art on top of art, masking the past with a fresh reality?

The tainted canvass suddenly had infinite potential to me, as if blank once more. I felt powerful enough now to reshape the past—confident enough to reflect on me.

My face was without a body, angry and incomplete. Beneath my intense eyes, a tear rolled over my cheek. An angry demon flashed his fangs, and in the background an unknown male figure like 'The Nightstalker' cast a shadow down a long, narrowing corridor, penetrating deeply along the path. One of my hands streaked desperately along the walls, as if clawing to break free. The center was torn at the seams, and my other hand was cast in a pool of blood that began to drip over a lovely, but melancholy woman's face.

It felt like I was falling, but struggling to hold on.

This painting was packed with imagery, both of my past and my imagined future. It expressed my desire to wrestle myself from the shackles of mediocrity and climb to the heights of greatness, despite the torment of my past, the inner demons that made me feel trapped.

When I looked at the canvass I had reproduced, I saw myself for the first time and knew that the only way for me to fracture the chain of mediocrity was through constant reexamination. The key to greatness in art was to be changing all the time, trusting that my imagination can take me farther than my fear of imperfection.

I flashed back to my first LACHSA audition. The panelist had instructed me, "Raymond, you need to draw from life."

And, while scrutinizing one of my own original works, I finally knew what she meant. Great art doesn't arise by fixating on objects and recreating them. It comes from letting go of the delusions of perfection and seeking instead to pioneer an even more intractable effort—the pursuit of personal growth.

Great art comes from looking inward, honestly, and having the courage to expose yourself to the rest of the world.

So, who was I? What was the picture that I'd become?

Perhaps I was lucky to be so physically unattractive. My tall, bulbous frame combined with my pimply skin and glasses made me a repellent sexual magnet. So when it came to interacting with others, there wasn't the slightest doubt that, at best, my relationship with other people would be strictly platonic. It didn't matter. To boys, girls, and goats alike, I was undeniably unsexable. Even if I were to begin looking into my own sexual desires, I would be guaranteed matelessness—my term for being devoid of a sexual partner.

Unsexable matelessness. It was an afflicting condition, but it was authentically mine.

One day for an assignment in painting class, I tried to express the predicament. For a few weeks, there was an object that I became particularly fascinated with. I drew a pear as part of a still life, and, in the subsequent days, I found myself, consciously or not, portraying the image repeatedly in my sketch book.

There was something fascinating to me about a pear.

First of all, the pear is a highly underrepresented fruit. Apples, oranges, and bananas all have notoriety. They are reputable. And in each, there is a symmetry—a sort of character and definite sexual orientation. Oranges are perfectly round, and, when peeled away, there is a strong definition to its soft, juicy wedges. They are complex and feminine in form. Apples too were gifted by their creator with oppositely manly qualities. They jut out from their center into a crispy, round, firm crescendo where a perfectly centered stem balances the design. And bananas require no explanation as to their sexual identity. The banana is the chiseled phallus of nature.

Each fruit has an identity.

But the pear has none. It is bulbous and lumpy. The apple is red and voluptuously crisp, while the pear is pale green and disappointingly squishy. On the inside, the orange is juicy and sweet, the pear mild and grainy. The narrowing point at the top of the pear is disproportionate to its base and often offset, misguided, and confused. The stem is of inconsistent height, breadth, and orientation. The pear is, in the family of fruit, the pitiful, lonely, sexless step-cousin.

And I can identify with that. Like a pear in the produce section, I am nobody's first choice. I am imposing in size, but unthreatening in character. I am unfortunately shaped and easily misunderstood. So, unlike most people in the world, I have lots of ideas when it comes to pears, and I have spent an unreasonable amount of time already discussing my romantic musings on the subject.

One such idea became inspiration for a homework assignment in painting class. I considered the irony involved in sexualizing and personifying pears. My vision was to create a swanky bedroom scene, in which two pears were locked in the '69' position on a cheap bed clothed in tacky satin sheets. In a stereotypical, '70's porn scene, I imagined two sexy, but over-the-top, people pleasuring one another. Then, I thought, if I replaced them with pears, people might see the contrast and get a kick out of it.

I began the painting on the opposite side of a masonite board that I had used for another assignment. After mixing the colors and building the scene, I realized that I didn't like the direction in which I was heading. So, just like I had learned in figure drawing, if you can do it once, you can do it twice. I quit painting the moment I realized that I could do better, and flipped the masonite board over to begin painting the *69ing pears* over a previous painting that appeared on the back.

And because of my willingness to let go and start over again, the second attempt went famously. I stayed up for two straight days, without eating or sleeping for a minute, to finish the painting on time.

When I brought it into class, I subjected myself to our routine process of critiquing and peer review. Each student was required to post their painting at the front of the classroom and sit and listen while fellow students explained what could be improved. Most times, the students ripped into each other's work, trying to simultaneously display their sophisticated tastes while attempting to argue why they are better. And every time prior, I was a nervous wreck. Each of those times, I was harshly critiqued for a variety of flaws, and, as evidenced by my past, I didn't have great experience with putting myself in front of others to be judged. On this occasion, however, I felt cool and collected. I was absolutely in love with my work, and, at least for once in my life, I didn't care what other people thought.

69ing Pears was great and I knew it. It was me.

I was the fourth person to present my work. When I placed the painting up on the wall, it received an enthusiastic reception. Several kids laughed, others sat idly smiling, with their hands covering their mouth.

It was always interesting to hear people's thoughts. There was a wealth of classroom politics at play. So each comment had to be taken in context. There were a few people who I really respected, and there were a couple who I didn't respect at all.

One such student, who had just presented his painting depicting a bag of Cheetos—enough said about my respect for him as an artist—was the first to chime in on my painting.

"The perspective isn't exactly correct," he said.

And immediately, the best artist in the class, Marius, cracked up laughing.

"Are you kidding, dude? You just painted a bag of *Cheetos* and you are criticizing Ray's perspective? In your wildest dreams, you couldn't paint something this good," he chided.

Marius was known for being the most critical, most outspoken, and most talented student in class. He had a certain authority that developed through other people's admiration of his talent.

And he continued defending me. He leaned forward aggressively in his chair, and said, "That is easily the best painting in this whole class," waving his hands expressively. "That painting is rocking and I love it and the perspective is brilliant."

That was an unbelievable moment for me because all year I had modeled Marius' work and tried to learn from him. He was an amazing painter who had all the tools to become a phenomenal professional artist, and hearing him outwardly praise my work was extremely meaningful.

Any remaining critics in the class were immediately shut down by his enthusiastic support, and a few others raised their hands to compliment my painting's style, content, and satire. Some commented on how vivid the satin sheets were and how risqué the subject matter was, while maintaining a sense of humor. I earned some positive, constructive feedback like never before.

Even the professor raved about my painting. He told me, "I don't feel that the perspective is at all intrusive or inhibitive toward the painting's meaning. I think this painting is incredibly evocative without being pornographic, which is a very difficult thing to achieve. And it's also very whimsical and fun. So all around, this is excellent work. Good job Ray."

I smiled, but only on the inside.

This particular painting represented so much about me—repressed sexuality, love, passion without reward. It was an enormous step in my personal growth process. It created an identity by which my fellow students could remember me. This one painting inspired me to create a whole line of pear-themed pieces, all representing something human through the bulbous, sexless fruit.

With every new pear project, the other students seemed to demand more. They developed an affinity for the humorous, yet meaningful theme, and, for the first time in my life, my art had a direction. It had a channel through which people could understand not only my work, but, more importantly, me.

I learned that the best way to make an impact with art was through developing a consistency, an identifiable brand. I had a niche and a newfound individuality that could express sex and evocative themes that people wouldn't have been receptive to had I not expressed them through the pears.

I now had something proud to show to the world. I now had a way to belong.

Near the end of the first semester, I had taken incredible strides in my classes. I had made the decision that I was going to attempt to constantly reexamine myself. I had learned that I wasn't, nor ever would be, perfect, and that courage and style were more important to success in the arts. And I found an individuality that allowed me to feel comfortable belonging to something larger than myself. At LACHSA, even though I was different, I felt that I could be myself, and as long as I was willing to prove myself through my work, people would ultimately respect me for it.

However, I had absolutely no idea how this might help me in my career, or what I wanted to do with my life. More than a few people in my family, and in Cypress Park, had criticized me for going to an art high school because it would never lead to a career, and, to this point I had no cause for refuting their argument. I simply ignored them because I felt that, for some reason, I wanted to be an artist—no matter what anyone said.

And, once again, opportunity unwittingly followed my conviction.

One morning in French class, I was sitting beside my friend Renee, trying to follow along with the incessant French instruction being given by our teacher, Madame Kleiger. It was always a nerve-wracking experience because she demanded that nothing but French be spoken unless she addressed us in English. The problem was that I didn't know any French. So there was a constant communication barrier. I simply tried avoiding eye contact and appearing busy, so that I wouldn't be subjected to any humiliating class participation.

Renee was flipping through a leather binder filled with her work, and, when a momentary respite from class lecture ensued, I asked, "What is that?"

Without making eye contact, she whispered over to me, "It's my portfolio. You know, for Portfolio Day next month."

My eyes rattled around briefly in their sockets. "What's Portfolio Day?"

The students continued along with busy work as Madame Kleiger sorted through papers at her desk.

"Portfolio Day. It's when all the art colleges from around the country send representatives here to recruit high school students," Renee said. Her tone of voice was insistent, as if she were sure that, somewhere in the deep recesses of my brain, I knew what she was referring to.

But I didn't.

"What do you mean art colleges?" I asked shyly.

"Art colleges," she declared. "Where high school art students go to received advanced training for a career."

"What?" I said, my face wrinkled in confusion.

Renee giggled loudly, then averted her eyes from Madame Kleiger's general direction. "Ray, everyone here is trying to get into art college, silly!" she whispered emphatically. "And next month you can present your portfolio to the school you'd like to go to."

"What college do you want to go to?" I asked audibly, my voice rising as a result of the novel concept.

Madame Kleiger's ears picked up on the disruption. "Raymond," she scolded. *"Arreter de parler."*

What the?

I assumed she meant, "shut up." So I did.

Through the ordinary motions of the class, my thoughts ran wild. I hadn't the slightest idea—not the teeniest little inkling—that there was anything beyond art high school. I guess I was so excited to be spending two years in high school at a place where I could focus on art that it never occurred to me that there was a next step.

After class, I asked Renee all about it. She was a senior, a year above me in school, and provided me with all sorts of valuable tips about navigating LACHA. She was a tall Hispanic girl with long dark hair, and her lifelong dream was to become a fine art painter.

In the hallway that day, Renee taught me about all the different schools that would be visiting for portfolio.

"Well, which one do you want to go to?" I asked.

Her face lit up like a fat cop in a doughnut shop, "Oh," She cooed. "The School of the Art Institute of Chicago is amazing. I've wanted to go there for years." Her voice was dreamy as she romanticized visibly.

Ignorant as I was, I responded. "Well, what the hell is that?"

"It's only like the Harvard of art schools," she said, dismayed that I'd been so openly uninformed.

"Really?"

Seizing on the opportunity to talk about the Art Institute of Chicago more, she continued into a long-winded rant about the merits and appeals of the school, while I listened politely. Based on her descriptions, I got the impression that the Art Institute of Chicago was utopia, where everyone was happy. Humans and animals alike coexisted peacefully in a plentiful orgy of art, enlightenment, and free expression.

"Wow, I'll have to give it a look," I said emptily, not wanting to stomp on her dreams. "Do you have to take Math or P.E. if you go there?"

"I don't think so," she answered. "It's just for fine art."

"Good. I hate Math and P.E," I said while hauling my backpack and Tide box down the hallway.

Renee and I meandered outside to hang out in the courtyard for lunch hour, and she taught me more about how to prepare for Portfolio Day. As a senior, she was going through a really intensive process of creating new art, organizing the applications, taking the SAT, and piecing her portfolio together, but for me there was no urgency.

When Portfolio Day arrived, I just decided that I would use it to see where I stood. I didn't stress out about it. I didn't try to cram a bunch of new, innovative stuff into my portfolio or research everything or plan out what I was going to say. Hell, I wasn't really convinced that I would even apply to a college. I just decided that I would use the day to go in, one year before I really needed to decide whether art college was an option, and receive some feedback on my work.

I put photographs of my paintings into the pleather-bound portfolio I had used at my LACHSA auditions, and, on the evening of Portfolio Day, followed Renee.

For as calm as I was, there was a lot riding on it for others. While I waited to visit with the Rhode Island School of Design, a girl bolted out of the room sobbing. Wearing high heels and a skirt, she buckled down on a bench in sorrow near a friend.

The group of students in line gathered around her as she moaned,

"They said that I wasn't a good fit. I don't know what I'm going to do. I'm destined to go to that school," she whinnied.

Not according to them, apparently. Drama queen.

Her wailing was tremendous.

As we consoled her out of delirium, I suddenly began to feel my stomach turn because I was next in line.

They are going to totally rip me a new one.

I meekly crawled into the room with my portfolio squashed into my sweaty right armpit.

I said, "Hello," and handed them my portfolio.

I told them that I was a junior, but wanted to come early and get some feedback on me work. As they perused my creations, my eyes winced, bracing for the hard truth.

And, to my everlasting surprise, the female representative, wearing a fine dark blue suit with a white blouse, said, "Hm. I really like what I see here. The pear theme is really interesting and there are some fascinating, surreal elements in your work."

I looked to my right, uncomfortable with the positive commentary.

"Well, do you have any advice?" I asked.

"Well, a good portfolio shows diversity and consistency. We look for an identity, a theme that renders you recognizable as an artist. There should be one or two observational pieces, but don't overdo it. We would prefer to see the bulk of your work as original abstractions. These stylistic, humanized pears are a good start to building such a repertoire. Keep this up and we will look forward to your application next year."

Just like that, the meeting with the Rhode Island School of Design, the number one fine art college in the country, was over. I awkwardly snatched my portfolio from the table where the recruiters were stationed and dazedly wandered out of the room holding my breath.

Over the next two hours, I met with representatives from Cooper Union, Otis College of Art and Design, and the School of the Art Institute of Chicago, and at each one, I was surprised by the complimentary receptions that my art received. My best experience was at the Art Institute of Chicago interview.

What was the most appealing feature of that school at the time?

The recruiters reassured me that they required no Math or Physical Education classes, and, to the eleventh grade version of me, that's all the convincing I needed to hear.

In one single year, I transitioned from a high school dropout to a kid receiving serious feedback from the best fine art universities in the nation. At night, I returned to Cypress Park, where I slept in the same room, thought about the same things, and waited for the sun to return, when my room would become painted with vibrant blue and yellow light again, when I could return to my other world on top of the hill.

For once, I was being challenged by life. I was challenged to be the best in school, challenged to compete for a finite number of placements in an art college. And it was terrifying. I became completely anxiety-ridden by judgment and confrontation. Every day at LACHSA, I was subjected to it. Between presentations in class, art critiques, earning grades, and daily homework assignments, I was constantly bombarded with an impending sense of doom and failure.

Yet, I felt the same when I was at Franklin High. The anxiety was like a slow steady drip from a leaky sink, echoing through my psyche, reminding me of an impending tragedy. In the neighborhood, it was an incessant stream of wasted drips, ticking seconds that transformed into minutes and before long into years of mediocrity, that made me believe that I would never do anything meaningful. It was the anxiety in my heart that forced me to seek change in my life, a fear of mediocrity that compelled me to get myself out of here, to make it end.

I thought that if I just got to a new place, the terror would subside. But it didn't. I still harbored plenty. I still suffered from constant fear that prevented me from sleeping. I developed a habit of throwing up in the bathrooms on campus at LACHSA. In class, I experienced nose bleeds, hot flashes, and dry throat.

But it was a different type of horror, a new brand of anxiousness now. Before, at home without future prospects, without challenges, I was depressed and hopeless. I ate, but compulsively. I was agrophobic, a loner, a shut-in. I had low self-esteem and felt that I was just a mouth breather like everybody else, sucking up oxygen, releasing carbon dioxide, and pretty much nothing else. And the cycle perpetuated. When the anxiety would subside I filled the void with self-doubt. I deprecated my worth as a human being and came to believe that I could never do any better.

When faced with challenges at LACHSA, however, the anxiety was followed by post-anxiety periods that were characterized by euphoria, relief, and happiness. I could stop for a moment, take a deep breath, and look up at the sky. And when I looked up, beyond the debilitating Los Angeles smog, I could see hope on the other side. I could see the infinite distance between myself and the sky and feel good about the contributions I was beginning to make.

Opportunity and success were no cure for the harrowing tales of my past. They were no cure for my negative self-image or my sense that I was a misfit in my own life. They were no cure for my art, which featured sexless people in the form of fruit, bloody handprints, tears, and long shadowy corridors.

Opportunity and success did not change me.

But they gave me hope that, someday, somehow, if I continued to constantly reinvigorate my imagination, I could figure out a way to change.

Chapter 27

I took two deep breaths.

My eyes opened slowly as my head lifted. My eyes focused squarely into a red velvet curtain. A white satin robe draped over my shoulders, my hands hanging dormant at my side. Static nervousness emanating from the cavernous hall transformed indiscernible chatter into a dull hush.

A rope quivered inside of a thick golden ring above me on the right before jerking heartily in a long, continuous motion. The red velvet curtains rocked suddenly and a sharp yellow light punctured through, dousing the wall behind me and to the left with glowing paint. The light billowed left and right, engulfing me from back to front as an atom bomb would suck up the faint blue sky beneath its wings.

I squinted to the unyielding shine, and when my eyes adjusted to the shock, I could see one thousand people standing in applause. Raucous hoots and hollers spouted off intermittently, interrupting the steady, booming chorus of collective acclaim.

My stomach fluttered at the sight.

I was on the stage at the Dorothy Chandler Pavilion, where the Academy Awards were given every year. The legendary hall glistened and gleaned, crystal chandeliers hanging high overhead and deep orange lights lighting the dusk walkways on each side. Two tiers of balcony seating to the back were packed with standing well-wishers.

A dangling red cord tickled my left upper lip. I raised my left hand to swat it to the side and adjust the mortar board cap perched above my brow. I turned to my left to find a sea of white caps and gowns adorned with red, yellow, blue, and green tassels and golden cords. In the midst of the fine decorations were the expression-filled faces of my high school classmates.

The moment was precious. It was surreal,

But it was not a dream this time.

My dreams never looked a bit like this. They were dark and restless, harrowing and melancholy.

This was, serene.

When the applause ceased, the front of my row filed orderly to our right, down a short flight of stairs, and into a row of chairs placed just for us. On cue, the speaker gave us the signal, and we sat in unison. I never realized how noisy an event sitting could be until that occasion, when just over 100 butts collided with a surface all at once. It was most certainly a rare event.

And for plenty good reason. I'd hate to see the time, energy, and creative potential of 100 people wasted frequently on an exercise as frivolous as organized sitting.

The lights dimmed. The pattering of footsteps and the squeaking of shoes halting on finished hardwood ensued, and the red velvet curtain unfurled once more, and behind it was a troupe from LACHSA's performing arts department. The music department began playing a soundtrack to their performance.

The audience hushed in anticipation of their culminating act.

Their performance was of an old Chinese fable called *The Stonecutter*. The protagonist of the story was a meager stonecutter, laboring his life away by carving and chiseling stone into more useful products. One day, he passed the immaculate home of a wealthy merchant, and, in reflection upon his frustratingly modest resources, wished inside himself that he might become a wealthy merchant too. He mused about how much better life might be if he had fine things and knew influential people.

Then, through some mystical stroke of divine transformation, the stonecutter found that his wish was granted. He became the wealthy merchant of his envious dreams.

Once it came to fruition, his life as a merchant became routine and his habits of mind returned, he encountered an even more desirable figure. In the streets, a procession of soldiers carried a high-ranking political official in a chair upon their shoulders. The high official was paraded around as a miracle in himself, and whatever he wished upon others would be done in an instant.

"How powerful is that official?" the stonecutter asked himself. "I wish I could be that high ranking official."

And suddenly, through another inexplicable metamorphosis, the stonecutter was now the high ranking official.

This series of unfettered wishes repeated time and time again. When the stonecutter looked up at the sun, he dreamed of becoming the sun and it was so. Then he looked down upon the world with unparalleled strength until his path of force was blocked by a mighty storm cloud.

He wished he could be the storm cloud and it too became so. He reigned over the Earth by drenching all beneath him until he remarked at the ascendance of a strong wind, imagining again what it would be like if he could be that powerful.

And he turned into the wind.

Once he toppled trees and houses, jetting speedily as an unstoppable catalyst across the landscape of the Earth, he encountered an object that was impenetrable to him. It was a stout, well-grounded boulder. Recognizing his powerlessness to its impressive girth, he fantasized once more about becoming the boulder.

And, while holding his new, almighty position as the boulder—an immovable mass pressing incessantly against the cool of the Earth's soil—he was approached by a new impetus. It was a stonecutter, who used a hammer and chisel to carve him away into small, unremarkable chunks.

As a stonecutter, he had been the original source of power. Yet, because of his unyielding desires, his tragic flaw, it was all sacrificed to a silly notion.

I've always remembered that story. Like the stonecutter, I was bouncing around in pursuit of an apparently unattainable idea. All I have ever wanted was to change. I wanted to change my home, change my school, change my culture, change my body, and change my image.

You can do it, Ray. Get yourself out of here. Make it end.

It was the central passion that had compelled me to this moment in the first place. Without that idea, I would never be seated in the auditorium where famous movie stars and celebrities gathered once a year to crown the highest achievements in their industry. I wouldn't be able to peer to my right at dozens of the most talented young artists in Southern California. I wouldn't have a letter sitting on my dining room table at home informing me that I'd been accepted to The School of the Art Institute of Chicago and offered a scholarship to cover fifty percent of my tuition.

And I wouldn't have made the decision to accept their offer.

You can do it, Ray. Get yourself out of here. Make it end.

Was I driving myself to do something based on a foolish desire to be powerful? Was I allowing my perspective to be clouded by a false façade of control? What did I really know at eighteen years old about the path to success?

I hadn't seen it done. I didn't have role models. I was venturing headlong into a foreign world based entirely on the idea that I wanted something different in my life. I constantly wanted more.

Maybe I am the stonecutter.

"Ladies and gentlemen, I present to you the Los Angeles County High School for the Arts graduating class of 1997!"

Jubilation erupted in the cavernous theatre. Tears welled up in my eyes as I looked around at the smiling faces. It was the first time that I realized I may never see these people again, and the first time I admitted that I was part of something truly special.

It was the first group of peers I'd ever had who challenged me. I don't mean that my peers in Cypress Park weren't a challenge. I was constantly challenged by my looks, my attitude, and my social status. I was challenged to socialize and integrate into the culture that felt foreign to me. With them, it was all about proving my respect and allegiance.

The peers around me on graduation day, my peers at LACHSA, had challenged me to become better, to work harder, and to prove that I could accomplish more. They challenged me to open my mind to new ideas and learn to respect the autonomy of others.

Among them were a slew of accomplishments and awards that would impress royalty. There were two perfect SAT scores, three Presidential Scholars, an unmentionable number of contest winners, including myself. I had won second place in the Gene Autry Museum Mural Contest.

We had eleven valedictorians with perfect GPA's, and thirty others were within one-hundredth of a grade point away from a perfect GPA. Ninety-five percent of us had already been accepted to college and sixty-five percent had earned scholarships.

The challenges at LACHSA had been of a very different quality than those of Cypress Park, and undoubtedly changed my life for the better. Almost instantly I became a better artist, and the surrounding culture of achievement allowed me to set my sights high without being ridiculed and alienated.

Outside the graduation hall, a series of manmade geyser's spouted water high into the air, and my fellow graduates scurried about to greet their friends and family. The three guests who came to see my

Dad said, "Way to go Ray," emptily, while looking convocation waited in a small, awkward cluster at the corner of the mob.

Among them were my mom and dad, who were an hour late on account of my dad's inability to get moving at any given time, and my middle school social studies teacher, Mrs. Boselly, who remained a personal mentor of mine over the years.

"Oh Mijo, I'm so proud of you! You did it!" Mom exclaimed. Her eyes were bursting with excitement, her knees bouncing excitedly.

over me and to the right, with his arms languishing on his side. He didn't shake my hand or hug me or anything. He never knew how to be emotional or congratulatory.

It was one of those moments when you don't realize how proud you are of yourself until you see your family. I did it, and it was all me. And, despite the generally unengaged look on Dad's face, I think that he realized my achievement too.

As much as the little family reunion meant to me, the absences were equally momentous. I was very disappointed that my godfather, Uncle Ray, wasn't there. I had invited him specifically and when I would confront him later about it, he would respond, "Oh. Was that today?"

Really? Is it that important to you?

None of my brothers were present either. It wasn't the least bit disappointing because I hadn't invited any of them. I was sure that they wouldn't have shown up anyway. At that point in their lives, things weren't tailored to ceremonies.

Richard had been pretty busy lately because his girlfriend Vanessa had their first child, my niece Destiny. They were both living with Vanessa's parents in a house just up the hill from Aragon Elementary. Richard worked part-time for Verizon, installing phone lines and cable systems, and they didn't have enough money to get their own place. It was a typical life in Cypress Park, but at least he had a job.

Mando too was living a similar, albeit unique, life in the neighborhood. He had moved in more permanently with his girlfriend Bee, who was just a little over than forty years old with a son who was my age. He didn't work or anything, but, true to his character, he was skilled at just going with the flow.

And Ruben's lifestyle had finally caught up with him. About a month before my graduation, I was in my parent's room working on science homework, when a whipping roar magnified above. The windows and walls of the room reverberated and it grew more difficult to focus on my work.

Mom, who was in the room at the time, asked rhetorically, "Oh shit. Who are they after now?"

Palpable nervousness always pervaded in these moments, as we all knew that it could somehow involve us, anytime the police were around. For just over ten years, we had been lucky. My dad's record was cleaner than an anus after using a bidet.

On this day, my mom noticed a crowd gathering down the street on Maceo and we ran out the front door to investigate the breaking news. Two police cars were parked in a haphazard formation on the street. My mom ducked and weaved in an attempt to get a glimpse between the legs and torsos of the gawking audience. When somebody stepped up and to the left, a lane was created, and Mom caught a peek of the scene. The police were crouching over top of a young man lying in the street. One cop had his nightstick unsheathed, and raised it high above his head, repeatedly stroking it into the back of the young man.

And when one of the cops shuffled right to get a better grip on the suspect, Mom recognized the young man's shoes.

It was Ruben.

Mom ran out into the street shouting, "That's my son! That's my son! Stop! That's my son! Stop!"

She called desperately as the police officer continued to plow into Ruben with his club. Another officer had his knee planted firmly in the center of Ruben's back.

"He's just lying there. Why are you hitting him? He's not even resisting!" Mom pleaded with an officer stationed at the front of the crowd.

He replied, "Ma'am, if you don't get back, we'll hit you with the baton too."

She stepped back as commanded, knowing full well what the Los Angeles Police Department was capable of. Six years prior, Rodney King became infamous for the videotaped beating that he received at the hands of the LAPD. The Rodney King beating became a symbol for racism in the police force, but it was less reported that Hispanics were offered the same brand of abuse.

The cops were known widely in our neighborhood for their vicious treatment of suspected criminals, but in that era, it was extremely rare to have any video evidence. It wasn't like people had camera phones back then. So they continued getting away with all kinds of police brutality. And now they were doing it to my brother.

The officers scraped Ruben up off the asphalt and dragged him into the police cruiser, his nose and cheeks bloodied up from the incident.

When the scene began to clear, Mom confronted an officer who was involved in the arrest and asked, "How do I get him out of custody?"

And the cop responded, "He's eighteen Ma'am. You don't."

The cars tore away and Ruben was gone.

The next day, my mom cried frequently throughout the morning, broken up after seeing her son beaten by the police right in front of our house. We had no idea how we could help or what we should do.

That afternoon, we heard a loud bang at the door. I opened it to find two white police officers looming on our front stoop.

"Hello son, may I speak with your mother?" one asked.

"Ma, it's the fuzz," I replied loudly enough for all to hear.

I pinched the door shut and asked Mom if I should let them in. She agreed. Mom walked over to the front door, invited the officers to enter, and they sat down at our dining room table. I sat in the living room acting somewhat disinterested.

These were the same two officers who beat and arrested Ruben.

Once seated, an officer said, "I know what happened yesterday was a hard thing to see. Nobody wants to see their son arrested."

The second officer leaned forward, placing both elbows firmly on the table and interrupted. "But we wanted to come here and tell you that it would be foolish for you to make issue of the events that transpired yesterday. If you report the things you saw in a negative way, we are going to make your life a living hell."

His voice came out in a gruff whisper and his eyes glared with intimidation.

Mom pinched her lips together and folded her hands together on the table. "How stupid do you think I am?" she replied. "I know what you guys do. These kids around here don't stand a chance against you. You think I'm going to report you so that you can pigeon-hole Ruben in jail? I'm not going to do that," she explained.

Mom inhaled audibly through her nostrils, her eyes intensely focused on the point between the ceiling and the wall. She flinched angrily and snapped, "Will you just leave now? I won't say anything, but I want you out of my home. Now."

Without further conversation, the men picked up their caps and showed themselves the door.

Ruben was sentenced to six months in prison for "Grand Theft Auto." He had stolen a car in the neighborhood and the cops caught him, leading to the arrest described previously. His girlfriend Jeanette was pregnant with their first child, and the baby would be born while Ruben was in prison.

Between my older brothers, none of them had left the neighborhood willingly and all of them were mired in a lifestyle indicative of the culture. They were young parents or unemployed or in prison, but either way, they were subjected to a life of diminishing choices—a life that painted on them a whole lot more than they painted on it.

And I was on my way to art college in Chicago, the first in my family to do so. I had a chance—a chance to make choices for myself, a chance to change the trajectory of my life. It would take place in a new city with new people and new challenges.

I had no idea what would happen next, but I'd never been more excited.

Chapter 27

You can do it, Ray. Get yourself out of here. Make it end.

The spectacular thing about youthful illusion was that I couldn't see what happened next. One thing always preceded the next. My love of art from elementary school led to "Night-in-jail" Junior High, where a crafts teacher taught me how to apply to LACHSA. My persistence, my self-induced zero-sum game of getting in or dropping out, compelled them to admit me as a student. A series of challenges that I met led to graduation from a school that sent ninety-five percent of its graduating seniors to top colleges around the country.

For most of my classmates, the transition from high school to college was as traditional and assumed as the chill on a well digger's rump. Generation after generation of LACHSA Goths, rich kids who acted gothic, and Trustafarians, faux Rastafarians with trust funds, went to college on the dole of their parent's enflamed bank accounts. Art was a fun, unique way to express the inner-angst of living in the northern valley suburbs in a big house with a big lawn with parents who didn't pay them enough attention.

If art college didn't work out for one reason or another, most of my classmates had a family business or a college fund to fall back on. They could go to law school or study medicine. I was the one who wouldn't have any second chances.

I had one. And the School at the Art Institute of Chicago (SAIC) was it.

I had no family support or connections. Once I moved to Chicago, I was on my own. There was no guarantee that, even if I wanted to, I would be able to afford returning home to Cypress Park.

That is why I marvel at the blissful ignorance of youth, because I don't know if I could go through with it again. I didn't genuinely understand the risk I was taking.

All year long, I had saved money from work to pay for my moving expenses. Uncle Ray, who lived alone, and failed as miserably to clean as most straight men, hired me to clean his house every week. I'd iron his shirts, scrub the floors, and wipe the countertops so that every time he returned home, everything was sparkling and neat.

Each time, he gave me a choice for payment. I could either take ten bucks or his change jar, and I always chose the change. Sometimes it was pretty light, but once in a while I received a big bonus. On one spectacular occasion, it contained one hundred and ten dollars. When I told Uncle Ray the following week how much money was in his change jar he stopped letting me choose.

Thereafter, ten bucks was my reward.

If I could offer some advice in life, it's this: always take the change jar. If you can't handle the risk involved in setting your sights higher, you may know what's coming on the other end. But how far in life can ten bucks really take you?

Ten bucks is a guaranteed path to mediocrity.

Mom helped me save money too. When I told her that I was applying to art college, she began stealing money from Dad's stash to help build me a savings account. Every week or two, she snagged twenty bucks when he wasn't looking, and he never had any idea it was missing. His money flowed so quickly between elicit exchanges that there was never a reliable count anyway—unless he smoked it down to zero.

Dad was terrified of change, and his response to art college was indicative of this condition.

I said, "Dad. I'm applying to art college."

"What? Where at?" he interrogated grouchily.

"My top choice is the School at the Art Institute of Chicago. It's one of the best art schools in the country."

He chuckled vigorously. "Yeah. Okay. I'll tell you what. If you get in there," he proposed, obviously implying that he doubted the possibility. "I'll pay for your rent."

He howled to a long, drawn out crescendo.

"Okay," I responded blankly, knowing fully that he would back out of the promise even if I succeeded.

I think it hurt him to conceive that we might not always be in the neighborhood. Somewhere deep down, without ever saying it, he thought I would always be in the neighborhood, living right down the block, just like his mom and brother. Community and family were at once everything to him, because he wanted us all there, and nothing, because he never did anything to warrant our trust and support.

In the end, he was another cynic in a long line of people telling me that I was bound to fail. From Grandma Chance to the bitchy girl in the Nighthawk Nest, it was an assumed truth that art was an impractical hobby. There was no money in the arts. And, as was becoming a pattern with me, it became another instance where I wanted nothing more than to prove them wrong.

I sat in the terminal of the Los Angeles International Airport with my mom. It was five days before the beginning of college. Mom had secretly saved up 500 dollars from Dad's wallet, most of which she spent on her airfare. And, after paying for my airfare, I had around 400 dollars total from my savings and a graduation party at my Aunt Lilly's house in the valley.

It was my second experience boarding an airplane, and when we took our seats, the monotonous roar of the engines and cool, steady burst of air rippling against my cheek brought calm. We sped down the runway with the promise of escape coming forthright. The pressure built, vibrating the cabin. The engines bellowed louder and louder, and, in an instant, a brushstroke like any other during the course of my life, the soft rubber on the little tires beneath the plane detached from the asphalt, catapulting me toward the sky and away from home.

I leaned my forehead against the window and peered down like an eagle soaring high above Los Angeles. Tiny clusters of homes connecting to one another grew smaller every second, each miniscule part representing a home, a family, a job—a life. The clusters coalesced to others, forming a web of little communities separated by a system of roads and freeways that functioned as veins through the sprawling urban network.

Scanning to the horizon, there was no end in sight. I wondered how many children there were down there—children like me—who felt deep in their souls that something more was beyond the asphalt jungle in their midst, above the stagnant grey smog hovering incessantly over their lives. I asked myself how many of them would find the things I found; how many would one day board an airplane to a faraway city and start a new life?

For a moment as liberating as mine, ascending from the depths of fear into a dream pieced together from hope, there was little joy. Joining me on the plane was the weight of my past, the weight that millions like me feel—that no matter where you go and how much you accomplish, there is a fat kid in grey sweatpants somewhere aimlessly wandering an asphalt play yard, wondering if he'll ever find a place to belong.

I think about the odds he's up against. And a tear rolls down my cheek.

After arrival at the Chicago O'Hare Airport, we grabbed my one small checked bag that contained everything my new life would possess, and hailed a cab. Cruising down the jam-packed freeway at a jarring speed of five miles per hour, I already sensed the cultural shift.

It was as if my life had switched from black and white to color.

To the north, a spectacular collection of skyscrapers were compressed so closely together that it appeared there was no ground at all. I mused that people must just walk from building to building to get around because the densely congested structures appeared to provide no negative space between them.

A silvery-grey train jetted past on our left between the opposing freeway channels. Onlookers by the dozens huddled in lines waiting for the next train to arrive. Cars darted quickly in and out of lanes as if professionals in navigating an impossibly busy thoroughfare.

There was a visible logic to Chicago—routes that people took, central buildings, well-kept sidewalks with swarms of foot traffic. Everyone was clearly on their way to, or in the middle of, something that mattered. It was a fascinating contrast to my home in Los Angeles.

L.A. was extremely different. It was a diffuse smattering of unnaturally segregated districts. The neighborhoods had lawns and beautiful homes that were often adjacent to vacant dirt patches. It was grungy and poorly maintained. Whereas Chicago seemed dense, logical, and safe, Los Angeles was sprawling, senseless, and fearful. Almost nobody just walked down the street in L.A. There was no great public transportation system. People used cars to fly in from the suburbs and jettison away in the evening, leaving a shell of a city to cool, unsupervised, overnight.

Once downtown Chicago, I realized that there was in fact enough division between the skyscrapers to drive a car through, although not a whole lot more. The sidewalks were flowing busily with pedestrians in business suits and blue jeans. A dirty-bearded old white man in a tattered Chicago Bulls jacket held a clear plastic cup out asking for my change. I averted eye contact and helped my mother squeeze out of the cab before something unexpected and chaotic swept her away into some unseen Chicago abyss.

We waddled down the sidewalk out of sorts and mesmerized by the imposing buildings and overwhelming business of it all. A penetrating wind deflected through the maze of airborne canals created by the gargantuan buildings erected between the tiny avenues, blowing Mom and I off of our natural strides. My ears whistled from the unyielding gusts.

Frustrated by the hectic uncertainty, Mom stopped to speak with someone on the street.

Mom, you're going to get us shot!

"Hello, excuse me sir," she said to a man in jean shorts and a Nirvana t-shirt standing at a bus stop. He raised his head and made eye contact with her. "Where is the Art Institute of Chicago?"

He smiled and pointed directly across the street, immediately in front of us. "It's right there," he said.

"Thank you."

"Oh, no problem at all," he said, giggling inaudibly beneath a friendly smile.

We had been right in front of the building and couldn't find it.

How can I possibly survive here?

The Art Institute was a baronial, stately building with spectacular stone arches lining the entryway. Two bronze lions, weathered into splotchy pale green were perched at either side of the walkway. Inside was one of the most impressive fine art collections in the entire world.

I was struck by a hint of inspiration when the hulking wooden doors to the Institute clunked shut behind us. My ears rang quiet, suddenly unencumbered by the nagging wind. The sound of high-heeled shoes tapping against the speckled marble floors echoed rhythmically through the lobby.

I approached the front desk, where a women in a white button up blouse sat, politely waiting to assist visitors.

I said, "Hi, I'm here to enroll as a student."

Her brow furrowed as she tilted her head bewilderedly to the right. "This is a museum," she stated, as if that was perhaps the missing piece of information that led me to confuse her.

"Yeah, I know. I'm a new student at the School at the Art Institute of Chicago?"

I fed off of her baffled tone.

"Oh," she quickly rebounded. "I'm sorry. The main building for SAIC is across the street."

"Thank you" I said, dragging my luggage back towards the door. I stopped, blinked twice and turned back toward the front desk.

Mom and I lumbered onto the bustling streets to find the college office.

It was undoubtedly a chaotic, transformational day. The cold, hard reality of being new in such a vibrant, energetic town was beginning to hit home. The adaptations I would have to make seemed infinite and I doubted my own ability to find class.

As I would learn at registration, then next day, classes would be held in a myriad of different buildings spanning a few miles of the entrenched urban landscape, and I was expected to find my own way there every day, alone, without the protective cultural surroundings of high school. It was fortunate that LACHSA had acclimated me to the college milieu, but it was nothing like this. Few classmates would be the same. The schedule was sporadic and allowed for down time in the middle of the day. The responsibility to manage all of my finances, work, and social time rested solely on my shoulders.

This would be exactly what I made of it.

The anticipation of my first day was overwhelming beyond belief. I experienced panic attacks, anxiety, and lost my appetite all together for four days.

Mom had stayed with me for only a few hours—enough time to buy me a futon to sleep on with the remainder of her money and help me drop it off at the first apartment we looked at. She had to leave unexpectedly because Ruben's girlfriend went into labor that day. Since he was in prison, Mom felt the need to get home immediately to help care for her second grandchild.

I chose an apartment, hastily, with a former LACHSA student named Renee. It was her second year at SAIC. She was from Whitier, California, a wealthy suburban town with no particularly defining features. Her parents were quite wealthy and paid for her rent and living expenses. This was a convenient arrangement because she agreed to pay for groceries on account of her shocking inability to prepare even the most basic food recipe—I'm talking, can't make Macaroni and Cheese without later filing a police report, bad at cooking.

We lived in a twenty-two story high rise on Lakeshore Drive, perhaps the most beautiful urban street in America, overlooking Lake Michigan to the east. For eighteen years, curtains shielded my view of a bleak lawn on a tight, unkempt street. With each passing day, I had the distinct impression that we were sinking lower and lower all the time, as if I would one day open the door to find a wall of sod blocking me from the exit because our house was buried, trapping us lifeless, overnight, six feet beneath the surface of the Earth. Now, I peered out a large picture window and could ponder my thoughts in silence while watching tiny little waves crest and explode into the concrete shore of Chicago.

Although magnificent, I feared that it wouldn't last.

Deep down, I thought that, upon arrival at college, everyone would be smarter, more creative, and more talented than me, and I would have to drop out of school on account of my inferiority. In the days before school, I dyed my hair from bleach blonde to black in an attempt to look as normal as possible. I combed it blandly to the side, and recited my voice into the mirror in an effort to drop my California accent. The thing I feared most was being foreign, different from the crowd. I worried that everyone would view me as the unsophisticated ghetto kid from L.A.

While I had gotten away without being judged by my appearances in high school, I thought that looks would be everything in college, and I was very uncomfortable with how I looked. In my own mind, I was a fat, sexless, towering, awkward kid with acne and crooked teeth.

On the first day of school, before I left the apartment, the same *wicked partners* who had accompanied me into "Night-in-jail," Franklin, and LACHSA were at my side and in my mind.

Fear told me that my new venture would end in failure, disappointment, and everlasting mediocrity.

Anxiety racked my brain with the idea that I would become an outcast, that I wasn't good enough to make it here.

Panic packed me with the creeping sense that, somehow, I was going to be irrevocably hurt.

I stood with my chest out, my head extended back as far as it might go, listening to this cast of characters fill me with the same self-doubt, insecurity, and terror that had always escorted me through life. And, just as I had so many times before, I took two deep breaths.

You can do it Ray.

I walked out the door.

When I walked into my first college class, Sculpture, I timidly took a seat in the back of the large, theatre-style room. I didn't want to mix in too quickly or make a big first impression. I just wanted to blend in and focus on my studies. I was prepared for the most challenging class schedule of my life.

Yet, when it all got rolling, the professor handed out the syllabus, and nothing was overwhelming at all. The assignments were clearly mapped out and didn't seem too difficult. The professor was a lot like any of my old teachers from high school. And the students, much to my surprise, seemed pretty ordinary. For all the hype of being the second best art college in the nation, I thought that everyone would be unparalleled creative geniuses. However, after a couple days of classes, I realized that they were pretty unprepared.

Some kids asked questions about art topics that I would have been laughed out of LACHSA for asking two years ago, and when the assignments started to come due, I was shocked at how much better prepared I was than most others.

For one of our first assignments, the class was tasked with creating a piece of art that represented our surroundings. It was an extraordinarily open-ended assignment, not requiring any specific style or medium. We were encouraged to create something very much our own.

So I decided to draw a series of symbolic vignettes that symbolized something peculiar about my new life. Among my little iconic drawings, I included little snippets of life that I encountered every day. I drew Renee's beige, stuffed dog that sat on our window ledge because it was indicative of living with a relative stranger. I also drew a Chicago sidewalk that I tramped along every day, detailing the unique cracks and imperfections that I traversed unconsciously.

It was a drawing to display the little things that we see every day without really seeing. Our brain hums away on our little selfish tangents, and we pass by the apparently ordinary details that unknowingly shape our outlook.

On the day of our class critique, it received very positive reviews, and just looking at it amongst the other pieces produced by my classmates, I realized how advanced I really was.

One student in particular stood out as a model for how far behind many others were. He was this little rat-like Chihuahua kid that looked like he weighed just a touch over five pounds when soaking wet. His "work" was about sixteen random photographs glued to a piece of poster board.

During his presentation, he explained, in an annoyingly dramatic tone, that, "I was walking down the street one night when I came across this big brown box. The lid had toppled over and, inside, I found these stacks of old pictures. There was nobody there, man, and it was like, 'wow,' these are the faceless people who I share a neighborhood. It was, like, a really profound moment."

I sincerely hope that he was stoned out of his mind. Because, if he weren't, that was about the most idiotic thing I'd ever heard.

I raised my hand immediately to make a critique. "You're telling me that you just found a musty box of pictures on the street, posted them up on a piece of paper, and now you're calling it your art? How is that art?"

My voice rocked with agitation.

"I mean, you didn't even create something to frame the pictures in the context of your *profound* epiphany. How is anybody supposed to look at these pictures and have any idea what your purpose or message is?" I added.

He swayed back and forth uncomfortably as I finished my critique.

His response was that, "I mean, it's cool man if you don't get it. I just think that there's something really deep, really beautiful about these pictures."

The rest of the class reciprocated my feelings, explaining that there was no creativity or context to his project. He hadn't framed the pictures with anything symbolic or representation of where they came from. He didn't add any of his own personal style or elements that highlighted the message. It was just a crappy photo collage that a third grader could have produced.

Admittedly, I had been harsh, but I was just shocked that somebody who got into the SAIC could produce such a remedial project.

Later, because of how personally he took my critique, he was gossiping about it with a girl from the class and dubbed me, "The Demigod of Art School."

The girl he told was Lauren Klopack. She and I had started talking a few times prior because of an embarrassing moment when I was asked to introduce myself to the class and say a little something about myself, and the only thing I could think to say was, "Hey, I'm Ray—from L.A."

And in the playful spirit of the triple rhyme, Lauren liked to heckle me every time we crossed paths by taunting, "Hey there Ray from L.A!" She drew out her words to highlight my error.

Great, I gave myself a stupid label in the first three weeks of school. I might as well just wear a t-shirt that says, "I'm special!"

It turned out to be all in good fun, as Lauren and I became good friends. And she told me about how the little Chihuahua kid was going around calling me "The Demigod of Art School." I developed a reputation for being a know-it-all, crass with an air of superiority.

Amazingly, I got a kick out of it. I wasn't embarrassed or mortified like I thought I might be. I guess it was because, even though it was sarcastic, it implied that I was one of the best—that I knew what I was talking about.

It was true.

Without sounding overconfident—which by this point in the book I hope you realize that I'm anything but—I was among the best students in all of my classes. The professors were assigning me things like color charts, shade studies, still-life drawings, and figure drawings that I had already done in the eleventh grade. Despite all of the pressure and build-up about how amazing of a school the SAIC was, I couldn't have been trained any better for it than I was at LACHSA. So, now, I wasn't just trying desperately to keep up like I was in high school.

I was trying to figure out how to be the best.

Unlike LACHSA, college was not presented to me as a challenge. I was constantly trying to prove that I belonged at LACHSA. Perhaps it was the high stakes involved—that if I didn't get in I would have ended up a high school dropout trying desperately to get a retail job to survive. Or maybe it was the pressure I put on myself after being rejected five times before finally being admitted. Or maybe it was that living at home made my choices, the dichotomy of my life between LACHSA and Cypress Park, appear so stark. Or it could have been that I was constantly trying to prove to my family that I could do it—that I could accomplish something extraordinary.

My time at LACHSA was a blur because I was so involved in the challenge that I didn't have time to stop and reflect. Now, I had all the time I needed. Classes didn't seem hard. My peers didn't impress me as much. So I had to challenge *myself* because I'm not the type of person that can do something half-assed. I either put everything into it or I don't do it at all.

I used my first semester of college to do things that I didn't know I had in me. I wanted to represent some things that I hadn't told anyone outside of my family with art, in an attempt to come to terms with the obstacles that I faced as a child.

One assignment from sculpture class afforded me a unique opportunity to take this on. The professor explained that we were to create a three-dimensional piece of art to create a self-portrait, using only found objects.

I interpreted this assignment very differently from the rest of the class, and this would become very clear during the presentations. I decided that I would create the 'self portrait' by creating an abstract depiction of my inner voice and psyche.

The idea began when our professor showed us a place where we could find a collection of useful found art materials. In it, there was a group of clear glass bottles that were misshapen and deformed. They caught my eye, primarily because they reminded me of the *pear* motif. So, for the assignment, I collected my favorite contorted bottles, and began plotting how I could use them to represent my self portrait.

I reflected on the tormenting idiosyncrasies milling around inside my head. I thought of the difficult conversations I'd had with my mother and how the little snippets from our relationship helped me to hold on when I felt desperate and alone. I relived the damaging self-image that I'd harbored about my bulbous physique and enigmatic sexual identity.

In an effort to put these features of myself on display, I decided that I wanted to have a set of ten queer bottles counterbalance one another. I created a small, awkward wooden base with a sturdy post erected in the center. From wood, I created a web that jutted out from the top on both sides. From the corners of the web, thin wire hung the bottles evenly on both sides. I filled each bottle with used cooking oil to signify my obese build and oily skin, representing my internal obsession with greasiness and fat.

On plastic strips, I painted meaningful fragments of conversations that had transformed into emotional self-talk. Among them were: *It's not your fault, I wish I could have been there, don't worry about it Mom, I'll be okay*, and *we won't let you get hurt again*. These were uniformly quotes I remember from the tenth grade, when I told my family about my abuse in kindergarten. I slid the plastic strips strategically into the bottles, where they were suspended in the oil.

At the base of the sculpture, four nails poked upward through the wood, and on top, I placed four black candles to heat and illuminate the bottles of grease. When they were lit, and the room dark, the oil inside the bottle glowed from the candlelight, inducing a luminescent clarity that made the plastic strips profoundly legible.

If anything were shifted on the sculpture, it would topple over. It was a fragile concoction, like me, placed into balance for all to see. It was a process of seeing myself through a different lens—analyzing the psychological toll that my childhood took on my life.

When it was time for me to present, I asked a fellow student to cut the lights after I lit the candles. Then, the class filed into a procession to come forward and view the unique abstraction of my damaged, ever-human psyche.

I told them that the bottles represent me because of their irregular shape and that the oil represented my insecurities about my weight and skin. The strips of plastic were my inner-voice. The four candles represented my brothers and I.

Through the sculpture, I told them about me. I showed them, me.

The procession of students slowly crept past the sculpture, leaning over to table in an effort to discern the inner messages depicted in the incandescent oil. Some groaned lightly, but painfully. Others gasped. A couple cried.

And I was completely shocked to witness the effect I was having on people.

I nervously stood and watched as a crowd of my peers examined every inch of me through the metaphorical representation. I felt nervous. I felt naked. But because of the medium I didn't feel hurt or tortured. I wasn't gripped in terror.

The students commented on how amazingly emotional the sculpture made them and how touched they were by its content. They congratulated me on a job well done.

They had seen me and nobody ran away. My confidence grew.

Weeks later, my professor nominated the sculpture for a grant award. Without question, the project was a success, but, more than that, it was a leap forward for me in my development as a person and as an artist. For as long as I can remember, I've been the kid who leaves his shirt on at the beach, who swims with a t-shirt, who can't show his exposed body to others. It was mortifying for me to imagine people seeing me naked or vulnerable. It made me sick to my stomach.

But when I showed that vulnerability, that inner voice, through art, I didn't feel sick in the least.

Chapter 28

There was liberty to being out on my own.

I imagine that many people struggle to be away from home for the first time—far away from their family, old friends, and the familiar rhythms of their hometown. It could be frightening to know that when things go wrong, there is nobody you can rely on but yourself. Maybe that is alienating. Maybe it's scary.

But I didn't see it that way. Being at college allowed me, for really the first time in my life, to take a step back and be alone, to reflect in quiet, to dictate my own schedule, and to explore my passions. Absent from the daily irritations of Cypress Park—the gunshots, the parties, the drugs—I found that I liked to build things. I liked taking a myriad of miscellaneous parts and turning them into something whole.

In 3D class, I found myself using tragic components that had already been tossed aside, and converting them into a meaningful totality. And, like the sculpture I made from the deformed bottles of oil, I reveled in the challenge of creating something that symbolized me.

Late in the semester, I was alone in the men's bathroom. I never use a urinal. If the facility is full, I will wait in line to use a stall and prefer to use the largest one available. I lock the door carefully behind me so that nobody can get in.

I was nineteen years old and couldn't coax myself to pee out in the open. So while I was standing there, doing my business, my mind floated off to dreamy topics. I lost track of myself, and the door unexpectedly screeched open. I heard footsteps clacking against the tile, and my heart began to race.

As I stared straight ahead, I saw a utility door at eye level in front of me.

I held my breath and tried to listen to what was happening outside of my stall. The door opened again. Though I was finished with my business, I remained in the stall, waiting to ensure that all was clear.

A voice rang out. "Damn, that test was easy huh?"

"Yeah, piece of cake," the other mentioned lightly.

My cheeks flushed in embarrassment. A drop of sweat surfaced beneath my hairline, as I turned to unlock the door. After I did, I looked back at the utility door and got an idea for my next art project.

The professor had given us an assignment to create a three-dimensional piece of artwork using a 2X4 piece of lumber. So I began by creating a frame the size of a textbook. Then I whittled away about a dozen sturdy slivers from the piece and glued the ends to the frame. I used a letter opener that I had at home with a decorative handle made of glistening abalone shell and carved a wooden outline of it that would serve as its case.

To finish the project off, I placed the letter opener, which was sharp and resembled a dagger, into its case, and suspended it in the center using the fragmented splinters of wood. The piece was designed to mimic the utility door in the bathroom.

When I presented to the class, I told them the story from my youth. I explained that a boy used to take advantage of me in the bathroom and that is why I cannot use a public bathroom.

"I wish that there was a weapon in every bathroom so that sexual predators would be scared away and innocent young people could prevent themselves from being hurt," I said. "This dagger is the thing I wish I had when I was in their situation."

Everyone was blown away by the emotion of the tale. Even the professor was at a loss for words. The sculptures I made during my freshman year were very powerful to me. It was clear that I was a step ahead of the other students, and I was gaining quite a reputation for my work.

But I wasn't satisfied. I didn't feel like I was going anywhere in visual arts.

In fact, by the end of the first semester, I was about ready to give up. Sure, I was successful in school, but then what? Was I going to become a professional sculpture? Was I going to open an art studio featuring a bunch of statues and models that represented childhood abuse?

One key reason for my disillusioned feeling was that I wasn't making progress with my greatest passion, painting. I had enrolled in a painting class with a professor who everybody thought was, like, the most amazing teacher in the whole school. Everybody talked about him all the time.

By all accounts, he was thebomb.com.

However, it was in his class that I reached a critical turning point. With all the anticipation, all of the love I felt toward painting, I expected big things. After all, my most notorious accomplishments in high school were paintings. It was the reason I wanted to come to the SAIC, because of its reputation as an *unbelievable* fine art school.

So I put everything I had into that particular class. My style had always been figurative, emotional, and surreal. The *pear* theme was a metaphor for my own ambiguous sexual identity. The melancholy painting was a reflection of my haunted past. I used figures to express topics drenched in human emotion and my own personal struggles.

Every time I produced paintings of this genre for my college painting professor, however, I was squashed by his unfavorable critiques.

By the end of the first semester, I had battled to conform my work to his critiques while maintaining my artistic identity. The painting I produced to bridge this divide was of a flower centered on the canvass surrounded by a series of women, all featured in a different nude position. The painting was intended to mean...

The professor totally ripped it apart. He said, "I want to see the emotion let loose on the canvass. Why can't you just put it all out there?"

I disagreed with him entirely, and it wasn't the first time. For the whole first semester, he criticized me for stuff that I loved. They were figurative, improvised realities in which the forms represented symbols of deeper, intrinsic meaning.

However, he was the type of guy who fixated on outlandish interpretations of totally abstract paintings, where there are blotches of paint splattered about the canvass. And he would rave about how eloquent it was. I thought those concepts were simple and mundane—just a bunch of stupid blobs. A kindergartner can hurl a can of paint at the wall and call it art.

I just didn't get it.

I left class after my last critique completely dejected. Was this really where I was meant to be?

A couple of friends from class caught up to me in the hallway as I lumbered slovenly along with a bag slung over my right shoulder. They picked up quickly on my dramatized disappointment.

"Hey, don't worry about it Ray," one of them said. It was Lauren Klopack, the girl who loved to call me 'Ray from L.A.'

"I'm just so fed up with that class. He tore my painting to shreds because it 'didn't have enough emotion,' but then he loved that stupid glitter painting with a bunch of girls asses on it," I pleaded.

My upper lip raised up in disgust and my cheeks scrunched up against my eyes.

"It totally doesn't make sense," Lauren said.

We continued walking down the hall and out into the streets of Chicago.

"I came here because I love fine art, but if this is all it is, I don't think I can do it anymore," I pronounced. "I used to love painting, but I kind of hate it now. I'm so frustrated."

The other girl walking along with us spoke up. Her name was Piper Gorsuch. She was taking the painting class with us as an elective, but her main focus was fashion design.

"Hey, well, I have an extra ticket to the SAIC fashion show tonight. You should come with us Ray," Piper suggested.

"Um," I stammered, taken off guard by the unexpected invite. "What is it?"

"It's the school's fashion show."

"Well, I don't know. Is it any good?" I asked, trying to buy some time.

Piper paused and said, "I guess we'll see when we get there, right? It'll help you get your mind off of painting for a while."

"Alright, I'll give it a shot," I responded blandly.

That evening, Lauren, Piper, and I were seated together in the balcony of the auditorium where the fashion show was held. The building was a classically beautiful performance space with architecture and adornments that exuded tastes from the turn of the Twentieth Century. Noisy chatter infected the air. The people seated on the floor were dressed formally, as if attending a black tie affair, and were shaking hands and intermingling with their neighbors. Tiny yellow lights bordered the stage, and a professionally crafted catwalk jutted out about twenty yards into the seating area.

To this point, I had no expectations. It was a college fashion show. Whatever. I was just happy to have something social to do after a disheartening day. I sat unenthusiastically in my seat, pointing out quirky little flaws in the people seated below us and gossiping about class with Lauren and Piper.

The lights in the auditorium flashed on and off intermittently and the collective jabbering began to hush. Soon, the lights began to steadily dim, the stage cleared entirely, and silence swept the hall. As the suspense climbed, music suddenly thundered through the speakers.

I'll never forget the song. It was "History Repeating," by *Shirley Bassey and the Propellerheads*. In an instant, the curtain swung away and model came strutting out into the catwalk, her steps synchronized mystically to the swanky song. She walked with purpose, her extraordinary dress dancing boldly over her shins. At the end of the catwalk, she halted, stuck her right knee out—her chin held proudly high—to welcome the attention and awe. With a fluidly quick pivot, she retreated honorably back to the stage and out of our view.

My heart pounded in excitement from the song and the spectacle. An aura of accomplishment and glory blanketed my senses as I hung on every step, every beat, every new item that emerged. Hoop skirts and corsets and shawls created with fresh ideas and totally unique aspects kept emerging from backstage on incredibly beautiful people, and curiosity flowered inside of me.

How did they do that? What's that made of? How is it put together?

I was fascinated by the stream of enviable items and people. I was entranced by the ideas provoked in the art. The fashion was creative, innovative, and new. Yet, it was practical in the same breath. Each model changed, looked like a totally different person, based on the next thing they wore. Their fashion became a part of them.

Their clothes recreated the image that they projected to the world.

In that moment, fashion represented something that I wasn't. It was gorgeous and unapologetic. It was creative yet entirely useful. The attitude, the image, and the unwavering self-belief that fashion implied inspired me in a way that I hadn't felt in my whole year at the SAIC.

And a new thought sprang forth when the designers, who were all students like me, came out to take a bow.

Amidst the whistles and applause from the swarms of people in attendance, I stood and thought, "Oh my god. I've gotta do this!"

Within the next week, it was my turn to register for my second semester classes, and, looking back, the timing couldn't have been more serendipitous. The SAIC was unique from most colleges because they didn't set forth requirements about any particular major or focus. So while I originally enrolled in all visual arts courses, there was nothing preventing me from choosing a whole new slate of disciplines, and ever since the fashion show, I had my heart set on taking some courses in fashion.

The problem was that, because I was only a freshman, I chose last. I had to pick classes from the scraps left behind by upperclassmen, and every single introductory course to fashion was taken. All of the course sections that I had written down before my appointment were filled.

The only available fashion courses were in very specific, more advanced disciplines.

So that's the path I chose. With me, it's *do it all or don't even bother.*

My arts courses for the second semester included: Handbag design, fashion illustration, hat making, knitwear design, and, finally, footwear design and construction. I totally threw out visual arts, and it was mainly because I had grown restless sitting in class, listening to a teacher tell me that I had to put dots and splotches all over the place to get my emotions out, even though that wasn't the type of painter I was. So I felt like I was spinning my wheels in fine art. To be honest, after spending so much time with visual arts in high school, the first semester of college visual arts just didn't live up to my expectations. It morphed from being this awesome expressive learning process to a series of drab and lackluster projects that I had to complete.

Ironically, the fashion course that was least appealing to me was footwear design and construction. When I read the course description, it said, "Learn how to make your own footwear and sandals by hand." And I immediately conjured up images of hippies sitting Indian-style in a circle making Jesus sandals from burlap and cardboard. I could practically smell the dreadlocks and patchouli oil.

Gross.

Needless to say, I wasn't expecting to change the world on my first day of footwear design and construction. In fact, I had half a mind to drop it after the first day and find something else. But, like many things, first impressions can be deceiving.

I sat alone near the rear of the classroom, which was a big, flat, tiled workspace with chairs organized at the center. To the side were workbenches with all sorts of machines and contraptions machines that I didn't know what to do with. They looked like implements of medieval torture, sharp objects and leather strapping devices—get me out of here.

When the teacher walked in, my impression changed a little. I half expected a scrawny red-headed hippie guy with a beard, wearing a bandana and a Bob Dylan t-shirt. The actual teacher, Gillian, couldn't have been more different. She was a little, prim woman with short, silvery grey hair in a boy cut.

She said nothing as she tottled into the room with a leather briefcase in one hand and a stack of papers under her arm, her chin held high in the air. She wore a black designer smock and a pair of ginormous, perfectly round black-rimmed glasses like Carrie Donovan.

She stepped with immediacy, and, without mincing words she got right to our first assignment. "I want you all to take off your shoes and place them on the table in front of you," she declared.

The class awkwardly fumbled around for a minute until everyone was set and ready to learn why they had to do this silly thing.

"Now, draw it," she demanded without explanation.

For whatever reason, nobody questioned her. Perhaps it was because she gave little impression that she was willing to answer questions anyway. So we did, with one socked foot cooling on the tile of the floor.

This was an awakening. I never, in all the years of drawing things, realized how difficult it is to draw a shoe. Finding a place to start, getting the shape right, and plotting out the proportions, turned out to be a shockingly daunting task. Shoes have no definite line. There is nothing on them that indicates how the other parts of the shoe piece together with it, like a puzzle made out of circles. It was like learning how to write the alphabet all over again.

As I finished, I popped my head up to see our teacher, Gillian, making rounds to inspect everyone's progress. She offered few nods and little encouragement. She simply scoured the work like an army sergeant inspects his new company of troops. When she passed me, she stopped.

With a serious, unemotional voice, she said, "Ah. You're going to be one of the good ones."

I didn't know what to make of that comment. It was just a shoe. I drew it. What was the big deal?

Gillian then spent the next half an hour of class measuring our feet. She then outlined what our task would be for the semester. During the next class we would all need to bring in twenty-five dollars, which was a lot of money for me at the time, and purchase a shoe kit from a particular store in Chicago. Over the course of the semester, the assignment was to create real shoes that fit our own feet.

Based on the measurements of our feet, she would use the twenty-five dollars to pay for a set of lasts—molds tailored to our feet that were required in making shoes—for each student. Using our shoe kits, the tailored last, and the machines in the room, she challenged us to produce a professional-looking pair of shoes—not some rickety set of Jesus sandals.

If it was hard to draw a shoe using a pencil and paper, how hard would it be to do it with leather and stitching and laces and rubber soles?

I became intrigued by the prospect—intrigued and terrified.

Gillian and I didn't get off to the best of start in our relationship. The class was set up so that she lectured in the beginning on the different steps and intricacies involved in designing and creating shoes, and the second half of the class was work time, when students could use the tools in the room to get to work on their projects. But I was the type of person who liked to get the information and go try to do it on my own. So, every time she finished her lecture, I packed all my stuff up and left.

However, since she didn't know, or trust, that I was going home to work on it independently, she got the impression that I wasn't fully committed.

One day before we got started, she asked, "Why are you always skipping out in the middle of class?"

I didn't understand where she was coming from. "What?" I asked. "Do you want me to sit in class so you can watch me?"

And she said, "Yes. That's kind of the point."

"Once you tell me how to do something I can do it on my own. I don't need to be here in order to work on the assignment," I answered adamantly.

"Can't you just stay a few times so I can track your progress?" She pleaded.

"I don't know. I guess."

Then, after her lecture in the next class I packed up and left again. I don't know what it was, but I felt like lecture was a challenge and, once it was over, I just wanted to go home and try it out.

For the whole semester, we kind of went back and forth in little spats. I would leave to work on my shoes at home, never spending more than a few minutes working in the classroom. Eventually, she sort of shut me out and stopped trying to help me because I was being so defiant. It made it hard for Gillian and I to see eye-to-eye.

Nonetheless, I became fixated on the challenge of producing a real pair of shoes. I would stay up late into the night in my apartment designing the shoe and piecing everything together. I created a drawing of a black leather loafer with a saddle top that had a jagged edge on each side and rounded off toward the heel. Like professionally made shoes, I specified a different type of leather for the toe and the heel on the upper of the shoe. I drew the sole as a pretty standard men's dress shoe sole, very thin at the toe with about a three-quarter inch platform at the heel.

With my shoe kit and some leather materials I obtained from class, I began the first steps. I hand stitched the two unique leathers together in the pattern that I designed. I dampened the leather and stretched it out over the plastic last. The last is used simply to create the shape of the shoe and is removed once everything is finished. When everything was stitched and punched and flattened out cleanly, I nailed the excess leather down before placing it in the oven.

This step was hilarious when I arrived at class because a bunch of people showed up with shoes that looked like cookies. If you bake the leather on the last for too long, the plastic will melt and the leather will mix right in with it and flatten into a plastic with leather-chip cookie. And all of them had to start all over again, or quit.

The next steps were to remove the nails and sand the leather like a frantic ninja until it is totally smooth and flush to the last. Given the lessons and books that I had, everything went surprisingly smoothly for me. Until, I had to put on the heel.

I had a miserable time figuring out how to make the sole adhere to the upper part of the shoe. So, in the middle of the night, during a fit of O.C.D., I called Gillian at home.

"Hello," she answered grouchily.

"Hi Gillian, it's Ray from class."

"Ray? What do you want. It's the middle of the night," she responded.

"Well, I'm trying to get the sole to stick to the upper and I'm stuck."

She was shocked that I was so far along. "The shoes aren't due for another three weeks," she said bewilderedly.

"I know. I'm just so close and I want to get them finished."

And I don't know what it was, but she warmed up to me. We stayed on the phone for forty-five minutes talking through all the steps I would need to take.

Apparently the problem was that I wasn't applying enough pressure to make the adhesive stick. So after spreading the glue (which was mixed with chopped cork), I lifted up the futon that Mom bought me, and set the legs down on the inside of the shoes. I bided my time for thirty minutes while the glue coalesced with the leather and the rubber sole.

Once solidly connected, I cracked the plastic last and pulled it out, placed four screws into the soles for stability, and cut out a sock shaped liner to add padding. On a quarter-inch wide piece of cloth I designed a fashion logo with *Raymond Serna* embroidered at the center, and after doing a final polish, I had created my first pair of handmade shoes.

The next week, on the day of our class critique, I brought them in to show off to the class. I purchased a shoe box at a container store on my way to class and neatly placed the new pair on the inside. As I walked in the building, one of my friends from another class spotted me and said hello.

"Oh, did you buy a new pair of shoes," she asked.

"Yeah," I answered with calculated deception. "Want to see?"

"Sure."

She pulled my shoes out of their phony box and said, "Wow, Ray. These are really nice."

Ecstatic from the sensation of showing off a pair of shoes that I actually created, I couldn't contain the secret for more than a second.

"I made'em," I blurted out, desperately trying to restrain my proud smile.

"No way."

"Yeah. I handmade every little detail."

"That is incredible," she gasped. "They literally look like you bought them in a store."

"Thanks."

I walked away with my chest swelling in pride.

Sauntering into class, I could hardly bridle my excitement. I had a good idea about other student's progress on the project, and knew fully that it was extraordinary to have a fully completed pair.

By the time it was my turn to show my product, I was confident that people would be blown away. Hell, I was blown away and I made them.

"Ok, Ray. Let's see what you have for us," Gillian announced.

I glided to the front of the class, unhinged the shoe box and gently pulled at the soft, smooth leather heels, placing them squarely on the desk at the front of the room. There was a collective gasp followed by denial.

"You just went to a store and had those made, right?" one student said.

Others chimed in to accuse me of cheating on the project.

Gillian interrupted. "I cannot believe this," she said with calm, definite repose. "Ray, would you like to have these shoes featured at the fashion show?"

I lost my breath. My eyes fluttered. "Uh. Yeah. I. Of course."

I nodded strangely, a couple times up and down and a few times robustly gyrating from side to side.

"They are really good," Gillian reinforced.

As it turned out, not a single other person in my class finished a functional pair of shoes by the end of the semester. I had done so with two weeks to spare. Some students made single shoe prototypes, and others simply presented their designs along with some leather stitching, but nobody was even in the same league as me.

I don't mean to make it sound like I'm full of myself, or that it was easy for me. It wasn't at all, and I would learn shortly that I was nowhere near the skill level of a professional designer. It was one of the hardest things that I'd ever done. Every little detail, and I mean down to a half of a millimeter, had to be perfect. Every stitch, every cut, every measurement had to fit just right or it would ruin the whole project, and I became addicted to the process.

Shoe design tested all of the skills I had developed in my life. I was forced to conceptualize and draw, imagine, and shape into form. A shoe, a simple shoe, had the power of expression. It allowed me to express my creativity, and feel good about something tangible that I contributed to the world.

I don't know anybody from Cypress Park who ever made a pair of shoes.

Chapter 29

As I reminisce about my move to Chicago and the transition into college, I think mostly about the good things that happened while I was there—the things I learned, the people I met, and the challenges I faced. I was given my first opportunity to independently explore the world on my own terms. I loved, and I mean L-O-V-E-D, living independently.

No matter what I was faced with, I got to choose my own path.

But the reality is that I worked my ass off. Ever since I arrived in Chicago, I was forced to walk from storefront to storefront filling out job applications. I struggled week-to-week to have enough money to survive, and every couple of months I had a fresh bill for thousands of dollars in tuition that I had to pay off. I racked up a bunch of credit card debt, and I basically didn't eat.

That's the dirty little secret.

Ever since high school, I had suffered from chronic bulimia and anorexia. The person who I presented to all my professors and classmates was sassy and confident, but it was all a big front. During my time at LACHSA, I had learned how to play the role of an art student. A certain level of arrogance— even downright bitchiness—earned me respect from peers. If you can't dogmatically defend your work to others, then they will rip you to pieces.

I played into a fictitious persona. I morphed into whoever I needed to be, in order to protect my work.

But, hidden beneath the veneer of outer strength, was the same old weakness and insecurity of the fat kid in grey sweatpants. He wore vogue new clothes and fit in with posh cliques, but he was still the one inside of me. I could change the way he looked, but I couldn't make him go away.

My everlasting disgust with my own body made it worse. If I had to eat for whatever reason, I would throw up in the bathroom at home. I couldn't stand the thought that I was making myself fatter. In my head, I knew I was revolting. I hated the way I looked, and I thought others hated it too. The only way that I could gain their admiration, I thought, was to be thin and beautiful like a model.

And from years of this cyclically destructive behavior, I had grown a scrawny. I didn't look flush and healthy, but, even when reduced down to an ordinary size, I still looked in the mirror and saw the same fat kid.

I tried to keep him a secret. I thought that I had to put on a show because if anyone saw what I truly was, learned about where I really came from, then they might reject me again.

So nobody knew about any of it. Nobody knew about my eating disorders. Nobody knew that I grew up poor. And nobody knew about my sexual orientation.

I hadn't even come to terms with these things.

Since I was such an unsexable person to begin with, I didn't have to deal directly with sexuality, but I knew that if I didn't lose weight, nothing would change. So I pinned it all on that. If I could only get skinny, then people might find me attractive.

These issues lurking shallow in the perpetual ramblings of my mind, gnashing in my heart as I fervently strove to make it in life.

At home, my brother languished in prison, and my dad continued to sell drugs at "Tokies." My mom was home, clinging as best as she knew how to the people to whom she'd dedicated her life.

And there I was, standing at the end of a long, velvet red carpet shaking hands with big time financiers of the SAIC at a champagne and cocktails reception. The fine guests exited from town cars and limousines and sauntered gleefully down the red carpet. It was my job to shake their hands, introduce myself, and welcome them to the fashion show.

For an hour, I mingled and chatted them up. I later realized that it had been the first time I'd ever interacted with rich people at an affair. I laughed and spoke elegantly about rich people things, while listening sociably as they talked about their fancy jobs.

I told the donors some superficial lies about how great I was, and that I had recently produced my first pair of handmade leather shoes. They all seemed impressed. So I walked small groups over to a large glass case situated adjacent to the red carpet where my work was on display.

Right beneath my shoes was a card that read, "Raymond Serna: Freshman."

It was a pretty cool feeling to be part of something like that. It made me feel important. It made me feel like I belonged. The affair was all of the things that I wish I had—glitz, glamour, achievement, and class. I yearned so deeply to find a way to maintain that sense of belonging.

Had my brothers watched me that day, they would have jokingly labeled me a *Faggot* on account of my bougie behavior.

After the final day of the fashion show, an opportunity to entrench myself in the fashion department emerged.

Plastic champagne glasses were strewn about the bar. Red cocktail napkins were crumpled up on tables next to messy h'ordeuvre plates. I was cleaning up the wreckage from the reception when my professor Gillian approached.

In her normally clinical tone, she said, "Good job on those shoes Ray. I've never seen a freshman complete a pair so quickly and have it look so professionally done."

"Thanks, Gillian," I responded modestly and continued to clear the tables.

"Listen, I need an assistant for next semester," Gillian informed me. "Since you seemed to grasp footwear design so well, I would like you to take the job. Are you interested in being my assistant?"

I stood erect now with a mayonnaise smattered plate in my left hand.

"Wow, Gillian. I hadn't thought about it. I didn't even know that was something a freshman could do."

"Well, normally it's reserved for seniors, but I can choose whoever I want for the job," she replied. "Will you do it?"

I gulped excitedly. "Of course I will. That sounds great."

"Excellent. I need you to show up at my office on Monday at noon and we can get started."

"Okay, I'll be there," I said.

And with that she left for the evening, and I finished cleaning up the plastic glasses and plates.

For the next two years, I served as her personal assistant between taking classes. It was an incredible opportunity because I got to sit in on every single one of her footwear courses for four semesters. Not only did I get to retake this class four times for free, they paid me for it.

With that task came not only two years of mastering the course material, but also free access to all of the supplies, which allowed me to work freely on projects of my own while she delivered lecture. As students needed help, I would offer individualized advice, help them plan out their sketches, teach them how to select and cut materials, and how to piece the shoes together. Essentially, I was the second teacher and, through teaching, I learned a lot of stuff that a student wouldn't normally learn.

I began mastering my own technique, not just the textbook version. This skill was invaluable because a huge part of fashion is figuring out for yourself how things work for you with the given materials. So I gained a new perspective on how quickly I can produce different elements of a shoe. I invented little shortcuts. Whether it was scything leather, gluing, or sewing, I figured out more efficient methods of operation. For example, I started using cardboard to test my sewing patterns to make sure the machine's tension was set properly. This helped save me time, material, and the added headache of having to stop everything to unjam the sewing machine because the tension was set too loose.

I experimented with new materials, like horse fur, and new constructions. I made a new pair of high heeled pumps for my mom, which I was able to do from scratch without any extra instruction.

I used the class to advance my own knowledge and experience, and it evolved me because, by the end of my two years working for Gillian, there was scarcely another student at the university who had more experience in footwear design and construction than I did.

During that second year, I received a late night call from Gillian.

She said. "Ray, I have a symposium tomorrow that I am speaking at. Do you mind teaching the class for me?"

"You mean alone?" I exclaimed.

"Yeah. We are working on sketching and you know as much about it as anyone. I really need you to cover for me. Do you mind?"

I agreed, though my chest filled with fluttering little butterflies that I didn't like.

The next morning, I stood panicky at the front of the classroom as the students poured in. Once they were all seated, I had to explain the situation.

"Gillian won't be here today because she is a guest speaker at a fashion symposium. So I'm going to be leading lecture today."

It was pretty cool because nobody seemed to blown away that I was going to be the teacher. They just got out their sketch pads, like normal.

When I turned to face the whiteboard, I had a flashback to the seventh grade. In my head, I could hear someone shout out at me, "You're fat!"

But, when I blinked my eyes and turned around, I realized that I had the respect and attention of eighteen college students who were waiting for me, the same kid who has been horrified of public speaking for his entire life, to lead them.

Oh, how things can change.

The class went exceptionally well, as I modeled different perspectives of drawing a shoe and the lectured about the benefits of each. A couple students even approached me after class to compliment me on how clearly I explained sketching. It meant a lot, not just because the students showed respect for me, but because Gillian trusted me enough, as a junior in college, to run her entire class for a day.

With each passing week, each project, each fashion show, I developed a strange feeling—confidence. I sensed deep down that, despite all of the other hardships and all of the insecurities that abounded in other parts of my life, I was in the right place.

In fashion, I knew that I belonged.

Over time, I became fashion. I embodied the designs, the ideas, and the mannerisms of the fashion department. That's how you play the game. From the model on the catwalk to the DJ at the fashion show to the makeup artists backstage to the fashion designers behind the curtain, there is an attitude, a swagger, about fashion. There is an aura that permeates the pores, through the soul, and into the mind of the fashion industry.

The aura, the culture, is hyper-critical, *holier-than-thou*, elitist, and fabulous. In order to belong, in order to gain respect, it becomes necessary to incorporate yourself into the culture. You have to know all the hottest designers and celebrities who wear their products. You have to be at the forefront of the trends, but unique enough to stand out. You need to be proud of your work and proud of your image.

Fashion is confidence.

So how can a person like me—insecure to the bone, with body hatred, eating disorders, a constant anxiety about social interaction, and an unaddressed sexuality—belong in fashion?

It's not like I sat down one day, had some zen-like meditation, and said to myself, "Hey, since you are so insecure and miserable, you should enter fashion to help with your confidence!" I think it's more about running against the current than anything. I remember when I was in high school, my Aunt Lilly said to me, "Ray, I'd tell you not to worry, but it seems like you do better when you worry. So, worry away." And there was something brilliant about that because, for my whole life, I've been running away.

"You can do it, Ray. Get yourself out of here. Make it end."

When I was growing up, the men in my family never talked about their emotions. They would plaster their brains with drugs and booze and masculine bullshit a thousand times before they'd tell me about their feelings.

So where did I run?

To art school, where you are required to constantly express your emotions.

As my own negative self-image poured over into debilitating eating disorders, what did I change my major to?

Fashion design, where you are required to project beauty and confidence.

Like my Aunt Lilly said, I think I'm better when I'm forced to worry, and, for whatever reason, I've always seemed to force myself into situations by running away from the things that seem normal. Perhaps it is an addiction that I have. I get a rush of euphoria every time I cajole myself into chasing something new that I want, something out of the ordinary. It produces anxiety beyond measure and I get sweaty and nervous until I feel like throwing up, but when I have completed my task and I can anonymously walk away unharmed, there is no greater feeling in the world.

The only thing that scares me more than change is the idea that, no matter how hard I try, I'll never change again.

So that's my best explanation for how, as a deeply insecure person, I could enter into such a judgmental field. I suppose that somewhere deep down I got a thrill out of making beautiful clothes and shoes and handbags because people used those things to project a new image to the world. People use fashion to make themselves more beautiful, to feel more sexy.

And that's exactly what I wanted for myself.

I wanted change, and I wanted beauty. I wanted the hope that I could morph into anything that I wanted to, and fashion allowed me to morph into something more confident, something more beautiful. I could change my hair color, change my glasses, or shift the genre of my clothing. I could be whoever I wanted to be on any given day, and people came to expect that of me because I was responsible for modeling different ideas through my image.

And it was that very concept of self-malleability that pushed me to make some radical changes. In fine art, your pieces stand for themselves. They are judged entirely separate from the artist. Many artists appear grungy and disheveled. They allow their work to speak for themselves, and oftentimes go out of their way not to look nice because they don't want to project the image that they are defined by outward appearances.

The fashion designer, however, is entirely judged by outward appearances. What you wear is indicative of what you might create. So your projections of self can be just as significant as your designs, your creativity, and your technique. As difficult as it was to make myself vulnerable to judgment, it forced me to do something that I always feared—looking in the mirror at the image I was projecting to the world.

In the mirror was a bulbous, confused degenerate with crooked teeth.

I had never explored my sexual desires. For my entire life, from adolescence through the first three years of college, I had presented an entirely asexual person to the rest of the world. Even though I had many girlfriends, or, to be more specific, platonic friends who were girls, I never talked with them at all about sex. Hell, I'd never talked to anyone about sex.

When I was a very young boy, perhaps five or six, my mom told me how babies are made and how women go through menstrual cycles, but, beyond that, I never discussed sex with anybody. My only faintly sexual experience was with Eric.

Some of my girlfriends, I think, even had crushes on me. We would hang out in my apartment and watch movies. Every once in a while, one of them would bring up a mildly sexual topic and I would always just change the subject. I never gave anyone an opening to learn more about me. I never lied to anybody and told them that I was attracted to women or pretended to have girlfriends. I just acted like I had no sexuality at all.

Of course, this wasn't true. When I was alone, I felt urges and did what any guy might do to satisfy them, but for all those years, I just never thought that I was attractive enough to experience such sensual feelings with another person. I sort of silently condemned myself to a life of sexual loneliness.

Once in a while, as I sat in class, I'd look over at a boy and wish that he'd come over to talk with me. I invented little fantasies in which he whisked over to me, said just the right things, and I was seduced into a whimsy of uninhibited sexual feelings for him. But it never happened.

Sex was the big elephant in the room, and I was terrified of it. So far, it meant pain, isolation, and uncertainty.

However, I was growing more comfortable with social interaction. In high school, and now college, I was having positive relationships with people. I had slowly begun to heal the wounds of distrust and the scars of abuse. I wanted to trust people, even though every fiber of instincts born from a childhood of fear and bullying signaled me not to.

I was growing more confident through my studies that, even if I wasn't attractive, I had a place to belong, a reason to exist. And I guess this confidence bled through into other areas of my life and allowed me to take the first leap in exploring my sexuality.

One of the jobs that I had as an extra way to make money was as a receptionist at the front desk for the SAIC. It was the easiest job ever. I just sat there and did homework until somebody walked up with a question or the phone rang. I literally did nothing, but talk to people and point them in the right direction.

One of the people who I saw on a regular basis caught my fancy. Every day or so, a boy named Reed walked through. I knew him from class and he would stop by to chat with me once in a while. He was a tall, skinny guy with curly dark hair. His smile was infectious and I always laughed a lot when we talked. I found myself, probably because my job was super boring, anticipating the next time he'd walk by. I knew that he was gay, and I felt a pang of electricity run through me each time he caught my eye.

And, on a day like any other, I mustered the nerve to express my feelings for him.

"Hey Ray," he said to me casually as he purposefully walked past toward the door.

I urgently stood up, forcing the chair to squeak loudly as it pressed along the tile floor.

"Hi. Reed. Wait a second," I blurted choppily.

He stopped where he was and watched as I circled awkwardly around the desk and grew near to him.

"This may be a little bold, but I was wondering if you'd like to go out some time," I said.

I rubbed my index fingers nervously against my thumbs. My heels swiveled around as I frantically awaited his response.

Reed smiled and cocked his head to the side. "Sure, Ray. That sounds like fun."

"Great," I responded a little too eagerly. "I'll see you around."

"Cool," he said suggestively.

Though it turned out to be an anticlimactic relationship, it was an enormous moment for me. I had never told any friends that I was gay. I hadn't told my mom. I hadn't even verbalized it or written it to myself. It was a big secret inside of me that I could feel pressing incessantly against my chest. It produced anxiety and panic, but it was unspeakable until that day when I asked Reed out.

We went out to dinner once and had some fun, but it didn't lead anywhere and just sort of broke off without event. However, the event inspired an excitement in me that I wanted to explore for the first time. It made me want to keep trying to make myself a more desirable person.

So I went to the dentist and scheduled an appointment. At the age of twenty-one, it was my first visit to the dentist's office. I went specifically to request braces because I hated my crooked teeth. A couple weeks after my initial appointment, they brought me in to get them.

No matter what I tried, from exercise to bulimia, I couldn't get rid of the pudgy bulge in my stomach. I did some research about liposuction, and found a doctor who was willing to perform the operation. Even though I didn't have money for it, I decided to put the liposuction surgery on my credit card when I had it done in May of 2000.

With a miracle of modern science, I was thin for the first time in my life, and my teeth were becoming straighter by the minute. I can't say the same about me.

I was doing everything in my power to prepare myself to play the part of a successful fashion designer. I was doing everything I could think of so that, if I were to open myself up to another person, they would find me attractive. I bought new clothes. I conjured up a new image of Ray.

I sat up as stiffly as I could. The jerky gyrations of the *El* train in Chicago irritated my scars every time I moved. The light painted the train bright yellow as it cruised between the apartment buildings blocking the sun. My hands were folded in my lap.

As the train rocked slightly from side-to-side, I accidentally set my eyes to the left and caught the glare of a man to my left. He smiled at me and I looked away, feigning the idea that I had something interesting to look at.

"Is there anything fun to do in Chicago," the man said.

I looked over at him, then at the window to my right and back at him. He was looking right at me.

"Are you talking to me?" I asked skeptically.

"Yeah. I'm new in town and I'm wondering if you know anything fun to do in Chicago," he replied confidently.

He was an incredibly handsome guy about my age. He had flowing dark hair and a cleanly shaven beard. His teeth were like finely polished ivory.

"Oh, yeah. There's tons to do here," I replied excitedly, before proceeding to list off a bunch of places that friends had told me about.

I had rarely gone out since moving to Chicago. When I turned twenty-one I went out with friends, but I'd never done much partying. I didn't want to make this known, however, to the devastatingly cute guy who was asking me what was fun. I finished my unintelligible ramble.

"Cool," he said with a deep look in his eye. "I'm so excited to be here. Do you want to show me around sometime?"

My heart pounded relentlessly, and my eyebrows perked up. I'd never been asked out before. Nobody had ever been attracted to me before.

I shrugged my shoulders, and said, "Yeah, I'd love to."

He smiled at me again with his big, pretty smile and pulled a piece of paper out of his bag. He leaned over for a moment before handing it to me. It had his name and number written on it in blue ink. On the bottom-right corner it said, "Call me!"

"This is my stop," he said as the train screeched to a halt. "Maybe I'll see you later."

I waved and smiled back at him.

When the train pulled away from the station, I winced in pain and grabbed my right side where a large bandage padded my scar. I dreamed a bit about the interaction, and felt a good stinging feeling in my chest. It was quite new to feel desirable.

Minutes later, the train reached my stop and I aloofly wandered off the train with my bag. As stepped toward the stairway, I clutched my right pocket and felt around. I reached in to feel only a set of keys. Then I grabbed into my left pocket, and felt nothing.

I had left the guys phone number on the train. I don't even remember his name.

School was finished for summer in the first week of June after my junior year, and it had been a very long time since I'd been home to see Mom. I booked a flight because I thought that I should be there in person to give her some big personal news.

It was time for me to come out... (story to be finished with Ray)

After arriving home from Los Angeles, I felt a weight lifted from my shoulders. Deep down, I always knew that Mom would accept me for who I am, but it still wasn't easy. I was the type that didn't confront my own sexuality until a very late age, and it all kind of happened at once. So it felt like a waterfall of emotions pouring out of me.

Now, I felt free to have some fun.

About a week after arriving home, I felt a sneaking inclination to get off seven stops early and walk into a club called *Spin*.

That was the night that I met my husband Ben.

It came on the heels of an extraordinary couple of years that passed like a blur. I had changed majors, gained a fashion mentor in Gillian, had liposuction surgery, and come to terms with my homosexuality. Yet, the most significant in this transformative series of events was falling in love for the first time.

I never thought it would happen to me. I never thought that anyone could bring themselves to love such a damaged person. I never thought that I would be able to trust somebody enough either. Even though I accused him of being a serial killer at first and resisted intimacy, I was ready.

Feeling the warmth of a man for the first time...(story to be finished by Jeff)

Ben made me feel honest with myself. I had somebody who wanted to learn about me, who listened to the stories of my youth and didn't turn away. I could share my darkest, deepest secrets with him, and he told me that everything would be okay. He encouraged me to go for things in my career, and told me that he believed in me.

Ben was the reason that I felt comfortable enough with myself to start eating with regularity again. He helped me gain the confidence in myself and my body to stop throwing up after every meal. As it turned out, love allowed me to step away from some of the destructive insecurities plaguing my self-image more than surgery or braces ever could have.

Love made it possible for me to look in the mirror, take a deep breath, and smile for once.

Chapter 30

The next year, Ben and I moved in together. We stayed in a monstrous apartment on Pine Grove in *Boystown* with our friend Joanna, and one other person. It was about 1,600 square feet with three bedrooms and hardwood floors, not bad for a college pad.

I spent senior year doing my best to hone my fashion design skills. I took classes that ran the gauntlet of fashion disciplines, from clothing design to accessories to fashion history.

My work was beginning to gain some recognition. I had won the Professor's Award, which was given to an outstanding student in fashion, and a major scholarship for a clothing line that I created. It was emblematic of people with body dysmorphia and eating disorders. The line was judged by a panel of professional designers. Each piece dealt with a different insecurity toward the human body and showed both how people look on the outside and how they feel on the inside when they are afflicted with an eating disorder.

I explained that I had battled with these disorders myself and knew firsthand how debilitating a negative self-image can be. The outfits turned out really cool because they had a combination of vogue elements, as well as these strange flaws that represented the flaws that the person wearing the outfit saw in themselves.

The panel awarded me $3,000 in scholarship money to help pay tuition.

It all went swimmingly, until about a month before the end of my senior year when I realized that I had missed an important memo.

While talking to a classmate, she asked me, "So where are you interning?"

"Interning? What the hell are you talking about?" I responded abruptly.

"You know, a senior internship?" she asked as if I was supposed to know. "I'm going to be interning with *Bettsy Johnson*," she said haughtily.

Sudden panic and terror streamed through my veins.

"I have no idea. I hadn't even thought about it."

After that conversation, I started asking other classmates if they had a summer internship lined up. Much to my chagrin, everyone, and their step brother, did.

I had unwittingly fallen behind, and didn't know what to do.

By this point, I had firmly decided that I wanted to be in footwear design, and it was based on a pretty simple idea. I was very good at clothing design, but, when I looked around the room at my classmates, I could estimate that about thirty percent of them were at least as good as me. There was a ton of competition in clothing design, and all of the jobs in that field required about five years of experience before you could start making a decent salary. You need a boat load of experience before anybody will actually hire you for a starting position.

It was kind of a *catch-22*.

In footwear design, on the other hand, I could look around at a group of my peers without finding anybody who was definitely on my level. I didn't think I was any better at shoe design than clothing design, but, in that field, I was in a class of my own. I had carved out a niche and wanted to keep pursuing it.

Since I hadn't even thought about an internship, though, I was willing to take whatever anybody was willing to offer because I was in a pretty desperate position.

"Oh, God! What if I get out of college and have absolutely nothing to pursue?" I thought to myself. If was pretty terrifying to think that I might have gotten this big, fancy education with nothing to show for it.

So, in an act of ignorant desperation, I decided to ask Gillian if she could help. The worst part of it was that, in two years of working as her assistant, I had never seen her send a recommendation for anybody. She even told me that she doesn't give recommendations because it puts her reputation on the line.

When I confronted her about it, my hands trembled.

I had a big knot in my throat when I began talking. "Gillian, I have been hearing around campus that it's really important to get a summer internship sometime before you graduate, but I don't know of anywhere that I might get one. I know you don't really give recommendations, but do you know of anybody who might take me as an intern?" I asked nervously.

"Honestly, it's kind of late Ray, but I'll call around and see what I can dig up," she said.

It was as simple as that. It was one simple question that only required the courage to ask.

A week later, I bumped into Gillian in the hall on my way to class, and she stopped me.

"Oh, Ray. I've been meaning to talk to you. I spoke with *Thea Cadabra* the other day and asked her if she has any use for an intern. She told me that she will be in China for about a month, before returning home for a two week window. She could really use your help during that two week timeframe. Can you make it?"

"Uh. Yeah, of course. I'd love to," I gasped.

I was shocked for two reasons. First of all, I couldn't believe that Gillian had actually found something for me. I was dreading the idea that I might graduate before gaining any real work experience. And secondly, I loved *Thea Cadabra*.

I met Thea briefly during Gillian's class as a freshman. Her last name, Cadabra, was a pseudonym for her design career. She came in as a guest lecturer, and held individual sessions with us to see how much progress we had made on our first pair of shoes and to offer suggestions. During her ten-minute session with me, she showed me how I could solve a problem I was having with stitching together the two pieces of leather that I laid out in my sketch. She taught me how to make a tack stitch, which is a thicker type of stitch, and said that if I create a triangular stitch pattern on both sides of the shoe, then I won't have an awkward-looking gap on it.

It was extraordinary advice, and I used it in constructing the pair of black leather shoes that appeared in the display case at the fashion show. Deep in the recesses of my mind, I hoped fleetingly that I would have a chance to work with her again.

Thea was an unusually soft-spoken person, so much so that it was difficult to hear what she was saying at times. She was petite, and, if you were to pass her on the street, probably wouldn't peg her as an awesome shoe designer. But her passion comes out when she talks about shoes, and she has a wild flare to her that you have to get to know her to extract.

I respected the hell out of Thea and was totally blown away that I was offered the opportunity to work with her on a professional level.

The following week, I received a call from her, and she informed me of the summer dates that my internship would cover. The company she worked for was called *AmAsia* and it was headquartered in Boston, where I would have to travel for the internship.

"Well, what do you want me to bring with me," I asked her over the phone.

"Just bring your portfolio and some clothes and you'll be good," she responded nonchalantly.

She had a casual nature about her that made me feel more comfortable about this unsettling journey. If you haven't realized by this point in the book, changes in scenery make me extremely nervous. You can never trust people in a new environment because everyone seems to be angling for one selfish thing or another.

"Okay," I said, still uneasy about the logistics of the trip. I was terrified that I was going to be cooped up in a creepy youth hostel for two weeks without money or food.

"Where am I supposed to stay?" I asked gingerly.

I could hear her laugh on the other end of the phone. "You're staying with me, of course. I have a guest room."

I was stunned. I couldn't believe that she was going to let me stay at her house. I couldn't believe that I actually landed an internship, especially in footwear design. And when I think about everything, starting back in middle school, I really can't believe any of it.

It all seems like a chain of impossibly unlikely events that, without any one link attached, would have fallen asunder to the *Cypress Park Trash Bin of Broken Dreams*.

Ben dropped me at the airport on calm, sunny June morning to catch my flight to Boston. One little hiccup with the internship was that I would have to find a way to survive for two weeks on the meager $200 stationed in my bank account. My credit cards were getting pretty inflated, and I had very little wiggle room to be away for two weeks without pay of any kind.

Fortunately, Ben worked for *United Airlines* at the time, which afforded me a free flight to Boston.

Oh, the perks!

However, once I arrived, I was going to have to be exceptionally frugal, or run into the awkward situation of needing to borrow money from Thea just to get home. Such pressures made my heart a little extra fluttery when the plane touched down on the east coast.

The only instructions that I had to this point were to get myself to Thea's apartment. I hopped a cab and sat in the back nervously while a Lebanese man silently drove me down an endless string of roads, spanning what I imagined was the entire state of Massachusetts. My knees bounced recklessly as

I watched the pay meter on the cab tick upward faster than the green glowing clock on the face of the car radio.

When the car jerked to a halt, the engine sputtered like a popcorn machine, and I owed the driver just a shade under sixty dollars. Great, there goes a third of my total money for the trip, and I haven't even met Thea yet.

After shuffling out of the dilapidated vehicle and lugging my gigantic suitcase to the curb, I approached Thea's door, where I knocked three times as politely as I could. I was relieved to hear the pattering of feet on the other side of the wooden barrier.

She opened the door with a welcoming smile, and a softhearted, "Hi Ray. Come on in."

Now that I had arrived, I felt a winnowing sense of relief. I had fretted over the logistics for weeks. What if I get delayed? What if I can't find her place? What if something suddenly comes up and she cancels the internship? What if my hair randomly falls out?

You know, rational fears.

Within minutes, however, a new generation of panic came over me, as I thought, "Oh shit. Now that I'm here, I'm going to have to prove myself. What if I can't cut it? What if she expects me to do things I can't do? Is she going to criticize my work? The myriad of insecurities never ends with me. I slip into my routinely burdensome anxieties.

Thea was unbelievably hospitable. From the second I walked in the door, she was welcoming and accommodating, doing everything imaginable to help me get comfortable in a new place. We spent most of that first afternoon, which was a Sunday, chatting on her back porch. She perused my portfolio casually and apparently without too much judgment. We talked about the SAIC and I troubled her with question after question about the shoe design industry. She offered tons of inside tips and entertained me with stories of her trips to China to direct the factories on shoe specifications.

I remember thinking to myself, "How incredible of a person is she? She travels to China all the time, and has this really high level, awesome job."

She was totally a role model to me from day one.

When the day came to a close, she had fed me dinner and already taught me invaluable lessons about the design industry. I went to bed that night in a comfy bed and imagined what was in store for me on this internship. The most exciting thing I could come up with was that, after getting people coffee for a couple weeks, they might ask my advice about a shoe they designed. Then, I could contribute a little bit professionally.

I had no idea what I was getting myself into.

It was sweltering in Boston when Thea drove me to work with her in the morning. I bordered on being late because I had packed every piece of clothing that I owned and tried on nearly every one, and I was sweating like a hog because she didn't have air conditioning. What you present to others is exactly what they will think of you, and I may have taken my clothes a little too seriously for my first day.

The morning drive was unusual when compared to Chicago. Boston is a little more like a small town. It's still busy and hectic, but a lot more quaint and the drive time seemed to cover a longer distance. We didn't talk quite as much on the ride to work as we had the previous day. I started to shrink up a bit, feeling the nerves setting in.

After settling into her downtown office building for no more than three minutes, Thea walked over to me, plopped three shoe constructions down on the table in front of me and said, "Alright, I need three patterns for each of these shoes. Start drawing."

On the exterior, I tried to hide the frantic sensations that were pulsating through my system. When I spoke, I was as methodical as possible so as to not seem unprofessional.

"When do you need them by?"

It was a question that represented the most unassuming way for me to say, "I have no idea what I'm doing! What are your rock-bottom expectations for me?" without giving my hand away entirely.

"A half an hour," she replied without sarcasm.

I gasped. My eyes widened as they might for a person staring up at a meteor the size of Texas freefalling unrepentantly in their direction.

"Ok," is all I said.

I started drawing, despite knowing that I would never have all nine drawings sketched and inked within a half an hour. I figured it was still better to at least give it a shot. After a few minutes, Thea walked by to see me all tied in knots over a loopy strapped high heeled shoe that could have doubled as a model for the planets orbiting around the sun.

"What are you doing?" she asked.

"I. Well, I started. Now," I struggled to apparently relearn the English language in three seconds. "It's really hard," I settled on as the most honest way to describe my embattled condition.

She calmly leaned over to me and gently suggested a way that I could check my work as I went along to avoid compiling mistakes and having to start all over again. Then, she retreated back to her desk. Every couple of minutes, I would try to inconspicuously look over my shoulder to monitor her progress. She was whipping it out faster than Anthony Weiner.

I dropped my head into my hands in frustration. My head spun into a vortex, and I began having trouble breathing. Everything moved so fast around me and I felt like I was descending into quick sand, like I was seeing my dream job and watching myself as I fell back into the abyss of my past.

I retreated to the bathroom in fear. This is where I had my first panic attack in a professional setting. It would be the first of countless many to come. I leaned over, with my elbows propping me up against the bathroom counter and took deep breath after deep breath. My eyes climbed to the top of their sockets beneath my closed eyelids, and I asked myself, "What am I doing here? How did I get here? I'll never be able to do this professionally."

Once I calmed down enough to breathe, I went straight to Thea's desk and said, "I'm not fast enough Thea. I can't do it."

She blinked and turned the corners of her mouth up sympathetically.

She said, "Don't worry so much Ray. You'll learn to get faster. Your hand will just automatically learn what to do, but you have to give yourself enough time. The only way to get faster is to do it, and do it under pressure."

I don't know if it was that I wanted to believe her, or the comforting softness in her voice, but I took all of the fear, all of the anxiety, that had agglomerated inside of me and set it to the side. I wanted to do a good job. I wanted it so badly.

I wasn't going to quit now.

It took me all day to create three patterns for three different shoe constructions and the inking, the finalized sketch over, was awful. I had smudged the ink because my hand dragged over the paper as I drew. Nine very imperfect drawings in eight hours were all that I could finish. Thea had just a touch over sixty and they were all extraordinary.

It was a rough day, and, to cap it all off, I got car sick on the way home. I thought Thea was going to just take me straight to the airport the send me back to Chicago because I had been such a complete and utter failure.

But she didn't. She took me home and we started all over again the next day.

The week went on pretty much like that first day, except Thea kept adding new caveats and responsibilities to my tasks. One such thing was to design new patterns over a three-dimensional plastic last of a shoe, which was a method I had never tried before.

It was really tricky at first, but I actually liked it more than merely sketching the shoe because it offered a realistic look at how the shoe would actually come out. A lot of times, designers will sketch a really cool looking shoe that simply won't work with the materials required for mass production. With handmade shoes that you can spend months crafting, you can create really unbelievable stuff, but if it can't be mass produced, you're wasting your time with most companies. And Thea wanted to test my ability to make my designs applicable to mass production.

I showed a lot of progress over the course of the two weeks. My sketches improved and the three-dimensional designs went really well.

In the last few days, Thea gave me a final assignment. She asked me to take three shoe constructions, design a few patterns for each, and provide detail descriptions for the factory. By this point, I was becoming somewhat accustomed to getting a lot of serious work at the internship, but this was really advanced. Completing this final step would mean that I went through every necessary step that a professional designer would go through.

The detail description was the step in the design process where you specifically outline details such as, how many millimeters is the heel, what type of leather is used on the upper versus the sole, how heavy the stitching is and what type of thread is to be used.

It was really overwhelming to, in my first two weeks of experience, go through the entire process of creating a shoe line. Thea helped me with some of the specifications because I really had no idea about how to present the information, but she also made me do a couple designs entirely on my own. Despite my trepidation, it was the most exciting two weeks of my life to that point.

I was actually producing something for a company!

On my final night in Boston, Thea took me out to dinner at a cute little café. It was dimly lit, with social chatter emanating throughout the room.

Looking back, even though we had developed a friendly rapport, the conversation was unusually serious for the final days of an internship. We talked about a lot of the technical details that I'd gone through over the two week timeframe, and how the process proceeded from there.

Sensing the gravity of our conversation, I decided to ask about her intentions. It seemed like she was going somewhere with the content of our discussion.

I asked, "So what are your long term goals?"

Her face rumpled a little, perhaps taken aback by the role reversal inherent in a twenty-two year old asking his boss about her future.

She laughed and said, "Well, what are your long term goals?"

"I'd love to be in the shoe industry as a designer," I responded without hesitation. "I want to get right in, get a job and try to learn from somebody who has been in the business for a while."

In retrospect, I realize that I was hinting that I'd like to continue with the type of work that I did over the course of the internship.

Thea sat back in her chair, folded her hands on the table and said, "Well, I'll keep my eye out for you. If I hear of anything, I'll let you know Ray."

"I'd appreciate that."

The conversation grew a little spotty thereafter, as I began dreaming of finding a job like the one I had just completed. It was so attractive to me, so filled with purpose, to spend every day working with a team on an inspiring project like a shoe line. Everybody worked so interdependently, yet it was extraordinarily creative.

"I can't imagine anything better than this," I thought to myself, as I exhaled into the muggy Boston air.

The next morning, Thea had a cab waiting outside for me at eight in the morning. I gave her a hug, thanked her for everything, and redundantly gave her a sheet of paper with all of my contact information—just to be sure that she wouldn't lose track of me. It was a cordial and uneventful goodbye.

As the plane arose from the tarmac, giving me a quick glimpse of the Atlantic Ocean off in the distance, a slight sinking feeling reminded me that I didn't want to leave. Then, I thanked my lucky stars that my destination was Chicago instead of Los Angeles.

I had come a long way.

Chapter 31

When I was little, all the neighborhood kids used to get together to play baseball behind our house on Loosemore Street. They wandered in, with ball gloves laced over a bat on their shoulder, from all different directions to congregate in the street. Somebody would throw their cap down and all the other kids followed suit. It was as if they all knew exactly what to do. The way they set down their stuff, the way they waited patiently in line, and conversed playfully with one another, gave the impression of purpose.

They all knew why they were there.

I would stand in line alongside them, swaying nervously from side to side, a good foot shorter than most of the other boys. And they would start picking teams.

"Jose."

I kept swaying from side to side waiting.

"Richard."

I stayed in my place.

"Carlos."

Over and over, the names kept coming out, and *Ray* was never among them. I was always the last kid to get picked. The same thing happened in middle school gym class. Every boy would get picked before me.

Now, I can't say that I don't understand. I am utterly despicable at sports. But, as the youngest, and as the one that always got picked last, I think I just got used to being left behind. Every time I tried to play ball, I screwed something up. I was no good.

I had no purpose.

Art was my attempt to pave a new way for myself. If I couldn't fit in with the boys in my neighborhood, if I couldn't be good at the things they liked, at least I could be good in my own little way.

At least I could try.

But it doesn't go away—that feeling of always being picked last. Deep down is an omnipresent fear that, no matter what you do, no matter how far you run, you're still going to be left behind.

That's how I felt at the end of college. After all the hard work, all the struggle, it would all come down to who gets picked to do something for real.

I flew home from Boston with a great new experience, one that excited me to the core, but one that ultimately provided no certainty, no promise. I had one more semester in the fall until I received my diploma, and, if nothing emerged by then, I had to go back to the drawing board to start all over again.

For my final semester in the fashion department, I had to create a senior collection. It was a clothing line to be produced for a runway production, and the quality of work would determine whether or not I would be allowed to graduate.

Since I was the type of person who really worked independently, I arranged with the department to allow me to work on the collection away from classroom supervision, and I had to check in periodically with a clothing design professor who would monitor my progress.

So, the semester started, like any other, and I began to work on my final collection. I modeled it around sustainability. The idea was that we live in a "throw-away" society with disposable cameras, plastic cups, and fast food containers that simply go to waste. The mission of my collection was to argue that fashion had the same wasteful nature. In that, people would rather be caught dead in the fashion industry than be caught wearing the same thing twice.

I sketched and designed all of the clothing in the collection to be made from natural, biodegradable materials.

Just a few weeks into my project, while I was at the apartment with Ben and Joanna, my phone rang. It was Thea.

"Hey, Thea. What's up?" I answered, sounding as surprised as I felt.

"Hi Ray. I'm calling to tell you something," she responded ambiguously.

"Oh, okay. What's going on?"

"Well, I just wanted to call and let you know that the bosses here and the owner of the company felt that you did such a good job during your internship that they want to pay you for it," Thea said.

"What?" I said in an awkward, borderline inappropriate tone. My eyes bulged widely.

"Yeah, they want to pay you $250 for the two weeks that you were here, and they really appreciated your work."

"How did they even see it?" I asked, trying to get to the bottom of this unexpected phenomenon.

"Well," she paused sneakily. "I quietly put a few of your drawings into the collection and they actually used them for mass production. When the VP accepted the designs, I told him that you were responsible for them. "

"Why on Earth would you do that Thea. I'm blown away right now. I thought that all of my work was just for practice," I said, exuberantly flabbergasted.

Thea cleared her throat and spoke even more gently than normal. "Because, I've been telling them for years that I need an Associate Designer, and we haven't been able to find anybody that's right for the job."

"Oh, my God, Thea," I said. "Thank you so much. I can't believe it." My voice became high and squeaky by the end of the sentence. "I guess I'll talk to you later," I continued.

She said, "Whoa, wait a second Ray. I have something else to ask."

"Oh, sorry. Yes?" I asked, now becoming a little disoriented by the excitement.

"How would you feel about moving to Boston?" she asked.

At that moment, I began to have an out of body experience. I remember that moment as if I were watching myself from the ceiling reacting to the conversation on the phone. I was entirely weightless, my body ringing numb.

For ten to fifteen seconds, during this unique out of body moment, I failed to make a noise of any kind.

Perhaps sensing that I wasn't about to answer the question she had posed, she rephrased.

"I'm offering you a full-time job in Boston, working as my Associate Designer. What do you think?"

It was all too much for me to process all at once.

All I could say was, "Wow, Thea. I can't believe this. I have to think about it. Can I call you back?"

"Sure," she said. "But get back to me as soon as you can."

I snapped my *Nokia* phone shut and exhaled so deeply that I could feel my lungs collapsing on themselves.

I turned to Ben and Joanna, who were sitting on the couch talking without any clue what that phone call was all about. I remember that the living room shone brightly, the brown cardboard moving boxes from our other room painted a pale yellow from the incoming sun rays. My mouth hung open.

Ben looked over me and said, "What's the matter sweetie?"

With an inexplicable frown and my eyebrows furrowed, I said, "I just got offered a job."

"Oh my God, with who?" he answered vivaciously.

"With the company I just interned with," I responded blankly. Shock had set in.

"Well, are you going to take it?" Ben inquired.

I scratched the top of my head with my right hand.

"I don't know. Should I?"

And, in shocking unison, Ben and Johanna gasped and said, "Yes!" in a pleading tone, as if suggesting that I were a total idiot for even asking.

"But it's in Boston. We'd have to move," I said, as if seeking a reason why I shouldn't take the job.

"Then, we're moving to Boston," Ben insisted.

I didn't know how to respond to that situation. That type of thing never happened to people like me. I was a college senior with zero practical experience. I was overwhelmed during the two weeks I was there. Why me? How did this happen?

I questioned the very premise, as if afraid to take that next step.

It was great news—perhaps the best news that I'd ever received. Yet, something about it didn't seem right. It didn't feel normal. It didn't seem real that they'd chosen me.

I was the kid who they always picked last.

The next day, I called Thea back and, despite my own nagging doubt, told her I'd take the job.

I asked her about the details, and she told me that they would want me to start in the next month. Even though it would mean that I would fall short of graduation, I agreed to make it work. It was too good of an opportunity.

Then, I asked about pay and we hit a potential roadblock. Thea told me that they were willing to offer me $24,000 per year in salary. Ben and I had done some research and we had come to learn that apartments in the decent areas of Boston were really expensive. So it gave me pause.

I said, "Thea, that's not enough money to survive. Can we negotiate that salary at all?"

"Ray, I'm not sure, but I'll put you through to Allen and you guys can talk about it, okay?" she responded.

"Okay."

When I got on the phone with Allen, I told him that I figured the salary was far too little and I would need more like $40,000 to live reasonably.

His response was, "Ray, that's a lot of money. I don't know if we can get you anything like that, but I'll ask. Let me call you back when I find out."

So we hung up, and the days ticked by. I started checking my watch more frequently and becoming restless. A week passed and I heard nothing.

And I thought to myself, "Oh no. I totally screwed it up. Why did I have to ask for more money?"

Then, one day, when I was working the floor at *Marshall Fields* selling shoes, my phone started buzzing in my pocket. I hustled off of the sales floor and into a supply closet so that nobody would see me on the phone.

"Hello?" I answered in a mousy tone.

"Hi Ray. It's Allen."

"Oh, hi Allen. I wasn't sure you were going to call me back."

"Oh no," he reassured. "It just took some time to figure out the budget of your request."

"Well what did you find out?" I asked.

"So here's the deal," he paused, as if bracing me for bad news. "I spoke with the owner, and he said that he's willing to pay you $37,500 per year and pay for the move. How does that sound?"

I nearly jumped out of my shoes, I was so thrilled.

"Great. That's great," I said, just to reemphasize the *great*.

"Alright then. We need you to report on the last Monday in September. Does that sound good?" Allen asked.

"Absolutely," I exclaimed. "See you then."

The phone call happened on a Friday in early September. That weekend, Ben and I took a trip up to Northern Michigan to visit with his family. They lived in this stately farm house on a 135-acre plot of beautiful land on the Leelanau Peninsula.

Let's just say it was a far cry from the type of home I grew up in.

Ben's mom Cindy married a man named Dean Robb, a celebrated trial lawyer, and they lived together in the farmhouse, along with their son Matt, Ben's half-brother, who was in high school at the time.

When I told Cindy and Dean about my new job they were thrilled. They were the most supportive family I could ever imagine. When Ben came out to them at his high school graduation, Cindy became so active in the local PFLAG (Parents and Friends of Lesbians and Gays), that she ended up becoming president of a four-state region spanning the Midwest. She was a member of the local school board while Mat was in high school, and every time my career has taken a step forward or hit a roadblock, she was always willing to offer her love and support.

We had a nice relaxing weekend in the quiet rural county, going shopping and hitting the beach. Matt was out playing golf or something with his friends and never seemed to have the time to spend with us.

And it was a dreary Tuesday morning that we were set to fly back to Chicago, when the nation was shaken at its very foundation.

Cindy came bursting through our bedroom door on the upstairs level of the farmhouse and switched on the TV.

"Wake up! Ben! Ray! Wake up!" She shouted.

Ben and I panicked.

"Mom, what's wrong?" Ben asked.

"Look! An airplane just exploded into the World Trade Center."

We watched together as the deep, dark grey smoke from the tower billowed into the Manhattan sky. The commentator's voice shook in terror. Scenes of chaos clipped across the screen, people running in fear and pointing up at the sky in disbelief.

And after no more than five minutes of watching the harrowing event, another plane burst into the screenshot and penetrated the tower, sending an unrelenting plume of fire and smoke across the other side. Sparks and debris rained down from the majestic silver tower, and any hope that the first plane had happened by accident dissipated in an instant.

September 11, 2011 was five days after I got my first real job.

We didn't know what to do. We didn't know what it meant or why it happened or who was responsible.

From that moment forward, for an indefinite period, time stood still. Everything grinded to a halt.

People did what people do during a time of crisis. They cried. They rationalized. They got angry.

Cindy went to the store to stock up on canned goods, preparing for an unrelenting war that might shut down all food suppliers. Ben called a rental car agency, knowing that we wouldn't be getting on a plane any time soon.

I called Allen.

"Allen, I just saw what happened. It's just horrible."

We talked about it incoherently for a few minutes.

Then, when I felt that the conversation had been polite enough to sufficiently recognize the horrific national tragedy, I asked, "What does this mean for us?"

"I don't know, Ray. I don't know. I'll have to get back to you later."

Days turned into weeks and weeks turned into months. All I was told is that *AmAsia*, like thousands of other companies, instituted a hiring freeze in the wake of *September 11*. In the meantime, I worked on my senior project at the SAIC and worked my two jobs at *Marshall Fields* and *Gap* to make rent. Ben had a job as a manager at an Italian restaurant called *Leona's*.

Allen assured me that, so long as everything got back to normal, they still wanted to hire me. It felt like a big *if*.

I was petrified.

Time and hope make a peculiar cocktail.

I watched the fall rain turn to a bitter winter snow. I listened as the mighty Chicago wind blustered during quiet moments and the way the *El* train clinked and swooshed monotonously through the city at scheduled intervals. I felt the weight of my body push my feet against the floor as I stood still, feigning the idea that if I stood there long enough I would begin to submerge—like a rock pressing through the soil.

Graduation made the feeling worse.

My senior collection went over fantastically well. It was featured at the fashion show. Along with a wealth of compliments, I received a piece of paper called a diploma that indicated that I wasn't supposed to come back anymore.

I was sent out into the world with a degree in fine art and a job selling shoes at *Marshall Fields*—hardly a fashion student's dream job. I had asked around about potential job opportunities elsewhere, but the scene was bleak. All across the nation, hiring freezes prevented fashion companies from bringing in new people, let alone entry level college graduates without experience.

I replayed the conversations with Allen and Thea over and over again in my head. All I had to do was wait until things got back to "normal," whatever that means. Their reassurances depleted in meaning over time. I began to think that I would never hear back from them. I began to think they had forgotten about me.

You just never know in the business world. An economic hub of the United States was struck down and the markets panicked. Perhaps things would never get back to *normal*. Perhaps they would just move on without me, like they had in years past.

Perhaps it just wasn't meant to be.

When the new daily routines set in, I grew more restless by the day. I sent out a new batch of resumes to fashion companies around the country.

I heard back from zero.

The snow melted and flowers began to bloom once more. Birds began to chirp. And so on.

Now that I was out of college, my contacts at the university began to wither. They had new students and new assistants, new people to help.

The part-time work became a battle for hard-fought hours and I began to fall short on rent payments, which Ben was loving and supportive enough to cover for me.

And by the time May came back around, five months since graduation and nearly a full year since my internship, time had done quite a number on the status of my hope. I was out of options, out of prospects, and wondered if all the doubters from back home, who had told me that there wasn't a future for me in art, were right.

Then, Thea called.

"Ray, do you have a second?" she asked.

"Uh, yeah," I said sarcastically, not wanting to admit that I'd literally been waiting for half a year for her to call.

"They just lifted the hiring freeze, and we want you to come out here in June so we can get started on the next collection. Can you make it?"

Relief, ecstasy, and triumph flooded my pores. I held my chin high in the air and inhaled flavors of joy through my nostrils in one long, quenching breath.

"Yes, Thea. I'll be there. If you only knew," I said with finality.

When we hung up the phone, I turned to Ben and gave him a big powerful hug. I didn't say a word—didn't have to. Tears dripped off of my cheek and onto Ben's tightly flexed shoulder. He too began to cry, caught up in the overwhelming emotion.

I unclenched Ben's shirt and looked into his watery, hazel eyes.

He squeezed my face and looked back at me lovingly.

"You did it Ray. You did it. Can you believe it's finally over?"

I looked down at the darkly polished wooden floors and began to sob uncontrollably. I pulled Ben tightly back into my chest.

We trembled in unison.

"I can't Ben. I truly can't."

Chapter 32

The ecstasy vanishes when the plane lands.

Perhaps it's the realization that I have to start all over again, prove myself one more time. Maybe it comes from a fear of change or the panic that comes over me when I wonder whether all my creativity was spent, washed up, during my feverish journey to get here in the first place.

Or it could be the *Ambien* and three glasses of wine that I coax down my throat every time I fly home from China.

I'm thirty two years old, and the *Tommy Hilfiger* spring collection is now complete.

My career has been like a torpedo since I moved to Boston to work with Thea at *AmAsia*.

Looking back, I realize how incredibly lucky I am to be at this point in my career. I would come to learn later that *AmAsia* skipped me from being an Assistant Designer to an Associate Designer, which fast-forwarded my career by about four years.

One year after starting my job there, I was hired by *Coach* as a Senior Designer of Women's Footwear, and, after working there for three years, *Nine West* hired me to be their Design Director of Women's Shoes.

I now hold that title with *Tommy Hilfiger*.

At practically every company, I've been the youngest in their history to hold the job title I've been assigned. When I tell people about my career, they treat me like a king, as if I were born into royalty—living a life predestined for greatness. They say, "You must be so proud," and "I can't even imagine how cool that must be."

But, unlike you, they don't know the whole story. They don't know what I went through to get here. And if I tell them about it, they respond dismissively and say something like, "But you're here now. Everything is great."

They deny that life is a lead-based paint.

The morning after I returned home from China, I roll over in bed, rub my eyes, and squint to protect myself from the unfriendly light. I'm hungover from a long night out in Manhattan with friends, but it's good to be back in America. It's good to be home in bed with Ben.

He wakes to the sound of me rustling in the covers and asks, "How are you feeling?"

"Shitty," I reply.

He giggles.

"It was fun," he argues emptily.

My mind drifts off as I stare up at the ceiling, my vision still swirling a touch from the gallon of vodka I ingested. An uninvited feeling of guilt infects my senses, and I furrow my brow.

"What's the matter, Ray?" Ben asks.

I try to place my emotion.

"Just thinking about my Mom. I haven't talked to her since I left for China," I reckon.

"Well let's go see her," he pleads.

Ben's been waiting for me to introduce him to my family for eleven years now.

"No," I resist. "We can't—"

"We can't what?" Ben interrupts. "You are finished with your line. Plus, you told me last night that Bornie would be happy to give you some time off. Let's do it."

Ben is always encouraging me to take spontaneous trips. I think it's an addiction.

"Ben, you know I don't like to go back there," I complain.

"I have never met your family—ever. You come up to my home every Christmas and my mom buys you all kinds of stuff, and we have a great time. And you haven't even introduced me to your family. Come on. Let's go."

It became more of a command than a plea.

Against all of my better judgment, perhaps still a little drunk, I said, "Alright, but you still have to see if you can get off of work."

It was one last attempt to stop the trip from happening. Ben is a manager at *Dave and Busters* in Times Square, and, of course, because Ben finds a way to get everything he wants, he called in and got approved for a week off to fly to Los Angeles and meet my family.

"Great, now I need to get another bottle of Ambien," I whisper to myself.

"I'm so excited to meet your dad and brothers, Ray," Ben shouts from the bathroom.

My eyes widen.

"I'd better get a bottle of Xanax too while I'm at it," I mumble incoherently

"What?" Ben shouts in response.

"Oh, nothing!"

Ben had to work for the next two days before he could get away to Los Angeles. So we worked it out that I would fly in a day before him, stay with my old friend Roz from LACHSA, and he would arrive the following day. I pitched this idea to him as a way for me to get to spend some quality time with my friend, but there was an ulterior motive.

I needed to do a walk-through with my family one day in advance.

For years, I fretted the idea of bringing a boyfriend home with me. I thought any guy would run away faster than a Republican at a pride parade. However, Ben and I were now married—in Canada because we live in a bigoted country that won't recognize our love—so I figured if anyone could handle it, he could. But I was still worried.

You see, my family doesn't change—under any circumstances. They will do what they do regardless of the company. So I figured that the best way to ensure decent behavior was to show up a little early, unannounced, and give them a day to get things in order, relatively speaking.

I try to always show up without warning. I love the look on my mom's face when she is surprised. She is the sweetest woman in the world and I revel in the opportunity to bring her a little joy. She doesn't get a ton.

After landing in L.A. and catching a cab to Cypress Park, my knee started to bounce and my hands got sweaty. I realized more vividly that this would be the first time I brought a man home with me. It would be the first time my dad and brothers would have to really see me as a homosexual. They knew already because my mom told them, but I never felt the need to tell them directly. Emotions never played much of a role in our relationship.

As the cab pulled up to the curb, I paid the exorbitant fee without thinking twice. Money was no longer the least bit of concern.

Yet, I felt the sky coming down upon me. My chest tightened and my heart raced when I stepped outside and looked up the old street that I used to travel to school. I remembered the terror I used to feel wondering if Eric was going to hurt me that day. My eyes slowly tracked up the trunks of four twin palm trees that stood unchanged in the back of our house. Walking down the gravel driveway, I stopped to kick around some stones in the spot where Squiggy had been shot.

My stomach grew queasy, and right before I walked in, I stopped to take two deep breaths.

"Is anybody still alive in here," I shouted crassly.

I could hear some rustling through the screen in my parent's room.

"Is that Ray?" Mando shouted in shock.

Suddenly, through the screen door, I saw Mom toddle frantically through the kitchen in red heels to open the door and let me in. She gave me a big, longing hug.

Then, Mando came out to say hello. He still lives in our old room, and works at the liquor store two blocks up the street. When he brought me into his big, bear-like embrace, my nostrils stung on account of his pungent essence. He smelled like a dead dog having sex with a nine-year old can of tuna. And our old room smelled about the same except with a poorer ventilation system. I literally gagged when I caught a whiff.

My dad was out at the bar. You know, at his "job?"

As I meandered about the house, I was shocked at how much smaller everything seemed than it did when I lived at home. The ceilings seemed lower, the refrigerator, the living room, and even my mom seemed tiny by comparison. It seemed like a little shack, and I wondered how I possibly lived there for eighteen years.

I chatted with my mom at our kitchen table and tried to get a little update on how things have been. She tried to put a rosy spin on things, but, as I scanned the room, I was shocked at the level of decay and degradation that had fallen upon the house. Paint was chipped on the walls, picture frames were antiquated and slanted to the side, the doors and cabinets were hanging off of their hinges, the bathroom tiles were chipped, grime engrossed the bathtub, and stuff was piled up haphazardly as if they hadn't thrown anything away since I left.

Basically, everything had hit rock-bottom. It was scary. I didn't realize how bad things had gotten since I'd been gone.

Then, Ruben wandered out from the bathroom, clearly inhibited by some mind-altering substance.

"Ray," he said incoherently, his head bobbling from side to side as if his neck had turned into a slinky. "Wus sup, brotha?" he asked strangely.

"Hey bro. I want a bike. Will you buy me a bike?" Ruben asked.

He started picking at his face with his fingernails. Blood streamed down from his forehead, where his skin had been torn away completely. He was frustrated.

"Fuckiiiiiin'," he dragged the word on. "Worms, man."

Ruben thought he had worms crawling under his skin. It was a symptom of his longtime abuse of PCP.

"Mom, what the hell is wrong with him?" I asked concernedly.

"Oh, don't worry Ray. He's better than he was," she insisted.

"God!" I said with disgust that I couldn't conceal. "What was he like before?"

"Never mind, Mijo. He just comes in and out. He's been in jail off and on for sixteen years now."

She waved her hands around to visually accentuate the chaos that was Ruben's life.

"Don't worry. He'll go to sleep soon. Please, tell me about your job!" she said, enthusiastically trying to pivot from the subject.

Even though I was sickened, I did my best to have a good conversation with Mom. I told her about everything in my life. I told her that Ben would be coming, and she was thrilled to get the chance to meet him. I started to calm down a little and it reminded me of being a kid. Mom was always the only *normal* around that house.

Mom and I ventured into her room to look at old pictures and reminisce, and when we came out, Ruben had left his bedroom.

Mom shouted, "Ruben?"

"Where did he go?" I muttered back to her as we stood over his bed.

We rushed into the living room, where we saw him swaying back and forth trying to keep his balance, while mumbling unintelligible nothings. He was cooking drugs on the stove. As I walked up to him to convince him to stop, I could see my dad through the screen door, stomping up the driveway.

Ruben had a spoon in his left hand filled with some kind of substance and a lighter in his right hand. Not wanting my dad to walk in at that particular moment, I snatched the spoon from his hand and threw it in the sink.

"What the fuck bro!" Ruben shouted angrily, thrashing his arms wildly.

"Ruben, just shut the fuck up. Ruben! Shut the fuck up!" I insisted.

When Dad walked in, he said, "What the hell's going on in here?"

Dad looked incredibly different too. The best I can explain his visual transformation is this: when I left, he looked like Benicio del Toro from the *Usual Suspects*. Now, he looked like Benicio del Toro from *Fear and Loathing in Las Vegas*. His hair and beard were graying and chaotically overgrown. He had grown fat and slovenly.

"Hi Dad. Good to see you," I said with completely unmasked sarcasm.

Dad looked at Ruben and into the sink, where his drugs were splattered, and started to yell.

"Are you all fucked up again, you deadbeat? What did I do to get such a loser for a son?" he shouted rhetorically.

I leaned over to my mom and said, "Ruben was cooking drugs on the stove. I've got to go."

"I understand my love. I'll see you tomorrow?" she asked meekly.

"Yes. Ben will be here, okay? So make sure that everybody's *ready*?"

"Yes, my love. See you tomorrow!"

As I walked back out to the street, I could hear Dad yelling at her, blaming her for Ruben's condition. It was a mess. I got out my cell phone, called Roz and asked if she could pick me up as soon as possible.

Night had fallen. I tried to just breathe as I peered up at the Los Angeles sky. The moon was shaded pale white from the smog. I pulled at the grass and wondered how this could possibly be my *home*.

My eyelids fluttered and my cheek twitched.

I felt myself waking up in Richard's apartment. At least I thought it was Richard's apartment. But I'd never seen it before. It was in Hollywood, and he was hosting a party. People were everywhere. The apartment was a swanky first floor flat, with avocado green shag carpet and plain white walls. It seemed like the set to a crappy old porn film.

I wander around through the party, watching all the people as they mingle and celebrate. But I'm not having fun. A panicky feeling intoxicates my senses. Nobody else feels like me.

They don't even notice that I'm there.

After the party runs its course, people trickle out slowly. Richard and his close group of friends retreat into his bedroom. They are smoking and partying. I could hear jubilant laughter, commotion, and chatter through the thin wall that separated them from the living room. Pink Floyd's album, *The Wall*, blared loudly.

I wanted to know what they were talking about. I wanted to know what was going to happen.

I was in the big living room with Ruben and my sister-in-law Vanessa. But they both fell asleep. I was all alone, sitting awake, alone on the couch, staring at the wall.

One light shone dimly by the window, lighting up the carpet on the other side of the room. Suddenly, it started to rain—drenching, unrelenting rain. It pattered on the concrete outside.

Pokey plop deep dough deep plop

Cook cook shhhhhhhhhhh cook shhhhhhhhhhhh

Thunder rang out in quick succession.

Then, there was a knock at the window. A shadowy figure stood outside with a black slicker in the pouring rain. And I stared out at him.

"Go home. It's raining. It's four in the morning. Just go home," I pleaded desperately.

Ruben lay fast asleep. Nobody could hear me yell.

I got up to go to the window, and the figure slinked away into darkness. The water freefell so quickly from the sky that it began pooling on the ground.

"Tick. Tick. Tick," the clock hissed uniformly in the background.

The water rose all the way above my chest. The window was now half way covered, and it squeaked from the unrelenting pressure of the rising tide, straining to maintain its integrity.

Suddenly, gunshots echoed off the mountain in the distance, as I stood at the window. I stared outside, curiously seeking answers. A barrage of bullets emerged. They were headed right in my direction, and I saw them nearing in slow motion.

Just before the bullets penetrated the window, I thought to myself, "Where's Ruben?"

In panic, I glanced over to see him sleeping like a lamb on the couch. The worry subsided.

"But, what about me," I thought, lightly placing my hand over my wrist.

I watched, head-on, as the bullets slowly burrowed through the single-paned glass before finally bursting through. The glass shattered violently and I watched as the tiny fragments suspended in the air all around me.

Without warning, time sped back up and the bullets whizzed by my head in all directions, missing me as narrowly as earthly possible. Then, quiet came, the rain stopped, and the water poured out onto the floor. I scanned the room in shock, terror, and, somehow, curiosity.

Nobody woke up. The party in Richard's room continued. I was the only one who noticed the bullets propelling headlong in our direction.

I exhaled, and blinked my eyes once.

That's when I awoke.

I was in Roz' apartment, sleeping comfortably in a bed adorned with four satin pillows.

I'll never forget that dream because it was emblematic, in so many ways, of my life. It was as if I was the only one who truly watched what was going on around me. To everyone else it seemed normal. It seemed ordinary.

But I felt—I always knew—that it was anything but.

I chose to watch as the bullets came my way. I refused to duck. I refused to cower with others. I didn't join the party. I didn't fall asleep on the couch.

I stood transfixed at the window of life looking out into darkness. And, somehow, the bullets missed. Somehow, I found my way through.

It was down a narrow path that I avoided the fate of my neighborhood, the fate of my dysfunctional home. Had it not been for five key people—a teacher who told me about a different school, a social worker who gave me a second chance, a Dean who rolled the dice on a self-taught kid from the ghetto, a professor who took me under her wing, and a shoe designer who offered me a job—I would still be in the crossfire, watching on as the bullets approached.

Every minute of every day.

When Ben arrived the following night, we checked into a hotel in Pasadena, and he wanted to go straight to my parent's house.

"No," I said in the fewest words possible.

"Why not?"

"You really don't understand. We can't go at night. It isn't a good idea," I said.

Fortunately, he agreed, and I called my mom to let her know that we would stop by the next afternoon.

When we woke up, I started having hot flashes and panic attacks. Not only was it the first time everyone would meet my husband, but, if it were anything like my first visit, my husband would realize what a disaster my family had become.

My second visit went a lot more smoothly. They acted like *The Walton* family by comparison. As we walked in, my mom was in the kitchen, cooking and wearing high heels. We sat in the living room and talked with her for about an hour. At about noon, Mando wandered out to show Ben his pet turtles.

Luckily, Ruben was still passed out in bed.

After the hour with my mom passed, Ben said, "Well, where's Peanut?"

I took a deep breath and thought, "Oh god. Here we go!"

I showed him into my dad's room, which is like a cave—darkly lit and eerie. Walking Ben through the dark hallway felt like escorting someone to meet Darth Vader or Oz for the first time.

As we entered, Dad was sitting on his bed next to a black light and a lava lamp.

"Dad," I shouted timidly. "I want to introduce you to Ben."

"Okay, well let him in," he shouted.

So I just let Ben go in, and I left them alone for a while. It is usually best to let people meet him alone. He's more receptive that way.

After fifteen minutes of nervously gnashing my hands together, I heard them laughing uproariously. So I walked into the room to join. Dad had a mirror on his lap and leaned over to snort a line of white powder. Ben sat in the corner calmly with a smile on his face, apparently enjoying the spectacle. They got along like best friends, and my worst fears about bringing him to meet my family were squelched.

I was shocked.

By the time Ben and I walked out of the room, my Dad had given him a geode rock, which he loved to collect, and his father's prom picture. My mom couldn't believe it.

"He gave those to you?" she asked Ben afterwards. "Those are like his most prized possessions! He must really like you Ben," she assured him.

From that point on, I was basically trying to push Ben out the door. It really can't get a whole lot better than that. However, my plan was foiled.

Ben said, "No, I want to meet Ruben."

"Ben, no. You really don't want to meet Ruben. Trust me," I begged.

"Ray!" he whinnied like a horse. "Let me meet him."

Again, I conceded.

We walked into Ruben's room, and I told Ben to shake him in order to get him out of his hazy stupor.

Ruben struggled for a moment, tossing and turning onto his side. Then, he opened his eyes cautiously.

"Oh my God," he said in a raspy voice with only one bloodshot eye opened. "It's Buzz Lightyear!"

Ben howled and smacked his thigh. It was, like, the funniest thing he'd ever heard. Ruben rolled back over and fell asleep instantly.

Mom said farewell to us as we walked out the door.

I had averted disaster. Ben liked my dad, and he liked Ben. The conversation with my mom went swimmingly. Ruben acted like a drunkard, but a rather charming drunkard. By all accounts, it was way above average for an introduction to my family.

Now, there was just one more night remaining in the trip, a dinner date with my parents and all of my brothers and my husband—all of us together as if part of one big family.

Ever since I was a little kid, I kept secrets. I have always had something to hide. Whether it was my Dad's occupation, my brother's gang life, my ambition to become an artist, my eating habits, or my sexuality, it always seemed like I had to do things in private, like I couldn't just let everything out into the open to be seen all at once. Piece by piece, bit by bit, I had to come to terms with all of the haunting little images that were drawn beneath the painting that I choose to show the rest of the world.

Only when I have processed the secrets, come to terms with them, and made art out of them, could I let the secrets go. I painted my sexuality and my fear of abuse. I made sculptures and clothing out of my insecurity with my body. I applied to art schools to get myself away from Cypress Park. I got liposuction to make myself feel sexually desirable.

And now, here I was, in Los Angeles with my husband to bring it all together. I had kept him separate from my family because I didn't trust that putting my two lives together would work. I didn't trust that I had changed enough. But I could feel something odd slipping away.

I was running out of secrets.

Everything was being put out into the open for the world to see. The layers upon layers of paint that life had stroked across my canvass were coalescing for the very first time. The two lives that I led were about to crash into one another and I knew that they could never be fully separate again.

The anxiety I experienced throughout the whole trip prevented me from ever really enjoying the culminating moment. I had been so consumed by the fear that something horrible would happen between Ben and my family that I was constantly on edge. It was the same feeling that I got every time I was in Los Angeles. The shame I felt about my past, regrets about the trajectory of my family, and the fear that I might somehow have to live in that world once again, made the confrontation grueling and stressful.

But something was different about that last night in town.

We arrived at a Thai restaurant in Glendale early in the evening. It was the same restaurant that we had gone to for special occasions when I was young. My dad was a desperate creature of habit, and, for whatever reason, he loved this particular Thai place.

I remember nights when I was young, when my dad received a particularly healthy amount of money, he would splurge on a night out, and the Thai place was his predictable choice. When we went there, we did it as a family. Richard, Mando, Ruben, and I would be there together with Mom and Dad, and, in a rare showing of generosity, Dad would order enough food for three days. We would laugh and eat and be merry. We forgot all about the stressors of life, and, if only for an hour, we felt like a real family.

After fourteen years away from home, it had been a long time since I'd felt that way. But on that night, perhaps because it was such a familiar place, the old fleeting sensation returned. Richard and his wife Vanessa brought my niece Destiny and my nephew Logan. Ruben brought his kids, Alexis, Shane, and his newborn Jade. Mando was there, and, most significantly, Ben. Nobody was absent. Nobody was high or drunk.

Everything seemed *normal*.

Right when we sat down, my dad hassled Ben like an excited child.

"Hey, Ben. How many police officers does it take to arrest a Mexican?" he bellowed loudly in the crowded restaurant.

Ben laughed and said, "I don't know Peanut. How many?"

"Two. One to cuff him and one to hold the bag of oranges!"

Dad smacked the table and enjoyed a hearty laugh.

He continued. "Hey Ben. Why don't Mexicans like to barbeque?"

"I don't know," he paused to wait for a punch line.

"Because the beans fall through the grill."

Dad, Ruben, and Ben cracked up laughing, and the horrible, distasteful jokes continued. Fellow restaurant patrons glared over at us with contempt, as my dad continued his onslaught of polite company. I was mortified, but, like I said, everything was *normal*.

At a random moment, Ruben blurted out, "Eh, so, what's gay sex like? How often do you do it and stuff? And who's the bitch?"

"God, Ruben!" I exclaimed. "We're in a restaurant."

"Well, I's just wonderin'," he said.

Realizing the innocence of his question, I thought up a response.

"I don't know, what's prison sex like Ruben? You tell me since you have so much experience."

"Aw, shit. Dick. I's just kidding," he responded with a hint of embarrassment.

He shut up after that, and, despite the obviously offensive nature of his question, it was a really cool moment. It's hard to explain, but Ruben asking about gay sex was more endearing than it seems. It's like when a crocodile eats his young—it's the only way it knows how to show affection. To me, it was a sign that Ruben accepted me for who I was.

I felt relief.

I always feared that my family would judge Ben, and, in doing so, they would be indirectly judging me. However, they treated Ben like they'd known him for years. Without the slightest verbal acknowledgment of homosexuality, my family showed their approval in an even more powerful way. They treated me the same as they always had.

And Ben didn't seem freaked out either. He watched my dad snort drugs off of a mirror. He listened to the inappropriate jokes and saw Ruben in one of his stupors, and he never tried to run away.

I felt comfortable with bringing my life out into the open.

That dinner capped off an exhausting process of steering my life full circle, from the neighborhood kid who left for art college, to the professional with a gay husband and a new life in Manhattan.

And when the conversation wound down, and the only thing being shared were the empty, dull murmurs of a group so full of Thai food that they appeared ready to burst, Richard asked, "So where's the bill?

"Don't worry about it. It's already taken care of," I said proudly.

And, as everybody stood up, I wished that the moment would never end. I scanned the faces of each of my family members, and everyone smiled. Everyone was full. Nobody was in need. We were all happy and together and satisfied. It reminded me of a time from my childhood when we were all young, too young to recognize that we were poor or that our family sold drugs. It reminded me of a time long passed when all of us seemed to have infinite potential, and my parents still had a bright, youthful glimmer in their eyes.

I wished that I could go back in time, seize that moment, and pull us all onto a different path in life. I wished that we had moved out of the neighborhood and my dad got a real job. I wished that we all went to better schools and that Ruben never joined the gang or went to prison.

But when we all walked out of the restaurant together, as a family, I began to realize how unreal my wishes were. I realized that Ben and I were going to get into a rental car, and the next morning we would be on a flight back to New York. I realized that my parents and brothers and nieces and nephews were going to get into two cars headed back to Cypress Park, where they would probably remain for the rest of their lives.

Would my nephews join the gang? Would my nieces go to Franklin High? Would Mom ever get out of that God forsaken house?

As the succession of car doors slammed, we were all in our separate little spaces, going off to our own separate little lives. The silence rang audibly through my ears, and I thought of the distance growing between us as Ben and I drove off toward our hotel.

In that moment, everything came rushing back—the parties, the fights, the gunshots, and the smog hovering perpetually overhead. I remembered the streets and the crumbling homes. I remembered Jaybird and the dozens of Ruben's friends who had since died from senseless violence and self-abuse.

Then I remembered where it all started, when my mother agreed to move in with my dad, when she decided to dedicate her entire life to a man and the family that they might raise together. And I remembered how her fierce loyalty would prevent her from ever walking away, even if she knew it was the best thing for her.

I could taste the salty stream of tears permeating the corner of my mouth, and began to sob uncontrollably—lost, like the child in me.

"What's the matter Ray?" Ben asked sympathetically.

"Why couldn't it have been different for her?" I cried. "She's so innocent. She doesn't have anywhere else to go."

"What do you mean?" he asked.

Quiet ensued, the kind of quiet that can only be produced when a person realizes that the topic being discussed is far bigger than any one person—when the answers pale in comparison to the questions:

Never let it happen to you. Never let it happen to you. Get yourself out of here. Make it end, Ray.

The sobbing strangled my throat as I grew inconsolable, shaking and rocking with my arms held tightly across my chest.

Even though I had gotten myself away from that house, away from Cypress Park, away from Los Angeles, the pain is yet to depart. I still remember everything. I still harbor the same fears, the same insecurities. I still long for purpose. I still long for the reassurance that I am part of something meaningful, something important, and something productive.

I can't make it go away. I can't erase the abuse. I can't erase the drugs. I can't erase the violence. And I definitely can't erase the choices that the people around me decided to make.

But the one thing that I appreciate most about this whole thing—whatever it is—is that, somewhere along the line, I decided to run away. I was too afraid to stay put, and when I saw an opportunities to take my life in a different direction, I took the chance.

I took the chance.

And now I sit here, driving away from Cypress Park with Ben, dreaming of something new for my family, something better for my mom.

I envision her living in a classical, two-story home in Old Pasadena, with a lawn and a porch and a breathtaking rose garden. I imagine that Ruben has fully recovered and he stays with Mom to take care of her when I'm not around, and that they live together in peace, never having to worry about money or food.

Maybe, somehow, designing shoes can allow me to buy them a place like that. Maybe, by staying persistent and seeking better things for myself, I can help them transcend a life of unfortunate choices and people who took advantage of their loyalty and kindness.

My greatest hope is that I can give them that gift—the most wonderful thing that anyone can have, and the things I crave more than anything else.

A. blank slate. A. clean canvass.

A. Chance to start anew.

Made in United States
North Haven, CT
11 March 2022

17026901R10264